RICK STEIN'S

TASTE

«OF THE»

SEA

RICK STEIN'S TASTE «OF THE» SEA

PHOTOGRAPHS BY
GRAHAM KIRK

BBC BOOKS

This book is published to accompany the television series entitled *Rick Stein's Taste of the Sea* which was first broadcast in 1995. The series was produced for BBC Television by Denham Productions and directed by David Pritchard

Published by BBC Books,
an imprint of BBC Worldwide Publishing
BBC Worldwide Limited, Woodlands,
80 Wood Lane, London W12 0TT

First published 1995
Reprinted 1995 (six times)
Reprinted 1996 (twice)
This paperback edition first published 1996

ISBN: 0 563 38781 5

Designed by Barbara Mercer
Photographs by Graham Kirk
Photograph on page 2 by Guy Newman
Home Economist Louise Pickford
Styling by Helen Payne

Recipe for *Crab Newburg* on page 177 taken from
Cross Creek, © the estate of the late Marjorie Kinnan Rawlings
courtesy of Scribner, A Division of Simon and Schuster Inc.

Extract from *The Chef Has Imagination, or It's Too Hard To Do It Easy*
on page 51 reprinted by permission of Curtis Brown Ltd.
Copyright © 1953 by Ogden Nash, renewed

Set in Jansen by Selwood Systems, Midsomer Norton
Printed and bound in Great Britain by Butler & Tanner Ltd, Frome and London
Colour separations by Radstock Reproductions Ltd, Midsomer Norton
Cover printed by Clays Ltd, St Ives PLC

CONTENTS

ACKNOWLEDGEMENTS

Special thanks to Paul Ripley, David Pope and the other chefs at The Seafood Restaurant for all the time spent recipe testing. Particular thanks to Jane Rees, who typed most of the manuscript. Thanks to Heather Holden-Brown, Anna Ottewill and Frank Phillips at BBC Books for all their expertise, and their considerable patience with my failure to meet deadlines; to Graham Kirk and Louise Pickford for their sensitive interpretation of my dishes in the photography and to Barbara Mercer for her attractive and clear page design.

Lastly, thanks to the director of the television series, David Pritchard, the source of most of the ideas for the series, and consequently the book, for many hours spent talking about fish, fishermen and seafood in the London Inn, Padstow – and the source of some irritation to my wife, Jill, who cannot see why men have to have a couple of beers before they can talk about anything!

1

WHY SHOULD WE EAT MORE FISH?

Imagine it is early spring and you have just arrived in Padstow. You have passed through the narrow lanes and slate walls of Cornwall, seeing only the odd tree, bent over to one side by the Atlantic gales, and the village churches across the open fields. You've taken more time to get there than you planned having stopped at St Issey and caught sight of the estuary for the first time. Then finally, here you are; the sky is a pale blue, the sand spreads all the way across the estuary with the Camel river to one side. Can you really still be in England?

Away from the quay, with its view across the estuary to the sand dunes at Rock, past the lobster pots with the smell of filmy seaweed still clinging to them, you walk into a seafood restaurant for *Sea Bass with Beurre Blanc*, *Moules Marinières*, *Helford Oysters* or some *Razor-Shell Clams with Garlic Butter*. You will be longing for some fresh ozone-scented seafood on such an optimistic sort of day before you've even sat down.

This book is about that sort of exhilarating experience. It encompasses not only recipes but my enthusiasm for fish cookery. I make no claims for a comprehensive coverage of all species of fish, only the ones that I love and the recipes that I think bring out the best in them: just a taste of the sea.

Since I started my own restaurant in Padstow, Cornwall in 1975 I have witnessed,

with amazement, how seafood has grown in popularity. At first I sold grilled plaice and lemon sole, sea bass, mackerel, lobster, crabs, crayfish and the occasional scallop – and that was about it. I would never have dreamt of selling fish like cod or haddock because that was what fish and chip shops sold. Now there is literally not a fish that swims in our waters that I can't sell. To give you an example, not long ago I went out on a trawler and found a species of fish called dragonets in the nets, a fish I didn't know about. They're a bit like monkfish in texture and taste, but very small and a beautiful yellow and blue colour. I brought some back, skinned them, filleted them, deep-fried them, put them on the menu with some chilli sauce and we sold them all that night. So a species, totally unknown to the people that were eating it, including a Michelin Guide inspector, was enormously popular. If I'd put the dragonets on the menu 20 years ago I'd have thrown them away. I can sell any fish now: gurnard, weever fish, conger eel, trigger fish and I put this down to the fact that people are at last beginning to appreciate how bountiful the mackerel-crowded seas around us are.

Coupled with an interest in eating seafood has been a growing understanding about the important part played by fish and shellfish in our diet. A book called *The Eskimo Diet* notes a correlation between the declining consumption of oily fish, like herring, in Europe and North America and the increase in diseases due to eating too much saturated fat. Fish is what you might call protein without tears, it's completely lean and easily digestible with none of the side effects of fatty meat. Indeed, it seems clear that oily fish might reduce high levels of cholesterol caused by eating too much meat and dairy products. Even non-oily fish, such as tuna, trout, salmon, mullet, sea bass, squid and even mussels and oysters, contain the cholesterol-reducing fish oil known as omega 3.

I must say I'm optimistic about the future of fish cookery and our continuing interest in fish, but we still have a long way to go. There are still an awful lot of people who are indifferent to seafood. I find it interesting to try to analyse why this is. I still think one of the main problems is one of perception. Fish and shellfish are still regarded as being, in some way, not quite a full meal. I noted a comment in Jane Grigson's excellent *Fish Cookery*, written in 1973, which is still, I'm afraid, all too relevant today.

The writer remarked that 'fish could not be served as a main course when men were present as they needed steak or some other red meat.'

The incorrect belief that fish is not as nourishing as meat persists.

Fish bones are another reason mentioned to me for why people don't like fish. Speaking as someone who's spent a whole morning in the Radcliffe Infirmary in Oxford having a kipper bone removed from his throat, I should have given up fish long ago. But I haven't, and anyway, there are plenty of fish which don't have any small, throat-stabbing bones in them: flat fish, monkfish and all of the shark family, to name but a few.

The smell of fish is a problem to some. I do a number of demonstrations in local schools every year and children usually complain about the smell. This could be where poor fishmongers or perhaps poor turnover

of fish is to blame. I'm always at pains to tell people that fresh fish doesn't smell fishy. But if you look round one or two fishmongers and even large stores at the quality of fish they have on sale I'd be tempted to agree with those people who dislike the smell. Poor, sunken-eyed, flabby fish all sold at astoundingly high prices are fortunately not representative but definitely not acceptable.

I think the main reason for our reluctance to eat more fish is a lack of handed-down information. I was brought up in Oxfordshire, about as far from the sea as you can get in the British Isles, and I recall the fish that we had to eat in those days being dull. The transport of fish then was far less efficient than it is now. Fish was what everyone ate on Fridays; it was something that no one really looked forward to. I imagine most people have had similar experiences, unless they were brought up on the coast. I was brought up on a farm. I knew how to pluck chickens, remove guts from various animals. I saw pigs being slaughtered and all the bits made into something: brawn, chitterlings, hams. We had rabbits, partridges and pheasants and ate them regularly; my mother is a natural cook. Apart from the odd salmon, fish was not a great part of my experience except when we went to Cornwall every summer for our long holidays. It was almost like going to another country; the fish, the lobsters, the crayfish, the enormous crabs were so exotic.

Through lack of handed-down information many of us suffer from ignorance as far as fish preparation is concerned, so that when we're faced with a whole fish we don't know what to do with it. And because we don't know what to do with it, we lack imagination about the possibilities it offers.

One of the fishermen who catches sea bass for us describes his favourite way of cooking fish as being to fry them with mushrooms and tomatoes, rather as though he were frying bacon and kidneys. I wouldn't be surprised if the majority of people in this country considered that to be appetizing. But there is so much more he could do to cook those bass so as to pass on the excitement and quality of a beautiful fish. Think of roasting the whole fish and serving it with some *beurre blanc*, or grilling it and serving it with some basil, lemon juice and virgin olive oil with maybe a bit of rough sea salt sprinkled over it.

But I do have every reason to feel optimistic. One day, while we were filming the television series that this book accompanies, we went into a café just opposite the fish market in Newlyn and, having been excited by all the beautifully fresh fish in the market, we asked if we could have some simply cooked cod for breakfast. 'We don't serve fish here, it's a fisherman's café,' came the astonished reply.

We left feeling a little despondent – but you can either respond by thinking, 'this is an example of how indifferent we all are to fish in these islands', and be generally depressed and demoralized about it, or, you could think, 'okay, this is how it is now, but it isn't going to last for much longer'. And the more I think about it, the more I realize the truth in the latter viewpoint.

We are going through a revolution in our eating habits in this country and within the next 25 years I am confident that you will be able to find shops selling fish anywhere in the British Isles where there is a fishing community as well as plenty of seafood restaurants. We tend to think there's something wrong with us as a nation because we don't appreciate and make use of our natural resources, like fish. I think over the past hundred years or so people forgot how to enjoy eating. We moved away from fish in our diets partly as a result of the Industrial Revolution when much of the population moved from the countryside and coast to the cities, leaving behind a whole tradition of living off the land and sea. Of course, some people still eat well off the land to this day but most of us have lost sight of our natural culinary heritage.

I want to reverse the unhappy situation on this island where three-quarters of the fish caught are exported. I want to show you the unrivalled advantages of a diet containing fish. I have already stressed the invaluable health benefits but really hope to persuade you to eat more fish through the dishes themselves. By sampling just one of the recipes in this book, I think you will be bowled over not only by the marvellous flavour and texture of fish but also by the simple pleasure, ease and satisfaction there is in cooking with fish. Believe me, a whole new experience awaits you!

A NOTE ABOUT MY STYLE OF COOKING

The success of British cooking depends on the very best ingredients being treated in the very simplest way and when that happens I think there is nothing to beat it in the whole world. The problem with British food is that it really doesn't lend itself to commercial cooking and its downfall has been that the most indifferent raw materials when cooked simply, taste boring. If you have to use indifferent ingredients then you need to have a more inventive cuisine to go with it. Nobody could claim that farmed carp has much taste to it, but put it into a Thai or Chinese context with ginger, garlic, chilli, soy sauce and lime, and something very acceptable is produced. In British cooking we always rely on the quality of the ingredients and if it isn't there, the cooking is not worth consideration. When indifferent ingredients

are badly cooked, you have something truly awful, and that is what a lot of British cooking ends up being.

But the basic idea is what influences my cooking: keep the cooking simple and keep the ingredients good. I spend far more time in my restaurant on checking the quality of the fish, shellfish and vegetables than I do on inventing new dishes or endlessly refining a stock or a sauce. Much as I enjoy elaborate French food, I enjoy, far more, dishes like plain grilled lobster with herb butter, turbot with Hollandaise sauce, salmon with mayonnaise, plain boiled crab and mayonnaise, skate with black butter and plain grilled Dover sole. If they're accompanied by a dish of freshly dug new potatoes and followed by a bowl of Cornish strawberries, I'm even happier.

My recipes reflect my enthusiasm. Most of them are easy to make and most of them are not over-endowed with ingredients. But they all require the very best raw materials and if you haven't got the very best raw materials, you'll wonder what all the fuss is about.

NOTES ON THE RECIPES

All weights and measures in the recipes are written in metric and imperial quantities. The translation, however, from one to the other is not precise, therefore you should use either metric or imperial, and not a combination of the two.

Any unusual cooking implements like mortars and pestles, conical strainers or fish scalers are described in Chapter 2.

Ingredients are listed in the order in which they are used in the methods.

BUTTER

Most of my cooking is done with unsalted butter these days. This is because salted butter tends to increase the amount of salt in a recipe and because I prefer the flavour. Nevertheless, sometimes it doesn't really matter which you use, in which case the recipe will say butter rather than unsalted butter. Salted butter is still significantly cheaper than unsalted because it keeps much better.

THAI FISH SAUCE

I use the South-east Asian anchovy essence called Thai fish sauce or *nam pla* in a large number of my recipes. It has a clean salty taste and I like to use it in place of salt because it enhances flavours without actually being noticeable itself. I use a brand called Squid which we have found to have the cleanest taste. It also seems to be the type most easily found in Britain.

Thai fish sauce has a much better flavour when it has been recently manufactured. You can tell how old it is simply by checking its colour. It is always dark brown in colour but the fresher it is, the lighter the brown.

If you can't get hold of fish sauce, just use salt. Alternatively, you can use anchovy essence.

CELERY HERB

This herb, a member of the parsley family, has the same flavour as celery leaves but is much stronger. So strong, in fact, that a little goes a long way but it is a valuable flavouring herb in stocks and robust sauces.

OLIVE OIL

In the recipes, I specify olive oil for general cooking when the flavour and expense of a fine olive oil would be wasted. I specify extra virgin olive oil when the aromatic flavours of a good oil are all-important.

By olive oil I mean general purpose blended

olive oil, by extra virgin olive oil I mean oil produced by the first cold pressing of the fruit. I use about five different oils for different purposes. I tend to go for a good extra virgin Italian oil for using warm in my fish dishes and a French extra virgin for dressings for salads. The Italian tends to be stronger and more vigorous in flavour, the French softer and more subtle.

CHILLIES

I've used Dutch chillies throughout this book because the heat factor is consistent. If you are not able to get hold of these, bite the very end of the tip off the chilli you use to taste for strength before using.

WINE ACCOMPANIMENTS

I have often suggested wines to accompany the dishes. They are all very reasonably priced wines, available from off licences and supermarkets – and won't break the bank. On the whole, I've recommended white wine accompaniments but occasionally a light red

wine instead that will go wonderfully well with that particular dish.

WEIGHING HERBS

I have been experiencing some difficulty in trying to describe a measure for herbs in my recipes. The expression 'a small bunch of parsley' smacks a little of 'how long is a piece of string?' So I have specified the amount of herbs in a recipe by the tablespoonful. This means that you will have to guess roughly the amount of herbs to buy to produce a tablespoon. This might be a bit frustrating for you but at least it does ensure that exactly the right amount of herbs are put into the recipe. As a guideline 25 g (1 oz) of parsley on the stalk generally produces 8 tablespoons of chopped parsley.

It is a good idea to invest in a salad spinner for washing and drying your herbs as well as your salads. Coriander and parsley both tend to be dusty and therefore gritty. They particularly benefit from being washed and dried.

A NOTE ABOUT THE CHAPTERS IN THE BOOK

One of the hardest parts of organizing a cookery book is trying to fit the dishes into logical chapters. The last time I wrote a fish cookery book, the chapters were based on the courses of a meal but this didn't work particularly well because so many fish dishes can be served as either a starter or a main course. I thought about making the recipes follow the seasons but this is particularly difficult with fish as seasonal variations vary in quality everywhere and I have always found cookery books based

on the seasons to be particularly irritating to follow. I thought about an alphabetical list of fish but that seemed so uninspiring, so finally I thought that perhaps, by being illogical, I might get a more logical order! So I have grouped the fish in ways that seem to fit together. Oily fish seem to be a group to me as do flat fish, and fish I associate with the Mediterranean, the sort I would cook on a barbecue. In one group I have considered appearance, in another their cooking qualities; illogical, but it seems to work.

CHOOSING, PREPARING AND COOKING YOUR FISH

HOW TO CHOOSE FRESH FISH

I know, because people often tell me, that choosing fresh fish is not as easy as it should be. I have always told people to trust their instincts – if the fish looks shiny and attractive, it will probably taste good. But it is a bit like asking somebody who doesn't know much about wine to comment on the quality of a new vintage. It is very difficult unless you have spent years and years tasting all kinds of wine and have built up a fund of knowledge of colours, tastes and smells. So let me run through a few general points you need to look out for when buying fish.

A food writer visited my kitchen not long ago and paid me, what I consider to be, a very high compliment. She said, 'it's extraordinary but your kitchen doesn't smell of fish.' Fresh fish doesn't smell fishy. It has a smell in the same sort of category as green fields in spring or indeed dried sheets, taken off the washing line in a country garden on a breezy day. The appearance of the fish should be bright and shiny, it should be firm to the touch and, perhaps most important, if you lift up the gill cover, the gills underneath should be a lustrous pink or red. There should be no sign of brown in them and they should not look washed out. The eyes of the fish should be clear and bright and not dull or red and the scales should be tight.

An extra bit of advice to add about choosing fresh fish is that it's much easier to make judgements about one thing by comparing it with another. I would suggest you look for the nicest looking fish on the slab and, when you have found it, use it as a yardstick to judge the others. You can then ask yourself, 'Why are the other fish less fresh-looking?' The fish that looks better than the others is the fish to buy. So don't be too dogmatic about choosing fish. On p. 221 I've listed all the fish used in the recipes and given some alternatives if the specified fish is not available or is not in the best condition. You'll get much better results, for example, by using haddock instead of cod in a recipe if the cod doesn't look too good, even if the recipe specifies cod.

If you see something on the slab which looks fresh but is unknown to you, go ahead and buy it, although I don't expect you to be quite as foolhardy as I was when I once bought jellyfish. I had had jellyfish in a Chinese restaurant where it was served as a salad with a *julienne* of chicken, cucumber with coriander, and soy sauce. So enthusiastic was I about this dish that I was determined to try and make it myself. I asked one of the net fishermen to bring me some in. They started off about the size of footballs but when I boiled them, they reduced in size by about 90 per cent. Then I thinly sliced what was left. When I ate them though, it was a bit like eating a bunch of stinging nettles, the whole of my mouth came up in a wild rash. But I would still suggest you try anything that you see in a fishmonger's because they're not going to sell you jellyfish that sting your mouth!

I know that, sometimes, fish can be startling in their uncouth appearance and I'm no less affected by the look of unfamiliar fish than anyone else. I have been taking winter holidays in Goa on the west coast of India for the last four or five years. I go to the same hotel, where the food is excellent and where I've struck up a very productive relationship with the manager, who used to be a chef. He has taken me round the local fish market a couple of times and I must say the first time I went round it I was overwhelmed by the sight of so many strange fish. I have to admit that the smell was pretty overwhelming too; not of stale fish but, on the one hand, of a dried fish which has a particularly pungent odour, and, on the other, the smell of tropically heated fish guts. Everyone has the same mixed feelings when going to markets in India; fascination and excitement about how exotic it all is, but also a dread of some of the smells and sights. Having been to the market a couple of times I began to see patterns emerging in comparison with our own fish and thanks to Rui, my guide, I soon began to feel perfectly at home there. What became clear to me was, that although the fish looked strange to me, it could be classified in the same sort of way as our own fish and, indeed, adapted to the same sort of dishes that appear in this book. I don't think there is anywhere in the world that I could now go and not feel at ease in buying fish and cooking it in ways that I know.

WHERE TO BUY FISH

It is always best to buy whole fish at the fishmongers where it can be filleted or skinned by an expert, and where you can get a good look at the quality of the fish before you buy. It is much easier to tell the freshness of fish from a whole fish than a ready filleted one. A whole fish is also fresher because once it has been filleted it tends to oxidize and will never taste as fresh again.

Anyone with a serious interest in fish will always find a dedicated fishmonger to supply them. I know that fishmongers have been closing in their dozens over the last few years but I don't myself think that this is so much to do with a waning interest in fish as the fact that people are now buying fish from other sources, notably supermarkets, which have had a radical effect on the way we all shop. Supermarkets have been responsible for the demise of many small shops but no one can deny the extraordinary improvement in the supply of good-quality and wide-ranging food that they provide. I think that a dedicated fishmonger will survive. You only have to compare the enormous variety of fish and shellfish in a good fishmongers with what is still on offer at most supermarkets to see what I mean. Both types of outlet can exist side by side, on one hand, the convenient pre-packed supermarket product, on the other, the skilfully prepared, carefully chosen fish and shellfish of the fishmonger.

Apart from actually buying fish and shellfish you can always go and catch your own. It always seems to me extraordinary how little shellfish is gathered from the beaches which exist around our coastline. I'm an avid picker of shellfish from the beach and what could be more satisfying than going and collecting your food, coming home and cooking it, appealing, I guess, to some deep-rooted hunter-gatherer instinct?

THE PREPARING AND COOKING OF FISH

I wrote, in my last book, that I find cleaning and filleting fish is a very relaxing pastime. It's a job where my hands and brain are working in complete co-ordination because I've done it so often before. The feeling that I'm doing something right when I'm doing this job is one of the great pluses about being a cook; there's something about working with my hands that makes one happy, optimistic and calm. I watched a Filipino fishmonger fillet a yellow-finned tuna in Sydney fish market once. I videoed it as well because it was so beautiful. He was like a surgeon, parting the flesh from the bone with such apparent ease that it looked like the simplest job in the world. I love to watch the filleting of large cod on the fish market in Plymouth, or the swishing off of sides of salmon in a salmon smokery with one sweep of a long-bladed, serrated knife, or watching fishermen at sea gutting flat fish. A single cut and a flick and all the guts are removed. All these things are so fascinating. At the restaurant, we never achieve the speed or perfection that these people do because they are doing one job all the time, whereas we have to do hundreds. Nevertheless, the preparation of fish in our kitchen is one of the most important parts of our jobs and all the chefs have to attain a pretty high level of skill to avoid wastage.

STORING FISH

Domestic fridges are not ideally suited for storing fish, they are usually set at about 5°C and fish should be stored at about 0°C with plenty of ice to provide a moist atmosphere.

Despite this, I have found that it is possible to keep fish quite successfully in a domestic fridge if it's only for a short time and if you follow this procedure. Put the fish in a shallow dish and wrap both the dish and fish in cling film. Then, dot cubes of ice around the top of the cling film and put the dish in the coldest part of the fridge.

Whole fish keep better than filleted fish which is why, at the restaurant, we always buy fish on the bone. Once a fish has been filleted the cut surface tends to oxidize and turn an unappetizing yellow colour. You can slow down this process by wrapping the fish as I've suggested, but the oxidizing and discolouring will still take place, albeit at a much slower pace.

It is not worth keeping fish for more than a couple of days. If you're going to keep it any longer, you would probably do better to freeze it. Some fish freezes better than others, the firmer the flesh, the better it freezes. So Dover sole, turbot and monkfish freeze very well and bass, lemon sole and plaice freeze less well. If you are certain that the fish is very fresh and no more than a day or so old when you get it, then I can see nothing wrong with freezing it, as long as you use what you have frozen within a week or two. Ungutted fish freeze best of all as long as they're perfectly fresh when you get them.

The problem with buying frozen fish is that you don't know how long it's been frozen for and over a period even fish stored at the lowest temperatures will deteriorate. This is particularly the case with oily fish like mackerel or herring. Something seems to happen to the oil in them, it turns slightly rancid even after a short period of freezing.

When defrosting fish, give it plenty of time to thaw. The best method is to put it in the fridge straight from the freezer.

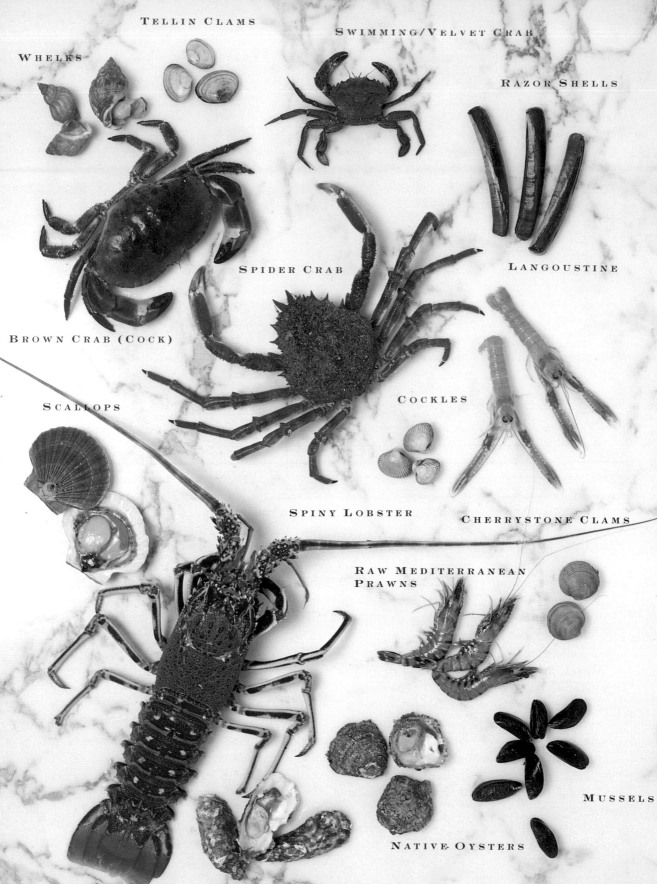

TELLIN CLAMS

WHELKS

SWIMMING/VELVET CRAB

RAZOR SHELLS

SPIDER CRAB

LANGOUSTINE

BROWN CRAB (COCK)

COCKLES

SCALLOPS

SPINY LOBSTER

CHERRYSTONE CLAMS

RAW MEDITERRANEAN PRAWNS

MUSSELS

NATIVE OYSTERS

ROCK OYSTERS

CUTTLEFISH

SHARK

OCTOPUS

SQUID

SHRIMP

NATIVE LOBSTER

WINKLES

SEA URCHIN

GREEN CRAB/SHORE CRAB

CLEANING AND GUTTING FISH

If you buy fish ungutted it is essential to remove the guts as soon as soon as possible otherwise they will start to taint the flesh around the stomach. It is not a bad idea to remove the scales at the same time, even if you're not going to eat the fish for a while. They're much easier to get off while the fish is still moist. If you let the skin dry at all, the scales are very hard to get off.

ROUND FISH

TRIMMING

Snip off the fins with kitchen scissors. This is particularly important with spiky fish like bass. There is not a chef in my kitchen who has not caught his knuckle on the spines of a bass!

SCALING

This is best done on several sheets of newspaper so you can catch as many of the scales as possible. They tend to fly everywhere. You can then wrap up the newspaper, throw it away and have a relatively easy job cleaning down afterwards. There is nothing worse than trying to clean down a work top with dried out scales on the surface.

Remove the scales by scraping the fish from tail to head using a blunt, thick-bladed knife, a special descaler or even a scallop shell. A descaler does the job best, if you can afford it. The one we use in the kitchen used to have a little plastic box on the back to collect the scales but, like a lot of natty implements in our kitchen, it disappeared a long time ago.

GUTTING

Having removed the scales, slit the belly from the anal fin (two-thirds of the way down the fish from the head) to the head and pull most of the guts out with your hands then cut away any pieces of entrails left. If you like you can also remove the gills at this time by cutting them away from the two places where they join the fish at the back of the head and under the mouth. Give the cavity a good wash. In salmon and sea trout you will need to remove the clotted blood on either side of the backbone. Do this by scraping at it with the point of a knife.

GUTTING ROUND FISH FOR STUFFING

If you intend to fill a whole round fish with a large amount of stuffing, you can either fill the gut cavity and sew the flaps up with string, which you cut away just before serving, or you can remove the guts through the gill cavity to form a natural container.

To stuff the fish through the gill cavity, cut away the gills, then, reaching through the back of the head, pull out the insides with your fingers. Make a small opening in front of the anal fin and wash the cavity through from the gills.

BONING ROUND FISH FOR SERVING WHOLE

You can remove most of the internal bones from a round fish so that when it is stuffed it can be eaten without the bones getting in the way. Gut the fish as normal, but slit it right along the belly, from head to tail, cutting through to the back bone and exposing the backbone along the whole length with your filleting knife. Snip the backbone with a pair of scissors where it joins the tail and behind the head, then pull out the backbone. We have a pair of thin-nosed pliers in the kitchen which we find ideal for removing bones. With the pliers, you can remove the bones around the gut cavity as well as from the backbone by pulling them out one by one.

FLAT FISH

TRIMMING

When cleaning flat fish snip off the side fins with a pair of scissors.

SCALING

Not many flat fish need scaling. Dover sole and brill are the only ones with serious scales. See p. 20 for instructions on scaling.

GUTTING

If you need to gut flat fish, make a small incision below the head where the guts cavity is. You can locate this by pressing on the white side of the fish where there will be an area that is much softer than the other side of this fish. Pull the guts out with your little finger. If you want to remove the roe at this stage, make a larger incision on the same side and pull it out too.

FILLETING FISH

I would expect you to get your fishmonger to fillet your fish. It's a bit of a specialist task really and not many people are any more adept at removing fillets from a fish than boning a large side of beef. However, from time to time you are bound to get hold of the odd catch of whole fish or feel like doing it yourself and the following instructions are designed to help you as much as possible.

FILLETING ROUND FISH

SMALL FISH: MACKEREL, HERRING OR TROUT

Lay the fish on a chopping board with its back towards you. Cut across the fillet of the fish through to the backbone, behind the head. Turn the knife towards the tail and cut the fillet away from the backbone right down to the tail in one clean sweep using the flat of the knife against the backbone as a guide. Turn the fish over and repeat on the other side.

A simple way to fillet small fish like mackerel or herring without using a filleting knife, is to cut off the head and make an incision from the gut cavity right down to the tail. Put the fish on a chopping board, belly-side down, and press the back firmly with the flat of your hand down into the chopping board, gradually flattening it out onto the board. Turn the fish over and pull out the backbone. Then remove any small bones left in the fillet with a pair of tweezers or pliers.

LARGER ROUND FISH

Lay the fish on a chopping board and cut off the head behind the gills. Don't cut straight through but rather follow the line of the gills in a V-shape to make sure that you don't lose any of the fillet. Now lay the fish with its back towards you and cut down the length of the back keeping the knife above the back bones and the blade horizontal against them. As you cut, lift the flap of fillet up with your fingers to make it easier to see where you are cutting. Lift off the top fillet, turn over and repeat on the other side. This sounds easy, doesn't it? I'm afraid it's not really. To start with your knife won't seem to go where you want it to and you'll find yourself cutting into the fillet. Practice makes perfect. The only really difficult part of filleting round fish is the cutting round the rib bones. The rib bones which surround the intestines are different on all fish. In some species like hake it is far better to cut around the rib bones but on others like salmon it is usually better to cut through them then remove the bones from the fillet afterwards. As I said earlier, filleting is tremendously satisfying

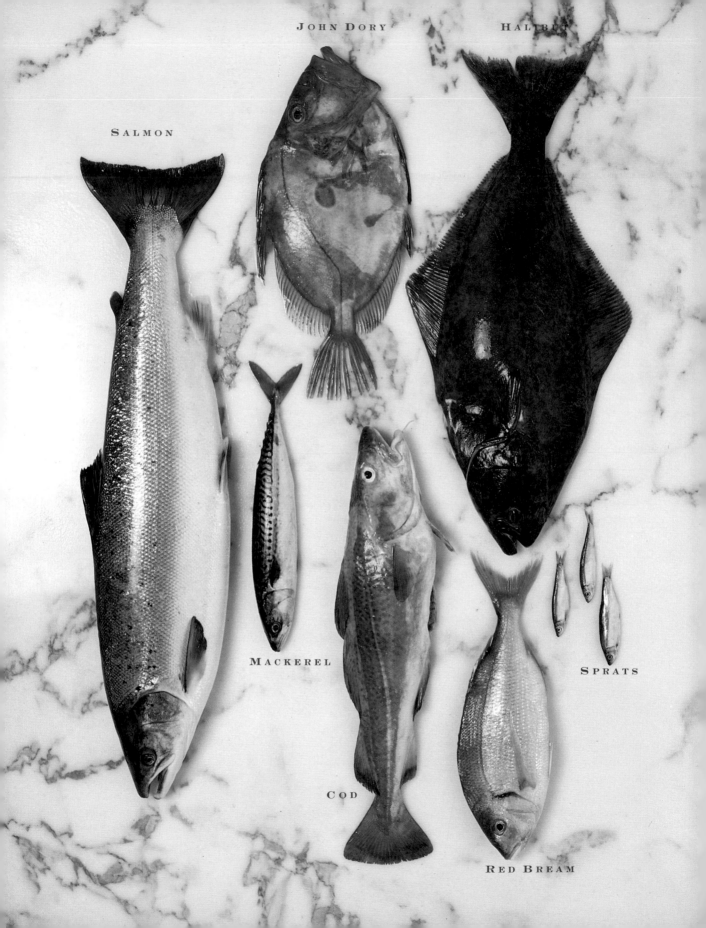

SALMON

JOHN DORY

HALIBUT

MACKEREL

COD

SPRATS

RED BREAM

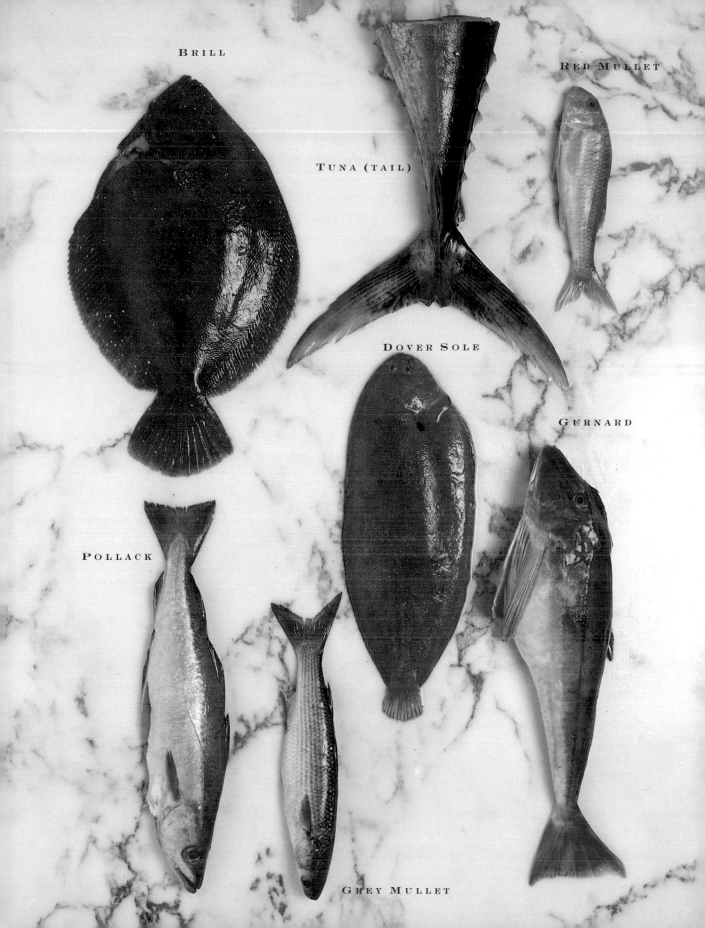

BRILL

TUNA (TAIL)

RED MULLET

DOVER SOLE

GURNARD

POLLACK

GREY MULLET

when you've learnt how to do it – if you've got plenty of fish and plenty of time, give it a try.

FILLETING MONKFISH

Cut the tail into two large fillets by running your knife against the spine. Monkfish has a membrane under the skin which should be partly removed otherwise the fillet will shrink and twist unattractively in cooking. The membrane is best removed by pulling as much as you can off with your fingers and cutting some off. I don't think it is a good idea to try and completely remove the membrane because you will lose a lot of fillet by cutting it off; as long as a fair amount is removed the rest will not be a problem. (See p. 25 for information on skinning monkfish.)

FILLETING FLAT FISH

This is much easier than filleting round fish because the bone structure lends itself to straightforward cutting. Slice through the fish from the head to the tail down to the backbone. Now slide the filleting knife under one fillet away to the side of the fish until the fillet is free. The angle of the knife is almost flat, using the long back bones as a guide. Do the same with the remaining three fillets.

FILLETING JOHN DORY

Because John Dory is actually a round fish rather than a flat fish, it has to be filleted in a slightly different way, even though it is flat! Lay the fish on a chopping board with its head facing you and insert the point of a knife into the right-hand side of the fish next to the tail and above the bony fins that run all around the body. Work right round the fish cutting away a little flap all the way around one side of the fish. Now, gradually work your way right across one side of the fish with your filleting knife flat against the central bones. Lift the fillet off. Do the same on the other side.

SKINNING FILLETS OF FISH

Place a fillet on the chopping board, skin side down. Grasp the tail end with one hand and with the other work your filleting knife up the fillet against the skin working away from your body in a series of short jerky cuts.

SKINNING DOVER SOLE

Lay the fish dark side up and cut the skin across the tail. Work a finger under the cut and loosen the skin down both sides of the fish. Sprinkle the tail end with salt to make it easy to hold. Grasp the flap of skin with a tea towel and pull the skin away from the fish right over the head holding the tail with your other hand. Repeat on the other side.

If the sole is particularly fresh, skinning it is tricky because it won't come away very easily. If pulling the skin away seems to be tearing the flesh it is a good idea to cut the skin through at the head and start at the other end.

SKINNING EELS AND DOGFISH

To skin eels and dogfish, you will need some strong string, pliers and somewhere to hang the fish. Cut the fins and tail off the fish, then cut through the skin behind the neck and continue this cut right round the back of the head so that the skin is parted all the way round. With the point of a thin-bladed knife, ease about 1 cm (½ in) of skin away from the flesh all the way round. Tie a piece of string around this cut, with a long enough loose end to attach to some anchorage point like a hook on the wall or even a door handle. Attach the fish, grip the flap of skin with the pliers and pull the skin towards the tail. Some of the flesh will start to come away with the skin but keep moving the pliers around different parts of the skin and pulling and you will find that the skin soon starts to pull away cleanly. Firmly and steadily pull the skin off the body.

SKINNING MONKFISH

Grasp the thick end of the tail in one hand and the skin in the other and pull away the skin. You will find that it comes away easily. (See p. 24 for information on filleting monkfish.)

STORING CRABS AND LOBSTERS

Cooked crabs and lobsters keep very well in the fridge for up to four days. Live crabs and lobsters will stay alive for three or four days as long as they were lively when you bought them. You should keep them in the bottom of your refrigerator covered with a damp cloth. They should be checked regularly to make sure they're still alive because once they have died their flesh deteriorates very quickly. If they have died they should be boiled immediately.

COOKING CRABS AND LOBSTERS

CRABS

Crabs should be killed before boiling. Take a small knife or screwdriver, turn the crab over and pierce it through the mouth straight up to strike the underside of the back shell, right between the eyes. Now pierce it again right in the middle of the under-shell beneath the flap which folds over the shell. This flap is small in a male crab and large in a female.

Crabs should be boiled in plenty of water salted at the rate of 150 g (5 oz) to 4.5 litres (8 pints/1 gallon). This is roughly the salinity of sea water (in which the shellfish are actually cooked at my restaurant). Cooking times for crab are as follows (timing begins when the water has come back to the boil after the crab has been added).

Crabs up to 550 g (1¼ lb)	15 minutes
Crabs up to 900 g (2 lb)	20 minutes
Crabs up to 1.5 kg (3½ lb)	25 minutes
Any larger crab	30 minutes

LOBSTERS

Killing lobsters presents a real problem in that it is impossible to kill them by piercing them in the same way as crabs. This is because they don't have a central nervous system but rather a series of nerves or ganglia throughout their body. Neither does the lobster have a brain. There is therefore no vital spot in a lobster to allow you to despatch it humanely. It is pretty unlikely, however, that the lobster feels pain in the way that we or most other animals do but we can't be totally sure about this. There was some talk a few years ago about manufacturing a small saline tank attached to the mains electricity supply in which a lobster could be painlessly electrocuted but nothing came of it. The RSPCA has recently suggested that putting live lobsters in the deep freeze for two hours before cooking them will kill them painlessly. It is likely that if they do feel pain, putting them in cold salted water and bringing that water very slowly to the boil will probably kill them as painlessly as any other way, since heating the water will gradually drive out all the oxygen and they will drown.

The two methods used at the restaurant,

WHITEBAIT

CONGER EEL

WHOLE MONKFISH

SEA TROUT

SARDINES

SEA BASS

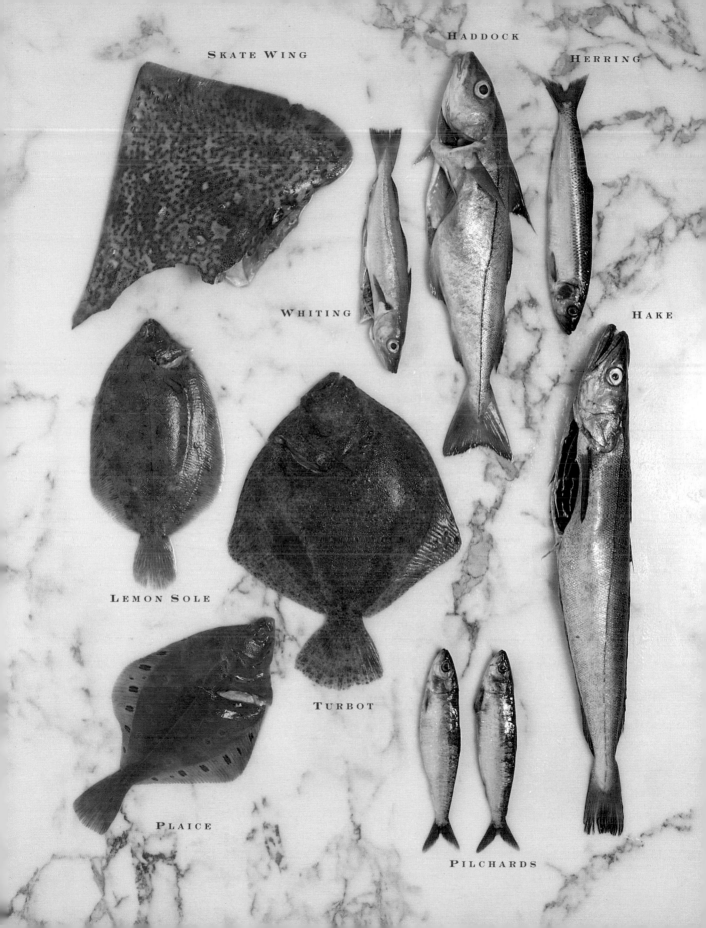

SKATE WING

HADDOCK

HERRING

WHITING

HAKE

LEMON SOLE

TURBOT

PLAICE

PILCHARDS

while not painless, are mercifully quick. We either drop them into a great deal of very rapidly boiling salted water, salted at the same rate as for crabs – 150 g (5 oz) to 4.5 litres (8 pints/1 gallon) – so that the time taken for the water to come back to the boil once the lobster has gone in is minimized. The other way is to take a very large kitchen knife and cleave them in two. To cut the lobster in half, place it on a chopping board and drive a large knife through the middle of the main body section, lengthways, cutting down towards and in-between, the eyes. Turn the knife round, place it in the original cut and bring the knife right down through the tail to split it in half. Pull off the claws, cut off the rubber band binding them and crack each claw open. Do the same with the other sections of the claws with a short sharp chop from the thickest part of your knife blade. Lobsters should be boiled for the following times. Again, as with crabs, timing begins when the water has come back to the boil after the lobster has been added.

Lobsters up to 750 g (1½ lb)	15 minutes
Lobsters up to 1.25 kg (2½ lb)	20 minutes
Anything larger	Boil for an extra 5 minutes per 450 g (1 lb)

CRAYFISH OR SPINY LOBSTER

These are killed and cooked in the same way as lobsters. Instructions for removing the meat from crabs, lobsters and crayfish is given in the individual recipes.

PREPARING SQUID, CUTTLEFISH AND OCTOPUS

SQUID

Gently pull apart the head and body, the intestines will come away with the head which is joined directly to the tentacles. Reach into the body with your fingers and pull out the rest of the insides which will be the plastic-like quill and normally some soft white roe. Pull the purple skin off the body – it comes away very easily. Remove the two fins and pull the skin off them too. Wash the body, cut the tentacles from the head in front of the eyes. Squeeze out the beak-like mouth from the centre of the tentacles and throw it away. You may like to keep the ink sac which is with the rest of the insides. It is easily identifiable being pearly white in colour with a slight blue tinge. The only other part of the insides worth keeping are two pieces of muscle running down either side which can be taken off and used with the body and tentacles. Discard everything else. You are now left with the body section, the fins, the tentacles, perhaps the ink sac and two pieces of muscle from the insides.

CUTTLEFISH

Cut off the tentacles in front of the eyes and remove the beak-like mouth from the centre of the tentacles. Cut the head section from the body and discard it. Cut open the body section from top to bottom along the dark coloured back. Remove the cuttle bone and the entrails. Skin the body and, with large cuttlefish, the tentacles. Cook in the same way as squid.

OCTOPUS

Cut off the tentacles in front of the eyes and, as with the squid and cuttlefish, press the mouth and beak out from the centre of the tentacles. Cut the head section from the body sac at the round openings in the body. Discard the head. Turn the body inside out and pull away the insides. Discard. Pull off the small bone-like strips sticking to the sides of the body and discard also. Bring a pan of water to the boil and simmer the body and tentacles very gently for up to 1 hour depending on the size of the octopus.

OYSTERS, MUSSELS AND OTHER MOLLUSCS

OPENING OYSTERS

Wrap one hand in a tea towel and place the oyster in it, put your hand on a work top, push the point of an oyster knife or small, thick-bladed knife into the hinge of the oyster and, using firm but not excessive pressure, work the knife backwards and forwards into the shell, breaking the hinge. As the hinge breaks, twist the point of the knife to lever the shell up then slide the knife under the top shell to sever the ligament that joins the oyster to the shell. The ligament is slightly off to the right of centre of the oyster. Lift off the top shell keeping the bottom shell upright at all times to avoid losing any of the juice. Pick out any little pieces of shell that might have broken off.

PREPARING MUSSELS FOR COOKING

Mussels should be washed in plenty of cold water. There is no need to steep them in buckets of cold water with or without oatmeal. Not only is this totally ineffective but more likely to kill them than anything else. None of the water in the bucket will get inside the mussel, they will remain tightly closed. Mussels only open their shells when they sense that they're in well aerated water, sea water or brackish water. The same advice goes for all bivalves like clams or cockles, a good wash is all they need. Having washed the mussels, scrape off any barnacles that are sticking to them and seaweed and pull out the beards. These are the threads called the byssus by which the mussel attaches itself to rocks. Raw mussels are excellent to eat as long as you accompany them with the *Shallot Vinegar* on p. 52. Without it the mussel leaves a bitter metallic aftertaste. To open a raw mussel, take a small, thin-bladed knife and force it between the two shells then run the blade right round to separate them. Carefully scrape the live meat from one shell into the other and pull out any remaining beard.

PREPARING COCKLES AND CLAMS

As with mussels, cockles and clams need to be washed in plenty of cold water by swirling them round and round in it. The cockles or clams that you buy will already be free from mud and grit but another wash does no harm at all. The easiest way to open cockles and clams is to steam them open in a covered pan to which you have added a little bit of water or wine. However, both can be opened raw by inserting the blade of a small knife between the shells and twisting them open. With both cockles and clams, unlike oysters, the knife should be inserted on the opposite side to the hinge not into the hinge itself.

PREPARING SCALLOPS

Like mussels, scallops too should be washed in plenty of cold water. Place the scallop on a chopping board, flat shell uppermost and slide the blade of a filleting knife between the two shells. Keep the blade of the knife flat against the top shell and find the ligament that joins the shell to the muscle meat of the scallop and cut right through it. The top shell will come off. Pull out all the material in the scallop shell except the bright orange coral and the muscle.

COOKING FISH

Fish cooks very fast and overcooks even faster so you really do have to be very attentive to get it right, particularly where you're dealing with very small pieces of fish. Whichever method of cooking fish you use, the one main point you need to remember is timing. These days recipes for fish in cookery books tend to be aware of this, but when you look at some older recipes which talk about boiling fish for 1½ hours or steaming scallops for 20 minutes, you wonder if there was anything left at the end that was worth eating. At the restaurant we use a temperature probe to gauge the internal temperature of the dish exactly but you can also use the following methods. Take a small knife and part the fillet in the centre. If it is cooked, the fish will have changed from a translucent colour to solid white. Alternatively, take a metal skewer, push into the centre and leave for 5 seconds. Remove and touch the tip on either your top lip or elbow. If it feels pleasantly warm the centre will be about 45°C (113°F), if it feels hot, about 65°C (149°F). If it feels very hot it will be overcooked and you'll burn your lip as well! If you are cooking whole fish, you can also check the gills. If they are cooked they will have turned a grey brown colour with no traces of pink in them.

BAKING

These days, the words baking and roasting are pretty interchangeable because what we actually do with roast beef is to bake it in a baking oven. Roasting means cooking in front of an open fire. However, I do see a distinction between roasting in a baking oven and baking in the same oven, in that I take baking to mean cooking a fish in a reasonable high-sided dish with flavouring ingredients around it. The flavouring ingredients to some extent permeate the flesh of the fish and the high sides prevent both the fish and other ingredients from burning. The temperature for baking fish is lower than that for roasting, about 180°C/350°F/Gas 4.

COOKING IN A BAIN-MARIE

Fish terrines, like the *Prawn Terrine with Courgette Salad* on p. 194 are cooked in a moderate oven 160°C/325°F/Gas 3. The terrine is then placed in a tray of boiling water and the tray and terrine placed in the oven. Cooked this way, the terrine cooks slowly in a very moist atmosphere.

BRAISING

Fillets, steaks or whole fish are placed on a bed of vegetables. Stock and white wine are added to come about half-way up the fish, herbs are sprinkled over and a loose-fitting lid or butter paper is placed on top. The dish can either be cooked gently on the top of the cooker or else in a moderate oven. When the fish is just cooked it is removed. The juice and vegetables are reduced down to make a thick sauce which is then poured over the fish.

BOILING

The only fish dishes that are cooked by boiling are stews where the idea is to force oil or butter to amalgamate with the liquid by rapid boiling. Most other cooking methods where fish is immersed in a liquid are described as poaching (see p. 33).

FRYING

SHALLOW-FRYING

This is the process of cooking small fillets or even whole fish in oil or fat in a shallow pan. You can coat the surface of the fish with flour or other starchy materials like semolina, matzo meal, oatmeal or breadcrumbs. You don't have to coat the surface of the fillets at all. If you are looking for a slightly oily finish, try frying them with some good olive oil and at a low temperature.

A couple of important tips about shallow-frying: first, don't overcrowd the pan, the object is to cause the surface of the fillets of fish to caramelize by cooking at a high temperature. If you overcrowd the pan you will lower the temperature and caramelization will not occur. (Caramelization is when the sugars present in all foods are burnt by contact with a fierce heat. The burning, if arrested at the right time, is full of flavour, if you take it too far it becomes like carbon.) The other important tip is not to let the oil burn so that it carbonizes the surface of the fillets before the fish has had time to cook or caramelize.

With regard to the second point, pure butter is a bad cooking medium because there are lots of solids in butter which burn at a much lower temperature than that needed to caramelize the fish. Burnt butter will give you black and greasy results. Either use clarified butter or vegetable oil with a little knob of butter for flavour. (For notes on how to clarify butter see the recipe for *Hollandaise Sauce* on p. 40.) If you are going to cook a large steak of fish or a whole fish, you would be better off caramelizing the fish by starting it on the top of the cooker then finishing it off in a moderate oven. In this way you will avoid the risk of burning it.

A lot of people complain that one of the main reasons they don't like frying fish is the smell. If you're cooking with an oven whose flues are connected to the outside like an Aga and Rayburn, you can avoid excessive cooking smells when frying fish by completing the operation in the oven.

Several of the baked dishes in the book call for colouring the fish by shallow-frying first, for example *Haddock Boulangère* (see p. 124). This shallow-frying not only enhances the flavour through caramelization but also gives the fish a pleasing colour which you would not otherwise get owing to the short cooking time of the fish in the oven.

DEEP-FRYING

Deep-frying is one of the most successful ways of cooking fish because, provided you use a good solid batter like the *Yeast and Beer Batter* on p. 53, all the flavour and moisture of the fish is sealed inside. There are a few points to watch out for when deep-frying. Don't be mean with the oil. Don't let it become too dirty before throwing it away, you will only ruin the food if the oil is bitter and black. If you only deep-fry things occasionally it is a very good idea to let the oil cool down in the fryer and then pass it through a sieve into a container that you can seal. Oil picks up moisture from the air all the time and spoils quickly. If you keep it sealed it will last a lot longer.

Another important part of deep-frying fish successfully is getting the temperature of the oil right. Temperature-controlled fryers are available relatively cheaply, as are thermometers, but if you can't afford to buy one, the best way of testing the correct temperature of the oil is to drop a small piece of bread into the oil when you think its shimmering surface is hot enough. If the bread browns within 30 seconds the oil is hot enough. If it blackens in the same time it is too hot. Fish should be cooked between 180°C (350°F) and 195°C (380°F). Big pieces of fish in batter, like cod, should be cooked at the lower temperature allowing the heat of the oil to penetrate right to the centre of the fish before there is any chance of the outer coating burning. Conversely, small pieces of fish like *goujons* or whitebait should be cooked at the higher temperature to allow the pieces to crisp very quickly.

STIR-FRYING

The Chinese way of cooking is ideally suited to fish. By cutting food into small pieces, vegetables and fish need not be cooked so thoroughly.

Many people find undercooked fish a problem because they are put off by the chewiness, unless the fish is thinly sliced and presented as obviously raw, like the sashimi on p. 165. But when the fish is cut into small pieces and stir-fried, nobody notices. What they do notice is the tremendous amount of flavour in the fish. As with shallow-frying, don't overload the wok. If you've ever seen the size of burner that Chinese and other South-east Asians cook over, you will see how little one should put in a wok using our puny Western burners. I will always remember a visit I made to a restaurant in the Sukhamvite Road in Bangkok a few years ago. The wok stoves they use there are like small volcanoes. Everything takes about 20 seconds to cook. The chefs are on show outside the restaurant. You go into a supermarket, choose your fish and vegetables, take them over to a chef and he cooks it in about a minute. The restaurant seats something crazy like 1200 people. It is one of the best dining experiences I've ever had.

GRILLING

One of the faults in my last seafood cookery book was that I was a bit over-fond of cooking fish in this way. This is because we use an overhead grill in our restaurant a great deal. It cooks fish perfectly every time and yet it is a method of cooking that you can walk away and leave for a minute or two without anything going wildly wrong – very important this when you've got maybe six different dishes all cooked in different ways on the go at one time. The problem is (as has been pointed out to me since writing the book) that the sort of grills we use at home are not as powerful, so I've tended to be a little less liberal in my use of such a method of cooking in this book.

However, if you do have a good grill it is such an excellent way of cooking fish, particularly fillets and whole fish, which should always be slashed right down to the bone so that the intense heat of the grill cooks the fish quickly before any of its juices have leached out and dried away. On the subject of juices leaching out, one of the most influential books on cooking I have read recently, called *On Food and Cooking* by Harold McGee, dismisses many cherished ideas about the science of cookery but none more so than the whole business of sealing meat or fish by searing. He proves conclusively that

when you apply intense heat to a piece of protein you do not create a barrier which locks in the juices, you simply enhance its flavour by caramelizing the outside but the juices continue to run through. The reason that it appears that the juices have been locked in is that the intense heat dries them up so quickly that you can't see them coming out but, as soon as you take that piece of meat or fish away from the source of heat and leave it to rest, out they continue to run. So when we are grilling a fillet of fish in the restaurant, we always leave the cooking of it to the last minute. Only when a customer has finished his first course and has actually ordered a piece of grilled turbot for his second, do we start to cook the turbot. In this way the most flavour is delivered to the customer and doesn't leach out onto the grilling tray.

BARBECUING OR CHAR-GRILLING

Barbecuing or char-grilling is one of my favourite ways of cooking fish. It is so popular at the moment, though, that we are in danger of being criticized for having too many char-grilled items on the menu at one time. But, not only do I love cooking fish this way, my customers enjoy eating it. So enamoured am I of charcoal cookery that for five years in the restaurant we had just that, a grill heated by charcoal. We bought charcoal by the ton and stoked up the fire every night because I love that little edge of flavour that you get from the gases that emanate from charcoal. That smell from hot balmy evenings in Greece, once experienced, is never forgotten. However, in the end we had to give it up because we couldn't keep the grill hot enough right through a busy lunch or dinner that could last as long as four hours. Although the grill was about a square metre in size, even building up one side with fresh charcoal as the other side died down didn't give us enough heat. Now we have an excellent gas charcoal grill. To get over the lack of charcoal flavour, we throw dried herbs and charcoal dust over the lava coals.

I'm sure most people are familiar with barbecue cookery. There's nothing much I can add except to say don't be mean with the charcoal. I remember when I was in Australia lighting my first outdoor barbecue using wood, the girl that was with us said 'You call that a fire? – this is a fire,' and produced enough wood for Guy Fawkes night. Mine wouldn't have cooked a single prawn. You must build up a really good fire then let it die down. When barbecuing you cook on the residual heat to achieve the best results because the great enemy of good barbecue cooking is flame. What you really need is very hot ash because then, providing that the barbecue is very hot (and therefore the barbecue bars are very hot) and the fish, even fillets, are well oiled, they shouldn't stick. We have found that the best way to prevent a whole Dover sole from sticking is first to brush oil all over the sole and then sprinkle it liberally with sea salt and put it straight on oiled grill bars. A lot of cookery books suggest that you shouldn't season anything before you put it on a charcoal grill because you won't get a crisp char-grilled surface. This is total rubbish; it works perfectly and anything cooked on a grill should be pre-seasoned.

POACHING

SHALLOW POACHING

Shallow poaching is the method used when fillets of fish, or perhaps whole flat fish, are laid in a shallow butter dish, perhaps on some chopped shallots or other finely chopped vegetables such as leek, fennel or celery. A little water and dry white wine is poured over the fish, it is covered with a butter paper and poached in the oven or gently on top of the cooker until it has barely turned white. To finish the dish, the fillets are removed, the cooking liquid is reduced and a little butter

or cream is added with whatever flavouring ingredients the dish calls for.

POACHING IN A COURT-BOUILLON OR NAGE

Court-bouillon is the word used for a flavoured cooking liquor in which fish such as skate wings or salmon are poached. *Nage* is the word for a rather more strongly-flavoured liquid used for poaching shellfish, in particular freshwater crayfish which are notably lacking in flavour, at least when compared with their marine equivalent langoustine. I find that the flavour of a *court-bouillon* or *nage* tends to improve after 24 hours or so of being left in the fridge with all the aromatic vegetables and herbs that went into making them. If the fish or shellfish to be poached is of the best quality I tend to favour either plain water with salt or the very simplest *court-bouillon* maybe with a couple of slices of lemon, a bit of salt and some peppercorns. Generally, the lesser the flavour of the ingredient to be poached, the more flavour one should put into the *court-bouillon*.

ROASTING

Thick fillets of fish, thick *tronçons* or whole fish like bass can be successfully roasted in the oven at a high temperature, even as high as 230°C/450°F/Gas 8. The object in subjecting the fish to such a fierce heat is to crisp the skin on the outside while cooking the inside as quickly as possible. It works very well and in terms of the appeal of dishes on the menu there is something rather special in an old English cookery sort of way about the idea of roasting fish. It has a sort of echoes of Elizabethan banquets.

Menu writing is a tricky business. The object is and always must be first to tell the customer what he can expect to eat, this might seem fairly obvious but it is not so at all. So many menus promise one thing and deliver something totally different but the second and equally important object of menu writing is to stimulate the customer's appetite. Words like roasting, baking and grilling are stimulating, words like boiling and steaming are not so attractive. If you're going to use boiling or steaming in a menu you need to be careful that you explain how the dish is assembled.

STEAMING

Steaming is a brilliant way of cooking fish. The heat never gets much above boiling point so that, as with poaching and boiling, the cooking is a comparatively leisurely affair compared with, say, roasting or deep-frying. In addition, because the fish is constantly bathed in moisture, it tends to come out moist and delicate.

In a busy kitchen it is a godsend, partly because of the need to get the cooking just right in fish cookery, which steaming allows, and partly because steaming is relatively slow so you're given a little bit more time to do other things before you start to run the risk that the dish will spoil. If I am tasting a new species of fish for the first time, I always steam it first because that is the best way of getting the true flavour of fish without being diverted by any additional flavours added through the cooking. The great experts of steam cookery are the Chinese – a visit to a Chinese kitchen is like entering a steam bath. The recipe for *Steamed Scallops with Ginger, Soy, Sesame and Spring Onions* on p. 212 is one of my favourites and taken straight from a Chinese restaurant.

STEAMING IN A PRESSURE COOKER

Cooking in a pressure steamer is faster because when the pressure is increased in a closed, sealed vessel, the boiling temperature of water is also increased and therefore, the water being hotter than boiling point, the food is cooked much more rapidly. As a matter of fact, if you're steaming or boiling food it cooks faster at sea level than it does at the top of a mountain, simply because at the top of a mountain water boils at a lower temperature. Since fish cooks so quickly anyway, there is not a lot of point in using a pressure cooker. Its great advantage is in drastically reducing the cooking times of long-simmering dishes like stews of tough cuts of meat. The only serious application for seafood would be for the tenderizing of octopus (see p. 204).

MICROWAVE COOKERY

I'm not an expert on microwave cookery because I don't use them in the restaurant. This is not because I have anything against microwaves, it is simply that they're actually too slow when it comes to commercial cookery. This seems a bit paradoxical but the advantage of a microwave is more in the speed of re-heating food rather than cooking it. In terms of cookery, good grills, stoves and steamers can do the job better and for larger quantities than microwaves.

But, for re-heating food a microwave is invaluable and some of the dishes in this book like the *Hot Shellfish with Garlic and Lemon Juice* on p. 205 require previously cooked food to be re-heated. In this case a microwave is the best piece of equipment. You can also cook fish in a microwave and, as long as you are aware that cooking continues after the microwave has stopped and you make the necessary adjustments for this, you can get very good results. Microwaves are also invaluable when it comes to defrosting prawns which you've forgotten to do earlier.

SPECIAL EQUIPMENT FOR COOKING FISH

The longer I remain a cook the less enthusiastic I am about gadgets. There was a time when whenever some new electrical whizzer or hand-operated shredder came on the market I was keen to buy it but, probably owing to the relentless grinding down of any equipment other than the most basic knives, spoons and fish slices by chefs in too much of a hurry, I now tend to think that most jobs are better done by hand. A skilled chef can do more or less all the work done by a machine in about the same time; there are notable exceptions, in particular the food processor. Thank goodness the days of making fish mousselines with a mincer and drum sieve have gone!

There are, however, some pieces of equipment you may not have in your kitchen which are particularly useful in fish cookery.

First is a **fish filleting knife**. Even if you buy all your fish filleted from the fishmonger there will still be occasions when you want to, say, remove some skin or slide a thin-bladed knife between the two shells of a scallop. I think it is an essential part of any kitchen.

Next, I would suggest that anybody who is serious about fish cookery purchase a **fish kettle**. They look rather decorative in a kitchen, apart from anything else, and most people are bound to poach salmon or a large sea trout from time to time. They also double up as a steamer if you raise the perforated plate on stands such as two egg cups, and bring a couple of inches or so of water in the bottom to the boil. If you don't want to go to the expense of a fish kettle, a fish up to 1.5 kg ($3\frac{1}{2}$ lb) will normally fit into a large oval casserole dish if you bend it. Or, you could remove the head and tail and fit it into your largest pan.

If you are going to cook a lot of whole fish, a **fish scaler** is also a wise investment as is a **wok**, which is a pretty standard general-purpose pan used not just for Chinese cookery these days.

I would earnestly suggest that you buy a **conical strainer** and a **ladle** for passing soups and stocks through, and a length of **muslin** through which you can pass sauces.

Perhaps the most valued piece of equipment I have in my kitchen at home is a **mortar and pestle**. If you want to grind or purée large quantities of anything then a food processor or liquidizer is fine, but there are many times when you only want to make up a little fresh spice or a spoonful or two of *salsa verde*, grind a few peppercorns for *steak au poivre* or make up some *aïoli*. On these occasions, a liquidizer or food processor is too big. You can buy small mini versions of food processors for doing small quantities but I've had about four and each one has soon broken. I bought my mortar and pestle in a Thai food shop in London and it's made out of granite. You could drop it from a great height and it wouldn't split, it never breaks down and it's dead easy to clean.

There are also a few other small items that would be worth buying too. If you don't have a **steamer**, there's a very simple petal-shaped perforated one which you can get at any ironmonger's. It expands to fit the pan you put it in.

A **second pepper grinder for white peppercorns** is also a good idea. I use white peppercorns or *mignonette* pepper (meaning dainty) a great deal in fish cookery.

If you haven't got **a large cook's knife** with a, say, 25 cm (10 in) blade, it's a good investment for cutting lobsters and crayfish in half.

A good pair of **kitchen scissors** for cutting off fins and a small pair of **long-nosed pliers** or **tweezers** for extracting bones from fillets of fish will make life infinitely easier as will some **lobster picks** and some **winkle pickers**. Curiously I've never seen the latter on sale in England but hat pins would probably do the trick.

A **mandolin** would also be a wise investment. There is a Japanese mandolin sold by Continental Chef Supplies, Unit 11, Hetton Industrial Estate, County Durham, DH6 2UE. It is made of plastic and is unbelievably sharp. Not only can you slice potatoes wafer thin but it also makes the thinnest of *julienne* vegetables.

A **pasta machine** is a wonderful invention and lastly a **cast-iron ribbed grill pan** for all the char-grilled dishes that I love. You can now buy a large double-sized grill pan to fit over two rings or burners so that you can do some serious char-grilling.

Basic Recipes: Stocks, Sauces, Flavoured Butters and Dressings

Stocks and Other Basic Preparations

You can make good fish stock out of any fish bones except oily ones. At the restaurant two stocks are made, first class and second class. First class is made out of any of the cod family and all flat fish and the second-class stock is made from anything else. The first-class stock is used for all sauces and the second-class for fish soup.

You can store stock in a covered container in the fridge for up to four days. You can keep it indefinitely if you re-boil it every four days or so. Otherwise, store it in small quantities in the freezer.

Fish Stock

MAKES 1.2 LITRES (2 PINTS)

Although a precise recipe for fish stock is given here, the quantities are actually not very important. By cooking the stock twice, more flavour can be extracted from the fish bones and vegetables. I have not included salt in the recipe because normally the stock will be greatly reduced and so could become too salty. The seasoning should therefore be added after the stock has been reduced.

1.5 kg (3 lb) fish bones, including heads
1.75 litres (3 pints) water
A handful of fresh white button mushrooms, sliced
1 large onion, chopped
1 large leek, chopped
1 large carrot, chopped
1 celery stick, including the leafy top, sliced

Place the fish bones in the water and bring to the boil. Simmer for 20 minutes, then pass through a strainer lined with muslin.

Return the stock to the pan and add the vegetables. Bring to the boil and simmer again for 45 minutes. Strain again, then use or store (see above).

SHELLFISH STOCK AND SHELLFISH REDUCTION

MAKES 900 ML (1½ PINTS) OF
SHELLFISH STOCK AND 150 ML
(5 FL OZ) OF SHELLFISH REDUCTION

50 g (2 oz) carrot, chopped
50 g (2 oz) onion, chopped
50 g (2 oz) celery, chopped
15 g (½ oz) unsalted butter
350 g (12 oz) whole North Atlantic prawns,
    small crabs or shrimps
1 tablespoon cognac
25 ml (1 fl oz) white wine
1 teaspoon chopped fresh tarragon
75 g (3 oz) tomato, roughly chopped
1.2 litres (2 pints) *Fish Stock* (see p. 36)
A pinch of cayenne pepper

A lot of shellfish removed from its shell is sold in the restaurant so we use the shells for making a basic stock which is used to flavour sauces, soups, terrines and mousses.

You can make this stock by using whole unpeeled North Atlantic Prawns or shrimps in their shells, preferably raw ones. The little shore crabs which you find all round great Britain also make excellent shellfish stock.

To make the shellfish stock, fry the carrot, onion and celery in the butter for 2–3 minutes. Add the prawns and the cognac and fry for another couple of minutes. Add the remaining ingredients and simmer for 40 minutes. Pass the stock through a strainer and muslin. To store see p. 36.

To make the shellfish reduction, liquidize the stock before it is strained. Then pass first through a conical strainer then through a fine-meshed sieve. Return the strained liquid to the heat, bring to the boil and reduce the volume down to about 150 ml (5 fl oz). Store as for the shellfish stock.

CHICKEN STOCK

I read a sad but amusing article about Agas and the dreams of ideal country living that such comforting cookers induce. The subject was that of making stocks using the cooler of the two Aga hot plates.

The stock in the writer's house was made from the left-over bones from roast chicken out of a sense of thrift. But it was destined to go sour and be thrown away. The fate of the stock was actually inevitable but never admitted. I thought this a poignant statement on the way we live today. The chicken stocks that you need for fish cookery are not to be made from the remains of roasts, you need fresh chicken trimmings or winglets (which you can now buy in supermarkets). You will find that if you prepare beautiful clear stock from fresh raw ingredients rather than old roast bones, you will end up with something you really want to look after. Making stock is easy, relatively cheap and only needs to be done periodically. I find it one of the most satisfying jobs in the kitchen. The quantities in this recipe are for the carcass, wing tips and other trimmings of one medium-sized chicken obtained after having removed the meat for use in another recipe.

MAKES ABOUT 1.75 LITRES (3 PINTS)

Bones of a 1.5 kg (3–3½ lb) chicken or 450 g
  (1 lb) chicken winglets
25 ml (1 fl oz) vegetable oil
1 large carrot, chopped
2 celery sticks, sliced
2 leeks, sliced
2 fresh or dried bay leaves
2 sprigs thyme
2.25 litres (4 pints) water

Put all the ingredients in a large pan and simmer very gently for a couple of hours. Make sure you do simmer everything gently as boiling stock will force the fat from even the leanest chicken into an emulsion with the water making it cloudy.

Pass the contents of the pan through a strainer lined with muslin. Set aside and leave to go cold, then chill. Remove the film of fat from the surface. For storing see p. 36.

COURT-BOUILLON

This is a general purpose poaching liquid for skate, salmon and any occasion when you want to cook fish with plenty of flavour. After poaching the fish, you can use the *bouillon* and vegetables as part of the stock for fish soup. You can also strain it for use as an unreduced fish stock.

MAKES 1.2 LITRES (2 PINTS)

300 ml (10 fl oz) dry cider
1.2 litres (2 pints) water
85 ml (3 fl oz) white wine vinegar
2 fresh or dried bay leaves
12 peppercorns
1 onion, roughly chopped
2 carrots, roughly chopped
2 celery sticks, roughly chopped
1 teaspoon salt

Place all the ingredients in a large pan and bring to the boil. Simmer for 30 minutes. To complete the infusion of flavours, leave to cool before using. For storing see p. 36.

A COURT-BOUILLON FOR POACHING SMOKED FISH

MAKES 900 ML (1½ PINTS)

300 ml (10 fl oz) milk
600 ml (1 pint) water
1 medium onion, thinly sliced
2 fresh or dried bay leaves
6 peppercorns
½ lemon, sliced

Place all the ingredients in a pan and bring to the boil. Simmer for 10 minutes before using to poach the fish.

VEGETABLE STOCK

This is also a good general purpose vegetable stock which you can also use for poaching lobsters or langoustine. You can then reduce the *bouillon* to a beautiful sauce with a little butter whisked in at the end. We do a poached lobster dish at the restaurant like this using a small lobster poached to order. We rapidly reduce the stock in a vast shallow copper pan, beat in

some basil butter (butter pounded in a mortar with basil), a handful of peeled, seeded and chopped tomatoes and a few small vegetables (tiny carrots, fennel, spring onions, beans and mangetout) and serve the lobster out of the shell.

MAKES 1 LITRE ($1\frac{3}{4}$ PINTS)

2 carrots, sliced
1 leek, white part only, sliced
½ medium onion, sliced
1.2 litres (2 pints) water
15 g (½ oz) salt
Zest and flesh of ½ lemon
2 garlic cloves

15 white peppercorns
5 star anise heads
1 small bunch parsley stalks
1 fresh or dried bay leaf
1 sprig of fennel
1 sprig of thyme
300 ml (10 fl oz) white wine

Place all the ingredients except the wine in a large pan and bring to simmering point for 30 minutes then add the wine. Bring to the boil

for 30 seconds then cool. Leave for at least 12 hours before straining. To store see p. 36.

SAUCES

VELOUTÉ

A good *velouté* should taste neither heavy nor floury, so the flour must be thoroughly cooked by long, slow simmering.

MAKES 600 ML (1 PINT)

600 ml (1 pint) reduced *Fish Stock* (see p. 36)
300 ml (10 fl oz) milk
50 g (2 oz) unsalted butter
40 g (1½ oz) flour

Place the stock and milk in a pan and bring to the boil. Melt the butter in a heavy-based pan and add the flour. Cook for about 2 minutes, stirring constantly, without letting it colour

too much. When it starts to smell nutty, remove from the heat and cool slightly.

Gradually add the hot stock, stirring all the time, until smooth. Return to the heat when almost all the stock has been incorporated. Add the remaining stock. Turn the heat right down and simmer for 40 minutes.

Pass the sauce through a conical strainer into a bowl, cover with a butter paper to prevent a skin forming and allow to cool. Chill if not using immediately. To store, place the sauce in a covered container in the fridge. You can keep it indefinitely if you reboil it every three or four days. Flour-based sauces don't freeze well.

HOLLANDAISE SAUCE

I like my Hollandaise sauce to be well-flavoured with plenty of lemon juice and cayenne, and well-seasoned. You will need a wire whisk, a stainless steel whisking bowl and a saucepan into which it will fit.

SERVES 4

225 g (8 oz) unsalted butter
2 tablespoons water
2 egg yolks
Juice of 1 lemon
A good pinch of cayenne pepper
½ teaspoon salt

Clarify the butter by heating it gently in a pan until the solids fall to the bottom. Pour off the clear butter and reserve. Discard the butter solids.

Half fill a pan with water and bring to the boil. Reduce to a simmer and place a stainless steel bowl on top of the pan. Pour in the 2 tablespoons of water, add the egg yolks and whisk the mixture until it is voluminous and creamy.

Remove the bowl from the heat and whisk in the clarified butter a little at a time, building up an emulsion as if making mayonnaise. Add the lemon juice, the cayenne pepper and the salt.

Hollandaise is best used immediately but you can hold the sauce for anything up to 2 hours if you keep it in a warm place (about 60°C/140°F) with a lid on. If the sauce does split, it is actually very easy to reform it. Just take a new pan, warm it and add one tablespoon of hot water. Then whisk in the curdled sauce a little at a time.

PASTIS AND FENNEL HOT BUTTER SAUCE

This sauce is very good with grilled fillets of fish; it's especially good with hake.

SERVES 4

1 tablespoon chopped fennel
120 ml (4 fl oz) *Fish Stock* (see p. 36)
2 tablespoons pastis, Ricard or Pernod
1 quantity *Hollandaise Sauce* (see above)

Put all the ingredients except the *Hollandaise Sauce* and 1 teaspoon of the pastis in a small pan then boil rapidly to reduce to about 2 tablespoons. Stir the strained liquor into the Hollandaise and add the remaining teaspoon of pastis.

MALTAISE SAUCE

This sauce is good with grilled fillets of red mullet.

SERVES 4

Juice of 2 blood oranges
Grated rind of 1 orange
1 quantity *Hollandaise Sauce* (see p. 40)

Mix the juice and zest of the oranges with the *Hollandaise Sauce* and serve.

MUSSEL SAUCE

You can serve this with thick, poached fillets of cod, halibut, brill, turbot or bass. Alternatively, you can place the poached fish in a gratin dish, cover with the sauce and glaze under a hot grill. Either will be perfect if accompanied with new potatoes and spring greens thinly sliced and sweated in a little butter.

You can also make the sauce using oysters. Open the oysters gently by poaching them in their own liquor with a little white wine, some shallots and a little parsley. Then proceed as for the mussels.

SERVES 4

450 g (1 lb) small mussels
A splash of white wine
1 small shallot, finely chopped
1 teaspoon fresh parsley, finely chopped
1 quantity *Hollandaise Sauce* (see p. 40)

Place the mussels, white wine, shallot and parsley in a pan and cover tightly. Place over a high heat shaking the pan occasionally.

Remove the pan from the heat as soon as all the mussels have opened.

As soon as they are cool enough to handle, remove the mussels from their shells and pull out any beards. Stir all but the last tablespoonful of the cooking liquor (the dregs will contain some grit) into the *Hollandaise Sauce*. Add the mussel meats to the *Hollandaise*.

SEAFOOD SAUCE

Serve *Seafood Sauce* handed separately or use as a glaze for fish, as with *Mussel Sauce* (see above).

Make the *Shellfish Reduction*. Mix the reduction into the *Hollandaise Sauce*.

SERVES 4

1 quantity *Shellfish Reduction* (see p. 37)
1 quantity *Hollandaise Sauce* (see p. 40)

BEURRE BLANC

There is nothing complicated about *beurre blanc*, neither is it particularly unstable. If it does separate it is much easier to reconstitute than an egg-based sauce like Hollandaise. All you do is add a bit more water and boil it vigorously to emulsify the butter and water. You may lose some lightness in having to do this but at least the embarrassment of producing a separated and greasy sauce will have been avoided.

Use with poached and grilled fillets of fish like turbot, brill, bass, lemon sole, cod.

SERVES 4

50 g (2 oz) shallots (or onions), finely chopped
2 tablespoons white wine vinegar
4 tablespoons dry white wine
6 tablespoons water or fish stock
2 tablespoons double cream
175 g (6 oz) unsalted butter, cut into pieces

Put the shallots, vinegar, wine and water in a small pan, bring to the boil and simmer until nearly all the liquid has evaporated. Add the cream and reduce a little more, then remove the pan from the heat and whisk in the butter a little at a time until it has all amalgamated.

You can also make the sauce by reducing down and adding the cream as before then adding a couple of tablespoons of water. You then bring the sauce to a rapid boil and whisk the butter in while boiling. This method will produce a perfectly acceptable sauce but it will be a little less light than if you choose the first method. This second method is also the way to reconstitute a sauce which has got too hot and separated. At the restaurant we replace the water with well-reduced fish stock which gives the sauce a roundness but it still tastes good made with water.

BEURRE ROUGE

This is excellent with any grilled fillets of fish from the cod family, like cod, hake or haddock.

SERVES 4

250 g (8 oz) red onions
150 ml (5 fl oz) red wine
85 ml (3 fl oz) *Fish Stock* (see p. 36) or *Chicken Stock* (see p. 37)
85 ml (3 fl oz) red wine vinegar
¼ teaspoon sugar
A pinch of salt
100 g (4 oz) unsalted butter

Place all the ingredients, except the butter, in a pan and simmer until the onions are soft. Beat in the butter as for *Beurre Blanc* (see above).

OLIVE OIL MAYONNAISE

This is one of two recipes I have for mayonnaise. This one is of the utmost simplicity and uses best extra virgin olive oil, while the second uses groundnut or sunflower oil and is strongly flavoured with mustard. You will find that using extra virgin olive oil for this mayonnaise produces a waxy, slightly green finish which tastes bitter. Too strong you may think but, like most sauces, mayonnaise should be a bit strong on its own. When combined with the rest of the dish, like poached salmon, or sea trout, everything falls delightfully into place.

SERVES 4

2 egg yolks
2 teaspoons white wine vinegar
½ teaspoon salt
300 ml (10 fl oz) extra virgin olive oil

Make sure all the ingredients are at room temperature before beginning. Put the egg yolks, vinegar and salt into a mixing bowl then place the bowl on a tea towel (to stop it slipping). Using a wire whisk, beat the oil into the egg mixture a little at a time until you have incorporated it all. Once you have carefully added about the same volume of oil as the original mixture of egg yolks and vinegar, you can add the oil more quickly.

The science of all cold and hot butter sauces is as follows. Oil or hot butter likes to stay in one large puddle. Beating separates it into millions of tiny droplets which reform into one large puddle as soon as you stop but if you add oil to egg yolk and whisk, the egg yolk will tend to coat each droplet of oil and prevent it from joining the rest. A little egg yolk will go a very long way with oil, provided you add a little oil at a time and beat well.

MUSTARD MAYONNAISE

This sauce goes particularly well with crab.

SERVES 4

1 tablespoon English mustard
2 egg yolks
1 tablespoon white wine vinegar
¾ teaspoon salt
Few turns of the white pepper mill
300 ml (10 fl oz) groundnut or sunflower
  oil

Make sure all the ingredients are at room temperature before beginning. Put the mustard, egg yolks, vinegar, salt and pepper into a mixing bowl then place the bowl on a tea towel (to stop it slipping). Using a wire whisk, beat the oil into the egg mixture a little at a time until you have incorporated it all. Once you have carefully added about the same volume of oil as the original mixture of egg yolks and vinegar, you can add the oil more quickly.

FENNEL MAYONNAISE

SERVES 4

Mix all the ingredients together

40 ml (1½ fl oz) Pernod
1 teaspoon chopped fresh chives
1 tablespoon chopped fresh fennel
1 quantity *Olive Oil Mayonnaise* (see p. 43)

TARTARE SAUCE

SERVES 4

1 quantity *Mustard Mayonnaise* (see p. 43)
1 teaspoon green olives, finely chopped
1 teaspoon gherkins, finely chopped
1 teaspoon capers, finely chopped
1 teaspoon chopped chives
1 teaspoon chopped fresh parsley

Mix all the ingredients together and use with deep-fried, breaded fish.

AÏOLI

SERVES 4

8 garlic cloves
1 quantity *Olive Oil Mayonnaise* (see p. 43)

Peel and crush the garlic and mix with the mayonnaise.

If you don't have a garlic crusher, mash a peeled clove of garlic with the large flat blade of a knife. Place the garlic on a firm, non-slip surface (a wooden chopping board is best), position the widest part of the knife on the garlic then hit it with the palm of your hand. Chop the flattened clove then sprinkle it with salt and mash with the knife to a purée.

SAUCE VERTE

SERVES 4

25 g (1 oz) spinach leaves
25 g (1 oz) rocket
25 g (1 oz) fresh mixed parsley, chervil, chives and tarragon, roughly chopped
1 quantity *Olive Oil Mayonnaise* (see p. 43)

Blanch the spinach and rocket leaves in boiling water for 1 minute. Refresh under cold running water and squeeze dry. Blend together in a food processor with the fresh herbs and mayonnaise. Best served with poached salmon.

ROUILLE

You can quickly make this fiery accompaniment to fish soup and bouillabaisse, if you mix mayonnaise with garlic and mashed seeded and chopped red chillies. But this version includes *harissa*, an aromatic, spicy sauce from Africa.

SERVES 4

Put all the ingredients, except the olive oil, in a food processor and blend. Then, gradually pour in the oil until it is incorporated into the egg yolks.

25 g (1 oz) dry bread soaked in fish stock
3 garlic cloves
1 egg yolk
2 tablespoons *Harissa* (see below)
¼ teaspoon salt
250 ml (8 fl oz) olive oil

HARISSA

Harissa is a chilli, red pepper, saffron and coriander sauce which comes from North Africa. It is available in small tins from good continental food shops but our own recipe has evolved over time and it is a lot more aromatic than the bought variety.

MAKES ENOUGH FOR THE ROUILLE RECIPE ABOVE

1 teaspoon tomato purée
1 teaspoon ground coriander
A pinch of saffron strands
1 red pepper, seeded, roasted and skinned
2 red chillies
¼ teaspoon salt
¼ teaspoon cayenne pepper

Place all the ingredients in a food processor or liquidizer and blend until well incorporated.

CHARMOULA

This is another hot aromatic paste from North Africa. Use it to marinate fillets and whole fish prior to grilling on a barbecue.

MAKES 175 ML (6 FL OZ)

2 tablespoons roughly chopped fresh coriander
3 garlic cloves, peeled and chopped
1½ teaspoons powdered cumin
½ red chilli, seeded and chopped
½ teaspoon saffron strands
4 tablespoons extra virgin olive oil
Juice of 1 lemon
1½ teaspoons paprika
2 teaspoons salt

Liquidize all the ingredients in a liquidizer or food processor.

SALSA VERDE

This sauce, used with the *Grilled Sea Bass with Straw Potatoes and Salsa Verde* on p. 116, is one of the most versatile sauces for fish. Its piquant herb flavour brings out the best in most fish, particularly the blander cod family. A thick fillet of poached cod with *salsa verde* is pure bliss. Also try it with skate wings or even a pile of boiled whelks or long simmered octopus.

MAKES 250 ML (8 FL OZ)

3 tablespoons roughly chopped fresh
  parsley
1 tablespoon roughly chopped fresh mint
3 tablespoons capers
6 anchovy fillets
1 garlic clove, chopped
1 teaspoon Dijon mustard
Juice of ½ lemon
120 ml (4 fl oz) extra virgin olive oil
½ teaspoon salt

Blend together all the ingredients in a food processor or a mortar and pestle to form a thick paste. (I use a mortar and pestle but I don't pound the ingredients too much as I like the sauce to have a coarse texture.)

FLAVOURED BUTTERS

These are perfect sliced into rounds and placed on grilled fish. They are also ideal for flavouring sauces and for stuffing fish fillets.

All can be easily made by simply putting the flavouring ingredients and the butter (which should be soft) into a food processor and blending until smooth. The butter can then be turned out onto a sheet of cling film or greaseproof paper, rolled into a sausage shape and chilled.

MONTPELLIER BUTTER

SERVES 4

Blanch the spinach and rocket leaves in boiling water for 1 minute, refresh in cold water then squeeze dry. Place in a food processor with the herbs, shallots, gherkins, capers, garlic, anchovies, egg yolk, hard-boiled egg yolks and softened butter. Season with salt and pepper then blend until smooth before adding the olive oil in a steady stream. Continue to blend until all the ingredients are thoroughly mixed then turn out onto cling film, roll into a sausage shape and refrigerate until firm.

25 g (1 oz) spinach leaves
25 g (1 oz) rocket
25 g (1 oz) fresh mixed parsley, chervil,
  chives and tarragon
25 g (1 oz) shallots
3 small gherkins
1 teaspoon capers
2 garlic cloves
6 anchovies
1 egg yolk
2 hard-boiled egg yolks
100 g (4 oz) butter, softened
½ teaspoon salt
Freshly ground black pepper
85 ml (3 fl oz) olive oil

ANCHOVY BUTTER

SERVES 8

6 anchovy fillets
1 tablespoon roughly chopped fresh parsley
Juice of ¼ lemon
175 g (6 oz) unsalted butter

Blend together all the ingredients then place on a piece of cling film, roll into a sausage shape and refrigerate until firm.

MUSTARD BUTTER

SERVES 4

This butter is good with grilled oily fish like herrings, mackerel and sardines.

1 tablespoon French mustard
100 g (4 oz) unsalted butter
Salt and freshly ground black pepper

Blend together all the ingredients then place on a piece of cling film, roll into a sausage shape and refrigerate until firm.

GARLIC BUTTER

SERVES 8

225 g (8 oz) unsalted butter
4 large garlic cloves
25 g (1 oz) parsley
1 teaspoon brandy
1 teaspoon lemon juice
A good pinch of salt

Blend together all the ingredients then place on a piece of cling film, roll into a sausage shape and refrigerate until firm.

PINK PEPPERCORN BUTTER

SERVES 4

Perfect served with grilled small dabs.

2 teaspoons chopped pink peppercorns
75 g (3 oz) unsalted butter
Freshly ground black pepper
½ teaspoon salt
1 teaspoon brandy

Blend together all the ingredients then place on a piece of cling film, roll into a sausage shape and refrigerate until firm.

GARLIC AND ROASTED HAZELNUT BUTTER

SERVES 8

75 g (3 oz) hazelnuts
1 quantity *Garlic Butter* (see above)

Turn on your grill. Roast the hazelnuts under the grill turning them to ensure even colouring. When the skins are dark brown tip them on to one half of a tea towel, fold over the other half and roll off the skins. Open out the tea towel and roll the nuts to one side leaving the skins behind.

Mix all the ingredients in a food processor, place on a piece of cling film, roll into a sausage shape and refrigerate until firm.

CORIANDER AND HAZELNUT BUTTER

This is excellent as a stuffing for mussels.

SERVES 4

Blend together all the ingredients then place on a piece of cling film, roll into a sausage and refrigerate until firm.

75 g (3 oz) roasted hazelnuts (see *Garlic and Roasted Hazelnut Butter*, p. 49)
225 g (8 oz) unsalted butter
25 g (1 oz) fresh coriander
15 g (½ oz) fresh parsley
25 g (1 oz) shallot
Juice of ½ lemon
Freshly ground black pepper

PRAWN BUTTER

SERVES 4

75 g (3 oz) prawns, unshelled
100 g (4 oz) unsalted butter
1 teaspoon lemon juice
A pinch of cayenne pepper

Mix together all the ingredients in a blender or food processor. Pass the butter through a sieve, pushing it with the back of a ladle or wooden spoon. Place on a piece of cling film, roll into a sausage shape and refrigerate until firm.

NOISETTE BUTTER

Once you're familiar with the taste of *Noisette Butter* (and you need to make it as per these instructions at least once) all you need do is heat the butter to taste and throw it straight over the fish.

120 g (4½ oz) butter

Melt the butter in a small pan. Pour cold water into a bowl which is large enough to take the base of the butter pan. Keep it ready nearby.

Heat the butter until it turns a golden brown and starts to smell nutty. Remove from the heat and immerse the base of the pan in the cold water to prevent any further cooking.

DRESSINGS FOR SALADS AND CONDIMENTS

A dressing is not a compot,
A dressing is not a custard;
It consists of pepper and salt,
Vinegar, oil, and mustard

Ogden Nash

There could, to my mind, be no more urgent a call to chefs to keep it simple than in the matter of dressings. Ogden Nash's title to the above verse is *The Chef has Imagination or It's Too Hard to Do it Easy*. No dressing tastes better in a salad than one made with good olive oil, good vinegar and, for me, just a little salt.

LEMON OLIVE OIL

You can buy a brand of extra virgin olive oil with natural essence of lemons which is superb for salads. I use it in many of my recipes as a dressing for salad leaves. With a little of this and only a faint sprinkling of salt and perhaps a little *Preserved Lemon* (see p. 52), you can make a perfect, and very simple dressing. You can also make your own, as follows, but use the best olive oil you can find.

| I lemon
| 600 ml (1 pint) extra virgin olive oil

Carefully pare the rind from the lemon with a potato peeler. Slice the rind into thin strips then add to the olive oil. Leave to infuse for 12 hours.

OLIVE OIL DRESSING

If I use vinegar in a dressing, I use the tiniest amount and I only make the dressing just before tossing the salad. Once the two are combined, the vinegar begins to knock out the fragrance of the olive oil. This is why in Italy they bring oil and vinegar to your table in separate containers. If you make the dressing there and then, you get perfection; if you make it some time before, the flavour of the oil fades. Only use the best olive oil you can find.

| 85 ml (3 fl oz) extra virgin olive oil
| ½ tablespoon white wine vinegar
| ½ teaspoon salt

Combine the ingredients and toss into the salad just before serving.

MUSTARD DRESSING

This dressing is a much more rugged affair than *Olive Oil Dressing* and goes very well with bitter leaves like chicory, dandelions and radicchio. It can also be made some time in advance of being used. Add some chopped chives for an extra dimension to the flavour.

| 85 ml (3 fl oz) groundnut or sunflower oil
| I tablespoon white wine vinegar
| ½ teaspoon salt
| ½ small shallot, finely chopped
| ½ small garlic clove, finely chopped
| I teaspoon English mustard

Combine all the ingredients by shaking in a screw-top jar. Serve as required.

PRESERVED LEMONS

This is a way of keeping lemons which makes them more of a condiment than a citrus fruit. Preserved lemons are much used in Moroccan cuisine.

10 lemons
1.2 litres (2 pints) water
275 g (10 oz) salt

Cut the lemons almost in quarters, leaving them joined at one end. Sprinkle a little salt into the centre of each then arrange them, tightly packed, in a plastic or glass container. Bring the water and the rest of the salt to the boil in a large pan. Boil until the salt has dissolved then remove from the heat and leave to cool. Pour the brine over the lemons, weigh them down with some sort of non-metallic weight and leave for 3–4 weeks. Use as required. They will keep indefinitely. Finely chop the flesh and skins and add to salads or dressings.

BATTERS FOR DEEP-FRYING

YEAST AND BEER BATTER

I don't think there is a nicer batter than *Yeast and Beer Batter*. It is a perfect combination of lightness, crispness and flavour and in my opinion the only batter for fish and chips. In addition to producing carbon dioxide which makes the batter light, yeast also matures the dough and gives the batter a flavour of hops and bread. The only drawback is that it needs to be made some time in advance.

MAKES ENOUGH FOR 4 SERVINGS

15 g (½ oz) fresh yeast
300 ml (10 fl oz) beer, or Guinness for a
   deep brown batter
225 g (8 oz) flour
1 teaspoon salt

Dissolve the yeast with a little of the beer. When they have been mixed to a paste gradually add the rest of the beer, stirring continuously.

Sieve the flour and salt into a bowl and make a well in the centre. Pour in the beer and dissolved yeast and whisk into a batter. Leave covered for 1 hour before using at room temperature.

TEMPURA BATTER

This is a very light, thin batter which barely coats the food. The secret of making good tempura batter is to leave mixing it to the very last minute and to have the batter ingredients really cold.

MAKES ENOUGH FOR 4 SERVINGS

200 ml (7 fl oz) water
1 egg
100 g (4 oz) flour
50 g (2 oz) cornflour
½ teaspoon salt

Chill the water and egg then whisk together the ingredients just before dipping the food. The batter should be only just amalgamated.

MISCELLANEOUS RECIPES

KACHUMBER SALAD

This is a great Indian salad that goes well with spicy fish dishes like the *Mackerel Recheado* (p. 91), *Tandooried Monkfish with Tomato and Coriander Salad* (p. 137) or the *Grilled Sea Bass with Straw Potatoes and Salsa Verde* (p. 116)

3 tomatoes, halved and thinly sliced
1 medium onion, halved and thinly sliced
2 tablespoons fresh coriander, roughly chopped
¼ teaspoon cumin powder
⅛ teaspoon cayenne
1 tablespoon white wine vinegar
½ teaspoon salt

Mix together all the ingredients.

SHALLOT VINEGAR

This is perfect with oysters and essential with raw mussels.

85 ml (3 fl oz) Red wine
85 ml (3 fl oz) Red wine vinegar
1 shallot, finely chopped

Mix together all the ingredients.

SALT COD

Put a fillet of cod in a plastic bowl or ice-cream container and completely cover with a thick layer of salt. Refrigerate for 24 hours.

After a day, most of the salt will have turned to brine with the water it has drawn out of the cod. The fish will be sufficiently preserved now to keep for up to a week.

To prepare the salt cod for cooking, simply soak it in plenty of cold water for an hour or two if only lightly salted, or up to 24 hours if it is very dried out.

BRANDADE

SERVES 4

100 g (4 oz) Salt Cod, soaked (see p. 53)
120 ml (4 fl oz) olive oil
120 ml (4 fl oz) double cream
4 garlic cloves

Poach the cod in a little water for about 10 minutes then drain and remove skin and bones.

Bring the olive oil and cream to the boil in a pan. Put the cod fillet and the garlic in a blender or food processor and turn on. Gradually pour in the hot oil and cream to build up a thick emulsion.

Serve with plenty of French bread.

QUATRE ÉPICES

¾ teaspoon freshly ground black pepper
1 teaspoon nutmeg
¾ teaspoon ground ginger
¼ teaspoon allspice

Mix together all the spices and store in a screw-top jar out of the way of direct sunlight.

EGG PASTA DOUGH

SERVES 4

100 g (4 oz) plain flour
A large pinch of salt
¼ teaspoon olive oil
1 egg
2 egg yolks

Mix together all the ingredients and knead until smooth. Roll the pasta to the thickness you want, then leave to rest for 10–15 minutes before cutting.

SOUPS, STEWS, PIES AND SEVERAL MIXED SEAFOOD RECIPES

I judge the quality of a fish restaurant by its soup and, to my mind, nothing indicates the talent of a cook better than his ability to make a fish soup.

When I started my restaurant 20 years ago, I didn't actually know much about cooking (not a great handicap to running a restaurant in those days!), but over the next ten years or so, I attended a large number of day-release courses at the local technical college which taught me a great deal about cooking; the rest I learnt through cooking, making mistakes, reading books and going to lots of restaurants. At the college, it was my extreme good fortune to be taught by a chef who had spent many years cooking for a famous fish restaurant in London, Madame Prunier. He was an inspiring teacher who was probably more influential in turning me into a proper chef than anyone else.

One day, the whole class was given exactly the same ingredients and told to make a fish soup. At the end of it, we all tried each other's. None of them were the same. Mine wasn't bad, but the best was cooked by a Chinese girl and, extraordinarily, it tasted oriental. It had a depth that none of the other soups had. She knew about concentrating flavours. The basis of fish soup is a concentrated flavour; it must be deep and powerful. More fish and vegetables than you might think are necessary to achieve that vital fullness of flavour.

Fish soups, shellfish *bisques* and fish stews are among the most well-loved of seafood dishes so nothing makes me happier than when a delighted customer remarks on the heady aroma of warm fish, peppers, tomatoes, garlic and saffron that seems to permeate the restaurant because this is the scent of our popular fish soup and *bouillabaisse*. Of all the dishes that we cook at the restaurant, this soup is the one that must never be allowed to grow tired, even though it is cooked every day, year in and year out. The recipes in this chapter include a *Bouillabaisse* (see p. 60), which uses lots of whole fish and is simple to make. It has been designed to be eaten with great gusto by people who don't mind a few bones. There are also recipes for *Cotriade* (see p. 65) and *Bourride* (see p. 64), where the fish is filleted.

To me both approaches to fish stew are equally valid. Sometimes I prefer the easy preparation and the simple cooking to produce stews that would be little different to those cooked by the fishermen who first invented the dish, and other times, I like to take the essence of the dish and enhance it to make a sophisticated dish. I think everyone has the same approach to fish, sometimes you want bone-free fillets with reduced, aromatic sauces and other times you want to pile into a great plate of *Fruits de Mer* (see pp. 197–201) using your fingers and throwing shells all over the place.

There is also in this chapter a fish pie (see p. 72), a seafood thermidor (see p. 76) which is just a rather up-market fish pie, and a fish pasty (see p. 77) dish that we sell in our delicatessen.

I have also included some mixed seafood dishes like risotto (see pp. 68–9), seafood salad (see p. 68) and a tremendous dish of mixed seafood deep-fried in tempura batter (see p. 73).

FISH SOUP WITH CROÛTONS

This French soup is Mediterranean in origin but you can find the same sort of *soupe de poissons* in virtually any French coastal restaurant. I love fish soup. I think it is one of those dishes, like roast beef and Yorkshire pudding, or *aïoli Provençal* or Chinese crispy duck, which are so deeply satisfying that they have a special place in everyone's heart. Produce indifferent roast

SERVES 6–8

1.75 kg (4 lb) fish
225 g (8 oz) prawns in the shell
2.25 litres (4 pints) water
150 ml (5 fl oz) olive oil
175 g (6 oz) onion, roughly chopped
175 g (6 oz) celery, roughly chopped
175 g (6 oz) leek, roughly chopped
175 g (6 oz) Florence fennel, roughly chopped
5 garlic cloves, sliced
Juice of 1 orange plus 5 cm (2 in) piece peel
400 g (14 oz) tin of tomatoes
1 red pepper, sliced
1 fresh or dried bay leaf
1 sprig of thyme
¼ teaspoon saffron
A large pinch of cayenne pepper
Salt and freshly ground black pepper

FOR THE CROÛTONS

1 baguette
Olive oil
2 garlic cloves, peeled
50 g (2 oz) freshly grated Parmesan
2 tablespoons *Rouille* (see p. 45)

beef or fish soup at your peril, you will not be forgiven.

The best fish for this soup are conger eel, skate, cod, dogfish, shark but virtually any other fish is suitable except the oily ones, like mackerel and herring. You can also use prawns and other shellfish scraps, like lobster, crab, langoustine and shrimps or mussels.

Fillet all the fish (see instructions in Chapter 2) and use the heads and bones to make a fish stock with the 2.25 litres (4 pints) of water.

Heat the olive oil in a large pan and add the onion, celery, leek, fennel and garlic. Cook gently for about 20 minutes without colouring until the vegetables are very soft. Add the orange peel, tomatoes, red pepper, bay leaf, thyme, saffron, prawns and fish fillets. Cook briskly, stirring, then add the stock and orange juice. Bring to the boil and simmer for 40 minutes.

Liquidize the soup in a liquidizer or food processor, then pass it through a conical strainer, pushing it through with the back of a ladle to extract all the juices. Return to the heat and season with salt, pepper and cayenne. The soup should be a little on the salty side, with a subtle but noticeable hint of cayenne.

To make the croûtons, thinly slice the baguette then fry in olive oil. When cool enough to handle, rub the croûtons with garlic. Serve the soup, Parmesan and *rouille* separately. The idea is that each person spreads some rouille onto the croûtons, floats them in the soup and sprinkles them with Parmesan.

SHORE-CRAB BISQUE

The little green crabs you find on the beach are almost as good as lobsters for making *bisque*. *Bisques* are soups made with both the shells and meat of shellfish. If you can't get hold of shore crabs, you can use any other cooked shellfish, including brown crabs, prawns, langoustines, shrimps and, of course, lobsters, either on their own or together.

SERVES 4

900 g (2 lb) shore crabs or other shellfish
50 g (2 oz) butter
50 g (2 oz) onion, chopped
50 g (2 oz) carrot, chopped
50 g (2 oz) celery, chopped
1 fresh or dried bay leaf
2 tablespoons cognac
4 tomatoes
1 teaspoon tomato purée
85 ml (3 fl oz) dry white wine
1 good-sized sprig of fresh tarragon
1.75 litres (3 pints) *Fish Stock* (see p. 36)
50 ml (2 fl oz) double cream
A pinch of cayenne pepper
Juice of ¼ lemon
Salt and freshly ground black pepper

Bring a large pan of well-salted water to the boil, drop in the crabs then bring back to the boil and cook for 2 minutes. Strain and let the crabs cool a little, then chop with a large knife.

Melt the butter in a heavy-based pan and add the chopped onion, carrot, celery and the bay leaf. Cook without browning. Stir once or twice then add the crab. Stir, then add the cognac. Allow to boil off then add the tomatoes, tomato purée, wine, tarragon and stock. Bring to the boil and simmer for 30 minutes.

Remove the tough claw shells from the soup before liquidizing in a liquidizer or food processor in two or three batches. Process in short bursts until the shell is broken into small pieces about the size of your finger nail. Avoid producing puréed shell, the aim is to extract all possible flavour from any meat left sticking to the shell, particularly in the body section, rather than to extract flavour from the shell itself. Strain the soup through a conical strainer pushing as much liquid through as you can with the back of a ladle to extract all the juices. Then, pass the soup through a fine strainer before returning to the heat. Bring to the boil, add the cream then season with cayenne pepper, lemon juice, salt and black pepper. Reduce the volume by simmering if you think the flavour needs concentrating.

MUSSEL, LEEK AND SAFFRON SOUP

This is one of three or four recipes I have included from my first fish cookery book *English Seafood Cookery*, published by Penguin, and which are what I would call classic dishes. This soup is quite special; mussels with leeks and saffron seem to combine so well.

SERVES 4

1.5 kg (3 lb) or 1.75 litres (3 pints) mussels
50 ml (2 fl oz) white wine
450 g (1 lb) leeks plus 5 cm (2 inch) piece
   of leek cut into matchsticks to serve
1 small onion
75 g (3 oz) unsalted butter
20 g (¾ oz) plain flour
450 ml (15 fl oz) *Fish Stock* (see p. 36)
A good pinch of saffron
50 ml (2 fl oz) double cream

Wash the mussels thoroughly, scraping off any barnacles, pulling out the beards and discarding any that are open and don't close when given a good tap. Place in a large pan and add a dash of wine. Cover tightly and cook over a high heat for about 5 minutes, shaking the pan frequently, until the mussels have opened.

Strain the liquor through a colander into a bowl, shaking the colander well to drain off all the juices lodged in the shells. Pull any remaining beards from the mussels and remove the meat from all but 12 of the shells.

Chop 450 g (1 lb) leeks and the onion. Melt the butter in a pan and add the vegetables.

Cook on a low heat in the butter for about 3 minutes.

Stir in the flour until smooth. Gradually add the mussel liquor, remaining wine and fish stock to the pan, stirring thoroughly until smooth. Bring to simmering point then add a good pinch of saffron and continue to cook for 25 minutes.

Blanch the matchstick leeks in a little salted water. Remove the mussel meats from all but 12 of the shells and set aside. Process the soup in a liquidizer or food processor and then strain through a sieve into a clean pan. Stir in the cream and re-heat. Just before serving add the mussel meats, the 12 mussels in their shells and the leek cut into matchsticks.

PANACHE OF JOHN DORY, TURBOT AND RED MULLET WITH YOUNG SUMMER VEGETABLES

I ate this recently at an excellent fish restaurant in Brittany. It is a typically French combination – extremely fresh seafood with plenty of crème fraîche and wine made into a rich fragrant sauce. Many English chefs, being much more eclectic in their search for ideas than the French, have tended to steer away from these simple but enormously popular creamy seafood dishes but I love them. They are what holidays in Brittany are all about – those and the heavenly platters of *Fruits de Mer* (see p. 197).

SERVES 4

25 g (1 oz) fresh broad beans
25 g (1 oz) fresh peas
1 small leek
25 g (2 oz) tender cabbage
4 very small new season's carrots
4 very small swedes
225 g (8 oz) John Dory fillet
225 g (8 oz) turbot fillet
15 ml (½ fl oz) olive oil

225 g (8 oz) red mullet fillet
Salt and pepper
85 ml (3 fl oz) white vermouth
175 ml (6 fl oz) *Fish Stock* (see p. 36)
175 ml (6 fl oz) crème fraîche or double
   cream
Sprigs of fresh parsley

Boil all the vegetables in well-salted water till just tender. Drain and refresh in cold water. This can be done some time before making the dish. You will need to construct some sort of steamer for this dish (see pp. 35 and 205 for some suggestions).

Cut the fillets of fish into 4 equal portions. Season with salt. Place the John Dory and turbot in the steamer and steam for about 6 minutes. Remove the fish from the steamer and keep warm. Put the vegetables in the steamer to warm through for a couple of minutes. While you are steaming the fish, take a frying pan, add the olive oil and season the red mullet with salt and pepper and fry for 4 minutes, skin-side down. Remove and keep warm with the other fish. Add the vermouth to the frying pan and boil off for 1 minute. Then add the fish stock and the crème fraîche and reduce to a sauce which will coat the back of a spoon. Lay the fish on 4 warm plates all together on one side of the plate and a pile of vegetables on the other. Pour the sauce over the fish, decorate with the sprigs of parsley and serve.

CLAM CHOWDER WITH COD

A simple, and perfect, creamy soup. Any clams will do and if you can't get fresh clams in their shells, frozen clam meats are acceptable. When we can get them, we use razorshell clams, so called because they look like old cut-throat razors. They have a beautiful sweet flavour.

You can make salt pork by simply sprinkling 15 g (½ oz) salt over a 50 g (2 oz) slice of pork loin 30 minutes before using. Because you need the starch to thicken the liquid, don't wash the potatoes after they are cut.

SERVES 4

16 large or 32 small clams
25 g (1 oz) butter
50 g (2 oz) salt pork or thickly sliced green
    bacon, cut into small dice
100 g (4 oz) onions, diced
225 g (8 oz) potatoes, diced but not washed
300 ml (10 fl oz) milk
120 ml (4 fl oz) cream
1 fresh bay leaf, cut into fine shreds, or 1
    dried bay leaf, crushed
Cooking liquor from the clams
100 g (4 oz) cod fillet, skinned and cut into
    1 cm (½ in) pieces
Salt and freshly ground white pepper
1 tablespoon chopped fresh parsley
2 water biscuits, chopped into little pieces

Wash and scrub the clams then place them in a large pan with a splash of water. Cover tightly and cook over a high heat. As soon as the clams open, take the pan off the heat and drain them in a colander, saving the cooking liquor in a bowl. When cool enough to handle, remove the clams from their shells and cut the meat into 1 cm (½ in) pieces.

Melt the butter in a pan then fry the diced pork or bacon until it starts to brown. Add the onions and fry until softened.

Place the potatoes in a large pan with the milk, cream and bay leaf. Bring to the boil then reduce to a slow simmer until just cooked but still firm. Add the pork, onions and clam cooking liquor and simmer for a further 5 minutes then add the cod fillet. Simmer until the cod is cooked, then add the clams. Warm through then season with salt (if necessary) and white pepper.

Pour the chowder into a serving tureen then garnish with the chopped parsley and crushed water biscuits.

BOUILLABAISSE

Fish stews, like *bouillabaisse*, are wonderful for big parties where everyone can sit around a large, deep tureen filled with all kinds of fish, adding lots of *rouille* to their bowls and mopping up the rich aromatic *bouillon* juices with crusty bread.

Any of the following fish may be used in the *Bouillabaisse*: wrasse, dogfish, black bream, red bream, monkfish, cod or hake, weever, trigger fish, gurnard, red mullet, bass, John Dory, bream, skate, conger eel, grey mullet. The more variety there is the better. Use either small fish or slices of bigger fish.

For the shellfish, choose between: lobster, crayfish, langoustine or prawns in their shells.

SERVES 8–10

85 ml (3 fl oz) olive oil, for frying
2 medium onions, roughly chopped
White of 2 large leeks, roughly chopped
4 celery sticks, thinly sliced
2 large bulbs of fennel, thinly sliced
10 garlic cloves, chopped
2 × 5 cm (2 in) pieces of orange peel
900 g (2 lb) tomatoes, skinned and chopped, skins reserved
½ red chilli, seeded and chopped
1 level teaspoon saffron
2 sprigs of thyme
4 fresh bay leaves
3.4 litres (6 pints) water
3.5 kg (7 lb) fish (see above)
750 g (1½ lb) or 75 ml (1½ pints) mussels, washed and scraped clean
1 teaspoon fennel herb, roughly chopped
1 teaspoon oregano
1 teaspoon fresh thyme
2 tablespoons Pernod or Ricard
750 g (1½ lb) shellfish, sliced (see above)
25 ml (1 fl oz) extra virgin olive oil
Cayenne pepper (optional)
Salt and freshly ground black pepper

FOR THE CROÛTONS

Olive oil, for frying
12 thin slices French bread
2–3 garlic cloves
100 g (4 oz) *Rouille* (see p. 45), to serve

To make the croûtons, heat the oil in a frying pan and fry the slices of bread on both sides until golden. Rub each croûton with garlic, set aside and keep warm.

To make the *Bouillabaisse*, heat the olive oil in a pan large enough to hold all the fish and the water. Add the onions, leek, celery, fennel and garlic. Cook until soft. Season with black pepper then add the orange peel, tomatoes, chilli, saffron, thyme, bay leaves and water and bring to the boil. Simmer for 10 minutes.

Add the fish, putting the firmer-fleshed fish like conger eel, dogfish and skate in first. Add the softer fish 3 minutes later and the mussels 1 minute after that. While adding the fish, put in the herbs and the Pernod (or Ricard). Continue to boil only until the fish is just cooked (about 8 minutes).

Finally, add the shellfish and boil for a further 1 minute. Strain the soup through a colander and place all the fish, mussels, shellfish and vegetables in a large warm dish. The mussels and shellfish should be served in their shells. Set aside and keep warm.

Return the strained *bouillon* to the pan, add the extra virgin olive oil and concentrate the flavour by rapid boiling. Check the seasoning and add cayenne pepper if you like it (I do).

Pour the *bouillon* over the fish and vegetables and scatter the croûtons over the top. You can separate the fish from the soup as they often do in France, if you prefer, but I like to eat fish and soup together served with a dollop of *rouille*.

Serve with a Provençal rosé. I would, ideally, serve Bandol.

LOBSTER, TURBOT AND MUSSELS WITH STAR ANISE NAGE

A *nage* is a *court-bouillon* that is specifically for fish. The word comes from *nager*, which is French for to swim.

This dish also works well with mussels, oysters, crayfish or langoustine. The only essential requirement is that the fish and shell-fish should be slightly undercooked. Allow 12 hours for the *nage* to cool and for the flavours to develop before using. Star anise is available from Chinese and Indian food stores.

SERVES 4

  175 g (6 oz) turbot fillet, skinned
  100 g (4 oz) cooked lobster meat, from a
    450 g (1 lb) lobster
  1 carrot
  8 French beans
  120 ml (4 fl oz) double cream
  1 quantity *Shellfish Nage* (see p. 39)
  4 mangetout
  24 small mussels, washed and scraped clean
  1 small courgette, thinly sliced lengthways
  8 small spinach leaves
  50 g (2 oz) cold unsalted butter, cut into
    pieces
  A pinch of ground star anise

Cut the turbot into pieces about 2.5 cm (1 in) wide and cut the lobster into 1 cm (½ in) slices.

Peel the carrot, slice it thinly, lengthways, then cut these slices into long thin straws. Top and tail the French beans and cut them in half lengthways.

Add the cream to the *nage*, bring it to the boil then boil rapidly to reduce the volume by half. While the *nage* is reducing, blanch the carrots, beans and mangetout in boiling salted water for 3 minutes, then refresh in cold water.

Wash the mussels, scrape them clean and pull out the beards. Place the mussels in a pan with a splash of the *nage*, then cover tightly and cook over a fierce heat until the mussels have opened. Add the resulting liquor to the *nage* straining through a sieve to remove any grit. When cool enough to handle, remove the meat from half the mussels, discarding their shells. Leave the rest intact.

Add the courgette, spinach and fish to the reduced *nage* and simmer for 1 minute then add the blanched vegetables, all the mussels and the lobster. Simmer for 1 minute. With a slotted spoon or fish slice, lift the fish, shellfish and vegetables onto four warmed soup plates. Whisk the cold butter into the sauce then add a small pinch of ground star anise. Pour the sauce over the fish and vegetables.

Sancerre is the ideal wine to accompany this soup, or a Sauvignon from the Loire such as Sauvignon de Touraine.

(TOP LEFT) Lobster, Turbot and
Mussels with Star Anise Nage (*see
page 61*), (ABOVE) Fish Soup with
Croûtons (*see page 56*) and (LEFT)
Mussel, Leek and Saffron Soup (*see
page 57*)

BOURRIDE OF RED MULLET, BRILL AND SALT COD

I make *bourride* with salt cod because it makes the unsalted fish taste delightfully sweet. In all my recipes, I look for ways of extending the complexity of the tastes, so in this dish I have included a recipe for croûtons spread with chilli and sun-dried tomato – an idea I picked up from none other than Keith Floyd. I think it is an inspired combination.

You will need a large shallow serving dish which can contain about 900 ml (1½ pints) of sauce.

SERVES 4

25 ml (1 fl oz) olive oil
1 medium onion, chopped
1 small leek, chopped
½ bulb Florence fennel, chopped
4 garlic cloves, chopped
2 strips orange peel
2 tomatoes, sliced
1 fresh or dried bay leaf
1 sprig of thyme
1.2 litres (2 pints) *Fish Stock* (see p. 36)
½ teaspoon salt
225 g (8 oz) red mullet fillet, with the skin left on
225 g (8 oz) brill fillet, with the skin left on
225 g (8 oz) *Salt Cod* (see p. 53)
225 g (8 oz) *Aïoli* (see p. 44)
Chopped fresh parsley to garnish

FOR THE CROÛTONS

25 ml (1 fl oz) olive oil
4 × 2.5 cm (1 in) slices French bread, cut on a slant
1 red chilli, seeded and finely chopped
4 sun-dried tomatoes in oil, chopped

To make the croûtons, heat the oil in a pan and fry the bread until crisp. Remove from the pan and set aside. Mix together the chilli and sun-dried tomato and bind with a little of the *aïoli*. Spread over the croûtons and keep warm.

To make the *bourride*, heat the oil in a pan large enough to hold all the vegetables, stock and fish. Add the onion, leek, fennel, garlic and orange peel and fry gently without colouring for about 5 minutes then add the tomato, bay leaf, thyme, fish stock and salt.

Bring to the boil and simmer for 30 minutes. Add all the fish, including the salt cod, and simmer very gently for 5 minutes. Remove the fish carefully and set aside in the warm serving dish. Strain the cooking liquor through a sieve into a clean pan pressing down with a ladle to extract as much flavour as possible.

Put the *aïoli* in a large bowl and whisk in a good splash of the warm stock then pour in the rest, whisking continuously (if you add all the stock at once the *aïoli* won't amalgamate properly). Return the sauce to the pan and, continuing to whisk, heat to the temperature of an egg custard (hot enough to be uncomfortable to your little finger) to thicken it. Pour the *bourride* over the fish, sprinkle with the chopped parsley and arrange the croûtons on top. Serve with boiled potatoes.
Serve with a bottle of white wine such as Cassis, a gutsy aromatic white wine from Provence, or a white Rioja.

COTRIADE

Cotriade is a fish stew from Brittany. It differs from other fish stews in that it uses oily fish, like mackerel, herring and sprats, along with the more unusual fish used in a stew. All fish stews are really very simple dishes that were originally concocted by fishermen using whatever fresh fish and vegetables were available. In the case of a *cotriade*, I believe it was quite common for the stew to be made on board ship. But although I had long known about *cotriade*, I had never been particularly interested in cooking what seemed to me to be a fish stew lacking any excitement until last year, when I went to Brittany.

I stayed at the hotel of one of France's top chefs, Olivier Roellinger, and, in the second of his two restaurants (the first restaurant has won many stars and is much fêted), I had a *cotriade* of such brilliance that I resolved to have a go myself. What really distinguished this dish was the astonishing pungency of the fennel in the bouillon. In the spring, the fennel is just appearing in the hedgerows everywhere in Brittany. Used in this dish with gurnard, mackerel, monkfish and bass, it seemed all the more romantic because it evoked the scents and flavours of spring on the coast of France.

Being very close to Brittany, Cornwall has exactly the same fish, so I decided that it was just the sort of dish that I should be serving at the restaurant. In my recipe, I have also added slices of sorrel and anchovy butter which is served separately so each guest can stir as much or little into the dish as they wish.

Because there is quite a lot of work involved I have written this recipe for eight people, making it suitable for a dinner party. But just one word of warning about using oily fish in stews: unless you are absolutely sure that the fish is extremely fresh, leave it out because the smell and flavour of the slightly-less-than-fresh oil in those oily fish will ruin the dish.

You can use almost any fish fillets in this recipe, but my suggestions are to use a few of the following: gurnard, lemon sole, plaice, brill, mackerel, herring, sprats, cod, hake, haddock, red mullet, grey mullet, red bream, black bream, John Dory, turbot and whiting.

Use the smallest new potatoes you can find for this recipe.

You will need a large, shallow serving dish which can contain the fillets and about 750 ml (1¼ pints) of sauce.

SERVES 8

900 g (2 lb) new potatoes, sliced in half
1.75 kg (4 lb) fish fillets
100 g (1 oz) unsalted butter
900 g (2 lb) mussels
Salt

FOR THE COURT-BOUILLON

2 carrots, chopped
1 leek, chopped
2 celery sticks, chopped
1 bulb Florence fennel, chopped
½ onion, chopped
2.25 litres (4 pints) water
Rind and flesh of ½ lemon
2 garlic cloves
1 fresh or dried bay leaf
150 ml (5 fl oz) dry white wine
2 tablespoons Ricard or Pernod
6 black peppercorns
15 g (½ oz) salt
100 g (4 oz) crème fraîche
50 g (2 oz) sprigs of fennel, including stems
   and leafy fronds

FOR THE SORREL AND ANCHOVY BUTTER

10 leaves of sorrel
4 fillets of anchovy
100 g (4 oz) unsalted butter

To make the sorrel and anchovy butter, put all the ingredients in a food processor and blend until smooth. Place on cling film and roll into a thick sausage shape. Chill until required.

To make the *cotriade*, put all the *court-bouillon* ingredients except the crème fraîche and sprigs of fennel in a large pan, bring to the boil and simmer for 30 minutes. Strain through a sieve into a clean pan, pushing the liquid through with the back of a ladle to extract as much of the flavour as possible. Bring the strained *bouillon* to the boil and continue boiling to reduce the volume by about half. Add the crème fraîche and all but one of the sprigs of fennel and simmer for 5 minutes before straining again. Add the potatoes to the strained stock and boil until just tender.

Pre-heat the grill to high. Brush the oily fish fillets with a little butter and season lightly with salt. Wash the mussels and scrape them clean, removing the beards with a sharp knife.

Put a generous splash of the *bouillon* in a large pan then add the mussels. Cover tightly and place over a high heat until they steam open. Remove the mussels from the pan and keep warm. Strain the mussel's cooking liquor through a sieve into the *bouillon*.

Grill the oily fish under a hot grill until just cooked. Poach the rest of the fish in the *bouillon* and try to keep the fillets in one piece. Cook them in batches until they are just firm. They will continue to cook after you have removed them from the heat. As each batch is cooked, set it aside and keep warm.

Serve in the large shallow dish. Unlike most fish stews it is important to try and keep the fillets intact and lay them out neatly. Add the mussels and pour over only enough *bouillon* and potatoes to cover half the fillets. Sprinkle with the chopped fennel and serve the rest of the *bouillon* separately. Serve the sorrel butter cut into thick slices on a plate.

A MEURETTE OF PLAICE AND LEMON SOLE WITH BEAUJOLAIS

This Burgundian freshwater fish stew calls for plenty of fruity red wine to produce a robust, full-flavoured dish.

SERVES 4

FOR THE CROÛTONS

2 slices white bread
25 ml (1 fl oz) groundnut oil
A knob of butter

FOR THE FISH

350 g (12 oz) plaice fillets, skin on
350 g (12 oz) lemon sole fillets, skin on
25 g (1 oz) unsalted butter mixed with 15 g (½ oz) flour (*beurre manié*)
Salt and freshly ground black pepper

FOR THE STOCK

25 g (1 oz) butter
225 g (8 oz) equal quantities carrot, celery, leek and onion chopped and mixed together
1 tablespoon brandy
1.2 litres (2 pints) *Chicken Stock* (see p. 37)
½ bottle Beaujolais
1 fresh or dried bay leaf
1 sprig of thyme or ½ teaspoon dried thyme

FOR THE PERSILLADE

1 small clove garlic
1 small bunch of fresh parsley

FOR THE MEURETTE

24 shallots, peeled
¼ teaspoon sugar
15 g (½ oz) butter

FOR THE MUSHROOM AND BACON GARNISH

1 rasher smoked bacon, rind removed
15 g (½ oz) butter
225 g (8 oz) button mushrooms, cut into quarters

First, make the croûtons. Using a 2.5 cm (1 in) round cutter, cut out 8 discs from the slices of bread and fry them in the groundnut oil, adding a little knob of butter to the pan to give them a golden colour.

To make the stock, melt the butter in a pan and add the chopped mixed vegetables (known as *mirepoix*) and fry them until they are just beginning to brown. Add the brandy and boil off the alcohol before adding 900 ml (1½ pints) of the chicken stock, the Beaujolais, bay leaf and thyme. Bring to the boil and simmer for 30 minutes.

Meanwhile brown the shallots with the sugar and butter in a shallow pan. Add the remaining chicken stock and simmer the shallots gently until they are tender then turn up the heat and reduce the shallots and stock until you have a shiny brown glaze. Set aside and keep warm.

To make the garnish, cut the bacon into thin strips and fry gently in the butter, add the mushrooms and continue to fry until soft. Season with salt and black pepper then set aside and keep warm.

Finely chop the garlic and parsley together, to make the *persillade*.

Strain the red wine stock into a shallow pan, bring to the boil and boil rapidly to reduce the volume by half. Add the fish fillets and cook gently until it is just tender. (This should take about 5 minutes.)

Remove the fillets from the pan and place neatly on a warmed serving dish. Break the *beurre manie* into small pieces and stir into the red wine sauce. Continue to stir until the sauce thickens. Add the *meurette*, the mushroom and bacon garnish and the *persillade*. Check the seasoning and add a little salt, if necessary. Spoon the sauce over the fish, top with the croûtons and serve. Serve plainly boiled new potatoes and French beans.

A bottle of good Beaujolais, such as Fleurie, is excellent with the Meurette.

THAI SEAFOOD SALAD

This dish is designed for large numbers and it is always a great success. The aromatic flavours of lemon grass, lime, fresh chilli and coriander are just the sort of positive and attractive highlights that make a buffet dish like this memorable. I made it for about 50 last May Day. In Padstow May 1st is known as 'Obby 'Oss Day', a pagan festival when the coming of summer is celebrated with dancing, singing, eating and just a little drinking!

SERVES 20

50 ml (2 fl oz) olive oil
900 g (2 lb) squid, cleaned and cut into strips (see p. 28)
900 g (2 lb) monkfish fillet, sliced
20 scallop meats, cut in half
175 ml (6 fl oz) water
120 ml (4 fl oz) Thai fish sauce (*nam pla*)
The juice of 4 limes
25 ml (1 fl oz) sesame oil
A 1.5 kg (3 lb) cooked lobster (optional)
450 g (1 lb) peeled North Atlantic prawns
2 cucumbers, diced
3 sticks celery, diced
3 bunches spring onions, sliced
4 sticks lemon grass, finely sliced
6 cloves garlic, peeled and finely chopped
75 g (3 oz) ginger, peeled and finely chopped
6 red chillies, seeded and finely chopped
8 tablespoons fresh coriander, roughly chopped
6 Kaffir lime leaves, very finely sliced (optional)
1 iceberg lettuce, thinly sliced

Heat the oil in a large frying pan and fry the squid in batches till it has turned brown and is beginning to take on colour. Use the same pan and oil to fry the monkfish. Again, do this in batches so that the fish fries and takes on some colour rather than sweats. Repeat the process with the scallops frying them for only about 1 minute. Set aside all the cooked seafood and leave to cool. De-glaze the frying pan with the water. Mix these pan juices with the fish sauce, lime juice and sesame oil in a small bowl. Set aside.

Cut the lobster, if using, in half lengthways and remove the meat from the tail and claws. Pick out the meat from the head section. This is done in the same way as for the body section of a crab (see p. 177). Set the meat aside and discard the shells.

To make up the salad, gently turn over all the ingredients in a large salad bowl.

SEAFOOD RISOTTO

Risotto is one of those dishes, like *bouillabaisse*, where stern warnings about correct ingredients and cooking abound. But like many a simple dish there is really very little to it. It reminds me of an essay by Elizabeth David called 'An Omelette and a Glass of Wine', where the omelettes of Annette Poulard, proprietress of a res- taurant on Mont Saint-Michel, were analysed and secret ingredients like *foie gras* and cream and special methods were ascribed to her delightfully light dishes. Years after she had retired she replied to a letter asking what was in her omelettes by saying, 'I break some good eggs into a bowl, I put a good piece of butter in the pan, I throw the eggs into it and I shake it constantly'. There's nothing to it, and the same goes for risotto.

This seafood risotto is very simple to make and makes a perfect starter. You can use any of the following risotto rices: Arborio, Carnaroli, Maratelli, Roma, or Vialone.

SERVES 4

450 g (1 lb) prawns, shell on
36 small mussels
100 g (4 oz) monkfish fillet, thinly sliced
50 g (2 oz) squid, cleaned and thinly sliced

FOR THE STOCK

25 ml (1 fl oz) olive oil
1 garlic clove, chopped
1 medium carrot, chopped
1 celery stick, chopped
1 small onion, chopped
1 small leek, chopped
¼ red chilli, chopped
1 tomato, chopped
⅛ teaspoon saffron
900 ml (1½ pints) *Fish Stock* (see p. 36)
Cooking liquor from the mussels

FOR THE RISOTTO

50 g (2 oz) unsalted butter
2 shallots, chopped
1 garlic clove, chopped
350 g (12 oz) risotto rice e.g. Arborio
120 ml (4 fl oz) dry white wine
25 g (1 oz) Parmesan
1 tablespoon olive oil

Peel the prawns, reserving the shells for the stock. Set the prawns aside until needed. Wash the mussels, scrape them clean and pull out the beards. Open by placing in a pan with a splash of water, covering tightly then setting over a high heat until they have opened. Strain through a colander to remove any grit. Save the liquor for the stock. Remove the meats from all but 8 of the shells, discard the empty shells. Leaving a few whole mussels in the risotto makes it look very appetizing. Set the mussels aside until needed.

To make the stock, heat the oil in a large pan and add the garlic, carrot, celery, onion, leek and chilli. Fry for 5 minutes without colouring. Add the reserved prawn shells and cook for another couple of minutes then add the tomato, saffron, fish stock and mussel liquor. Bring to the boil and simmer for 30 minutes then push through a conical sieve with the back of a ladle to extract as much flavour as possible.

To make the risotto, melt the butter in a heavy-based pan (this will lessen the chance of the risotto burning on the bottom as it cooks) then add the shallots and garlic and sweat until softened. Add the rice and stir for a couple of minutes until well-coated with butter. Pour in the wine. Bring to the boil then remove from the heat and let the rice absorb all the liquid. You can make the risotto to this stage some time before completing the dish. The final cooking time, about 20 minutes, is reduced to about 10 by doing this.

Return the pan to a medium heat and add the shellfish stock to the rice in three stages, allowing the liquid to be absorbed each time before adding the next amount. Stir continuously until the stock is almost completely absorbed.

When the rice is just tender but still firm to the bite (*al dente*), add the Parmesan. (The small amount of stock left at this stage will be absorbed by the cheese.) While the risotto is cooking, brush the rest of the seafood with olive oil and grill for 3–4 minutes. To serve, carefully mix the seafood including the mussels into the risotto. Leave a few pieces on top to garnish.

(LEFT) Bourride of Red Mullet, Brill and Salt Cod (*see page 64*), (BELOW LEFT) Seafood Risotto (*see page 68*) and (BELOW) Cotriade (*see page 65*)

CHARLES FONTAINE'S FISH PIE

Charles Fontaine is a French chef who loves English food. He runs the Quality Chop House in Farringdon Road, London. The restaurant has had quality English food like chops and fish pies on its menu for over a hundred years. While making the television series, we filmed him making a fish pie. This recipe is a bit more elaborate than a basic English fish pie, made with hard-boiled eggs and parsley, but it is very much in the same tradition and extremely good.

SERVES 6

75 g (3 oz) unsalted butter
3 shallots, finely chopped
100 g (4 oz) button mushrooms, cut in half
25 ml (1 fl oz) dry white wine
900 g (2 lb) mussels, scrubbed and bearded
300 g (11 oz) monkfish fillet, skinned
300 g (11 oz) cod fillet, skinned
300 g (11 oz) lemon sole fillet, skinned
100 g (4 oz) peeled prawns
40 g (1½ oz) flour
50 ml (2 fl oz) double cream
Salt and freshly ground black pepper

FOR THE COURT-BOUILLON

150 ml (5 fl oz) dry white wine
600 ml (1 pint) water
2 slices onion
1 carrot, sliced
2 slices fennel
1 celery stick
A few fresh parsley stalks
2 bay leaves
6 black peppercorns
1 teaspoon salt

FOR THE MASHED POTATOES

1.5 kg (3 lb) mashing potatoes, such as King
    Edward, Wilja or Maris Piper
50 g (2 oz) unsalted butter
2 egg yolks
120 ml (4 fl oz) milk
Salt and freshly ground white pepper
A pinch of freshly grated nutmeg

Pre-heat the oven to 200°C/400°F/Gas 6.

Melt 25 g (1 oz) of butter and cook the shallots gently until soft. Add the mushrooms and cook for 1 minute. Add the wine and simmer until the liquid has evaporated. Season. Place in a shallow ovenproof dish and keep warm.

Place the mussels in a large pan with a splash of water, cover and place on a fierce heat until the mussels open. Drain, reserving the liquor. Remove the mussels from their shells and add to the mushrooms.

Simmer the court-bouillon for 20 minutes. Strain and return the stock to the pan. Cut the fish into 2.5 cm (1 in) pieces. Add the monkfish to the court-bouillon and poach gently for 2 minutes. Add the cod and sole and poach for 2 minutes. Transfer the fish to the dish and add the prawns.

Melt the remaining butter in a pan, stir in the flour and cook for 2 minutes, stirring and not letting it colour. When it smells nutty, remove from the heat and stir in the hot court-bouillon and mussel liquor until smooth. Return to a low heat, add the cream and simmer for 15 minutes, stirring. Pour over the fish.

Boil the potatoes in salted water until soft. Drain, then mash until smooth with the butter, egg yolks and milk. Season. Pipe over the fish using a piping bag and a large star nozzle or spread with a spatula and decorate in a wavy-line pattern using a fork.

Bake in the oven for 30 minutes then serve hot with mushy peas.

TEMPURA OF SEAFOOD WITH ROASTED RED CHILLI AND ONION PICKLE

This recipe is best served as a first course because it makes heavy demands on the deep-fryer and if you tried to cook it as a main course for any more than a couple of people you would find you were cooking an awful lot of batches. However, it is extremely popular; deep-fried seafood always is. The batter recipe given here has the enviable quality of remaining crisp for a very long time.

To give the best possible visual impact, I have chosen seafood which can be cooked partly in the shell and partly out. Only the tail shells are removed from the prawns and only one half of the shells from the mussels. This makes the finished dish look much more attractive than if you just served the mussel meats or prawn tails in the batter.

SERVES 4

8 Mediterranean prawns, shells on
16 mussels, cleaned
4 scallops
100 g (4 oz) lemon sole fillet
Vegetable oil, for deep-frying
1 quantity *Tempura Batter* (see p. 53)

FOR THE PICKLE

25 ml (1 fl oz) vegetable oil
3 garlic cloves, finely chopped
5 cm (2 in) piece ginger, finely chopped
1 medium onion, finely chopped
2 red chillies, seeded and finely chopped
2 tablespoons sugar
50 ml (2 fl oz) white wine vinegar
2 tablespoons oyster sauce
2 Kaffir lime leaves, very finely sliced
   (optional)
1 tablespoon Thai fish sauce (*nam pla*)
3 spring onions, sliced into thin rounds

Carefully remove the shells from the tails of the prawns taking care to avoid separating the tail from the head. Grip the sides of the tail with your thumb and forefinger and push the bottom edges together to crack the shell. Gently peel the tail shell back the other way. Try not to put any pressure on the prawns where the tail goes into the body section.

To open the mussels, place them in a small pan with just a splash of water. Cover tightly and set over a high heat until they open. Discard any mussels which don't open when cooked. Remove from the pan. Strain through a fine sieve to remove any grit. When cool enough to handle carefully remove one shell from each mussel, leaving the meat in the other. Also remove any stringy beards still attached to the meat. Prepare the scallops by cutting each one in half and the sole by cutting the fillet into 8 small pieces.

To make the roasted red chilli and onion pickle, heat the oil in a pan then add the garlic and ginger and fry until the garlic is beginning to brown. Add the onion and reduce the heat, allowing it to sweat for 5 minutes. Add the chillies, sugar, vinegar and oyster sauce and cook gently for 30 minutes. Add the lime leaves (if using), fish sauce and spring onions and cook for a further 3 minutes. Leave to cool.

To deep-fry the fish pre-heat the oil in the deep-fryer to 190°C/375°F. Drop the scallops and sole fillets into the batter then remove and drop immediately into the hot oil. Fry for 3 minutes. Remove and drain on kitchen paper. Next, cook the prawns for 2 minutes and, finally, cook the mussels for 1 minute.

Assemble the seafood onto four warm plates with a dollop of the extremely hot aromatic and delightful chilli pickle. Serve immediately. *Serve with a Chardonnay or Sémillon Chardonnay from Australia.*

(LEFT) Fish Pasties with French Tarragon (*see page 77*), (BELOW LEFT) Hake and Potato Pie with a Garlic, Parsley and Breadcrumb Crust (*see page 76*) and (BELOW) Tempura of Seafood with Roasted Red Chilli and Onion Pickle (*see page 73*)

SEAFOOD THERMIDOR

This is a star attraction at our deli.

SERVES 4

15 g (½ oz) butter
1 medium onion, finely chopped
85 ml (3 fl oz) dry white wine
300 ml (10 fl oz) *Fish Stock* (see p. 36)
75 g (3 oz) fresh button mushrooms
600 ml (1 pint) *Velouté* (see p. 39)
120 ml (4 fl oz) double cream
175 g (6 oz) lemon sole fillet, skinned
175 g (6 oz) monkfish fillet, skinned
4 large scallops
Melted butter for brushing over fish
100 g (4 oz) shelled North Atlantic Prawns
1 tablespoon made English mustard
75 g (3 oz) grated cheese
25 g (1 oz) breadcrumbs
A pinch of cayenne pepper
Salt and freshly ground black pepper

Pre-heat the grill to high. Melt the butter in a pan and fry the onions until softened. Pour in the white wine and boil to reduce a little, then add the fish stock and 25 g (1 oz) of the mushrooms. Simmer for 10 minutes then boil to reduce the stock by two thirds.

In a separate pan carefully heat the *velouté* then add the reduced stock to it. Stir in the cream and leave to simmer on a very low heat while you prepare the fish.

Cut the lemon sole and monkfish into 1 cm (½ in) pieces and slice each scallop into three. Put all the fish in a large, shallow gratin dish. Sprinkle the rest of the mushrooms on top. Melt the butter and brush over the mushrooms and fish. Season with salt and place under the grill. Remove when the fish is white but still a little undercooked. Sprinkle over the prawns.

Add the mustard to the sauce so it is slightly hot but not overpoweringly so. Pour the sauce over the fish and mushrooms.

Mix together the grated cheese, breadcrumbs, cayenne pepper and a couple of twists of black pepper and sprinkle over. Place under the grill until it is golden brown.

HAKE AND POTATO PIE WITH A GARLIC, PARSLEY AND BREADCRUMB CRUST

I'm very fond of this simple French fish pie.

SERVES 4

450 g (1 lb) potatoes, cut into 5 mm (¼ in) slices
100 g (4 oz) butter
450 g (1 lb) hake fillet, skinned
2 slices white bread
2 garlic cloves
15 g (½ oz) fresh parsley
Salt and freshly ground black pepper

Pre-heat the oven to 200°C/400°F/Gas 6.

Par-boil the potatoes for 2 minutes and drain. Grease an ovenproof dish with half the butter. Cut the hake into 2.5 cm (1 in) slices and layer in the dish with the potato slices. Season and dot with the rest of the butter. Cover and bake for 15 minutes, basting with the butter twice.

Process the bread, garlic and parsley to crumbs. Season, then sprinkle over the pie and bake, uncovered, for 15 minutes or until crisp.

FISH PASTIES WITH FRENCH TARRAGON

Use the cheapest fish fillet you can find for this dish. Ling, coley, pollack or pouting (in that order of preference) are all fine. This is the recipe I use in our bakery and very good it is too!

MAKES 5 PASTIES

  150 g (5 oz) leek, cut into 1 cm (½ in) dice
  150 g (5 oz) onion, cut into 1 cm (½ in) dice
  225 g (8 oz) potato, cut into 1 cm (½ in) dice
  425 g (15 oz) fish fillet, cut into 2.5 cm (1 in) pieces
  25 ml (1 fl oz) white wine vinegar
  25 g (1 oz) butter

  25 g (1 oz) mature cheddar, grated
  ½ teaspoon chopped fresh French tarragon
  ½ teaspoon freshly ground black pepper
  1 teaspoon salt
  900 g (2 lb) flaky pastry or shortcrust pastry, chilled

Pre-heat the oven to 200°C/400°F/Gas 6.

Mix all the ingredients, except the pastry, in a bowl. Roll out the pastry to about 5 mm (¼ in) thick. Using a pastry cutter, press out 5 × 19 cm (7½ in) discs. Divide the filling between the five discs. Moisten the edges of the pastry then pinch them together to seal. Crimp the edges then place on a lightly greased baking sheet and bake for 35 minutes. Serve hot or cold.

FISH CAKES

You can use any white fish or, indeed, any oily fish to make these fish cakes but cheaper white fish like ling, coley, pollack, whiting and pouting (also known as pout or bib) are ideal for this dish. I have included a couple of teaspoons of anchovy essence in this recipe because it improves the flavour dramatically. You can also use *nam pla* (Thai fish sauce) if you want to but if you don't want to use either, just add more salt to the recipe.

SERVES 4

  450 g (1 lb) cooked white fish
  450 g (1 lb) mashed potatoes
  2 eggs
  25 g (1 oz) melted butter
  2 teaspoons anchovy essence or Thai fish sauce (*nam pla*)

  2 tablespoons chopped fresh parsley
  1 teaspoon salt
  10 turns of a black pepper mill
  50 g (2 oz) seasoned flour
  2 eggs, beaten
  150 g (5 oz) fresh white breadcrumbs

Break the cooked fish into small pieces removing all the skin and bones. Mix the mashed potatoes with the eggs and melted butter, then fold in the anchovy essence, fish sauce or salt and pepper and parsley.

Mould the mixture into fish cakes using your hands and a palette knife. Coat each cake with flour, then beaten egg, then breadcrumbs. Shallow or deep-fry as you prefer.

Serve hot with a green vegetable or a salad.

5

OILY FISH: HERRING, MACKEREL, SALMON, SEA TROUT, WHITEBAIT AND EELS

Oily fish are rich in omega-3 fatty acids which have the benefit of reducing cholesterol levels. We should all eat more mackerel, herring, salmon, trout, whitebait, sprats and pilchards. Not only are they healthy and nutritious but their oil creates a delightful flavour when the fish are perfectly fresh and served simply grilled, fried or barbecued. They all lend themselves to being preserved in salt, smoked or pickled, too.

HERRING

The maritime countries of Northern Europe have made use of herring in as many diverse ways as the rural people of France have used the pig. Just think of the different ways that herring is served up: kippers, bloaters, buckling, red herrings, rollmops, Bismarck herrings, salt herrings, soused herrings, matjes herrings.

Large ports have built up over the years, particularly in the Baltic, the East Coast of England and Scotland, and Holland, from the earnings made from the fishing and processing of herrings. Yet, because they have always been so cheap, I tend to think we underrate them. I once asked a very good food-writer friend of mine, Linda Brown, why she thought that we underrate herrings and she came up with a novel and, I suspect, truthful answer, that people really don't like the lingering smell of oily fish in their houses after they've fried them. I remember doing some research on pilchards in Cornwall in the last century and reading an account of someone visiting the cottages of the poor at that time. They described the appalling smell of pilchard oil in every house, which was used to light lamps in those days.

If you don't like the smell of frying oily fish, but love the taste, here are three suggestions: get yourself a better extraction system, get an Aga or Rayburn or any cooker with an oven vented to the outside of the house, start frying them then transfer them to the oven, or get yourself a little bottle-gas barbecue and cook them outside! We barbecue fish outside the kitchen door even in the middle of winter. All of the herring family – pilchards, sprats and herrings – when cooked perfectly fresh are amongst the best things you could ever eat.

MACKEREL

The best way to eat mackerel is to cook it on the day it is caught. For this reason, I wouldn't suggest cooking the *Fillets of Mackerel with Dill and New Potatoes* on p. 92 with anything but the freshest mackerel. Apart from that exception mackerel from the fishmonger will be fine for all the other recipes. Make sure that the mackerel have some traces of blue or green in their skin. If they look grey they won't be particularly interesting to eat. When we were filming for the television series we took my youngest son out mackerel fishing. He complained, having never been in a boat on the open sea before, about the rocking until we gave him a fishing rod and he had his first bite. He was totally absorbed from then on. For this I feel most grateful to mackerel: first, for being such a delicious fish when fresh; and second, for being in such abundance in in-shore waters so that small boys can catch them.

On the whole I've tried to keep separate the writing of the cookery book and the making of the TV series (which includes about 40 recipes from this book). However, once in a while the experiences of making the cookery series are so interesting as to make me want to mention them in the book. This is very much the case with mackerel.

David Pritchard, the producer, wanted me to do some voice-overs. These are little introductory pieces to various episodes in the series. We were particularly tired as we'd been up since 5 a.m. at the market in Newlyn and had just finished three days of pretty hard filming, so I suppose we were all a bit half-baked.

David said, 'I want a piece about mackerel. If you remember there's a scene where Charles [my youngest son] is seen pulling in his first mackerel and then we cut to those same mackerel on a chopping board by the cooker. I want you to say, in line with what we have already been saying, that mackerel are, shall we say, ubiquitous. Let's call them the Mini Metros of the sea.'

So I started, 'One of the great joys about mackerel is that they make themselves so easy to be caught, they're everywhere, they're a bit like the Mini Metros of the sea.'

'Hang on a minute,' said Julian, the cameraman, 'they're not Mini Metros at all, they're Ford Escorts.'

There was a pause of aggrieved silence from David.

'Okay,' I said, 'Ford Escorts.'

'No, Julian,' said David. 'They're not Ford Escorts, they're Mini Metros. What I mean is that they crop up everywhere.'

'Okay,' I said. 'Fine. Mini Metros.'

'Well they're not Mini Metros to me,' said Julian.

'Look,' I said, 'does it really matter? Can't we just call them the Skodas of the sea?'

'That's not the point,' said Julian. 'Mini Metros are squat little cars, mackerel are sleek and shiny, much more like Ford Escorts.'

'I don't think that Ford Escorts are particularly sleek or shiny,' said David. 'A Mini Metro's a far better car to compare them with. You just don't understand, do you Julian?'

'Look,' I said, 'we're all getting a bit tired, can't we just call them Ford Escorts, just for a quiet life?'

'Anyway,' said the sound engineer, Tom, 'what the hell's wrong with Mini Metros? My wife's got one.'

'Okay,' said David, 'let's forget the whole thing.'

SALMON

Well-produced farmed salmon is perfectly acceptable but even more delightful is wild salmon and the fishermen who catch it. There's a salmon fisherman in Cornwall called Charlie Bettinson who catches fish on the higher reaches of the Camel or Tamar at places like Golitha Falls. The single-mindedness, obsession and skill that he puts into catching a 5.5 kg (12 lb) salmon out of a pool where you would never have believed anything was swimming is a joy to behold.

When I see how much time and care it takes to get wild salmon from the water, I am filled with a sense of value of the fish. It is a real prize; firm flesh and the taste of fresh nuts.

Fish farming is vital if we wish to continue eating fish at all in view of the inexorable over-fishing that is going on in the seas around us. Inevitably, the taste of farmed salmon is not as good as wild. Don't worry about using farmed fish in any of the recipes. I'd far sooner you cooked them with farmed fish than not at all.

SEA TROUT

In Cornwall sea trout are called salmon peel. I've had to start calling it sea trout on the menu at the restaurant because people just don't know what I'm talking about otherwise. But I think I might go back to the local name and keep explaining it – it has more colour and excitement.

The salmon peel is a brown trout which has exchanged its habitat of rivers for the open sea. Its flesh develops a pink colour from a diet of crustaceans but is slightly less pronounced than the salmon. If better known and more widely available I'm sure it would rank very highly amongst people's favourite fish because it is so sleek and good-looking. It suffers even more than salmon from overcooking and tastes far better if eaten slightly underdone. Some fish are inedible when undercooked, John Dory in particular, and monkfish, but those fish with soft flesh like salmon, salmon peel, whiting and hake really benefit from being slightly under-cooked.

WHITEBAIT AND SAND EELS

There is no such fish as whitebait. They are the young of fish in the herring family, normally sprats, herrings or pilchards. As you eat the whole fish, guts and all, it is important not to buy them too big or the bones, intestines and scales become unpleasant. The largest they should be is 5–6 cm (2–2½ in) in length. Wash the whitebait after you have bought them in case there is any sand clinging to them; it's not very pleasant when mixed with the flour and deep-fried!

If you are lucky enough to get sand eels, treat them in exactly the same way as whitebait.

EELS

I think we ought to eat more eels but having been the recipient of a polystyrene cup of jellied eels in a London pub on more than one occasion I can see why we don't. It wasn't until I started buying fresh eels and cooking them myself that I realized of what value they were. Of all the oily fish, I think eels have the finest flavour; a perfect contrast of delicacy and rich-ness. The flesh is firm and any stock made from eel trimmings is flavoursome and gelatinous.

HOT SMOKED EEL WITH LENTILS, SAUERKRAUT AND PINK FIR APPLE POTATOES

Smoked eel is one of my favourite smoked fish. This great warm salad makes a good first course if you halve all the ingredients but you can also serve it as a main course. I really love this sort of central European food – totally wizard!

SERVES 4

450 g (1 lb) pink fir apple potatoes or new waxy potatoes
100 g (4 oz) smoked eel fillet
50 g (2 oz) Puy lentils
1 sprig of thyme
100 g (4 oz) sauerkraut
25 g (1 oz) unsalted butter
25 ml (1 fl oz) white wine
85 ml (3 fl oz) *Mustard Dressing* (see p. 51)
1 bunch watercress, stalks removed

Wash the potatoes well and peel as much as possible (it's impossible to peel pink fir apple potatoes totally because of their knobbly surface). Slice them lengthways and boil in well-salted water. Drain and keep warm.

Slice the eel fillet into little finger-size pieces (being hot smoked, it is already cooked). Boil the lentils in salted water with the sprig of thyme until soft, drain and set aside. Gently stew the sauerkraut in a separate pan, with the butter and white wine for about 20 minutes.

Place the eel, potatoes, lentils and mustard dressing in a pan and warm through, turning carefully. Finally, add the watercress before dividing between four warmed plates. Serve with a portion of sauerkraut on each plate.

FILLETS OF EEL WITH TERIYAKI MARINADE

You can use almost any fish to make this dish but it does seem to go particularly well with eel which, being oily, responds to grilling or barbecuing well. This dish is designed to be cooked on some sort of charcoal grill or grilling pan but, like most of my char-grill recipes, it can also be cooked under a grill, not quite so exciting but still well worth doing. Teriyaki is Japanese and uses two unusual ingredients, sake and mirin. If you can't get hold of the rice wine sake, use dry sherry. Mirin is a syrupy sake and I have increased the amount of sake and sugar in the recipe to allow for its omission.

SERVES 4

750 g (1½ lb) skinned fillets of eel

FOR THE TERIYAKI MARINADE

150 ml (5 fl oz) soy sauce
150 ml (5 fl oz) sake or dry sherry
25 g (1 oz) sugar
1 garlic clove, finely chopped
1 teaspoon finely chopped ginger

Boil all the marinade ingredients in a small pan for 5 minutes. Leave to cool. Brush the eel fillets liberally with the marinade.

Pre-heat the grill to high and cook the fillets for 2–3 minutes on each side. Brush the eel fillets with the marinade twice more on each side during cooking. Serve the eel accompanied by the marinade as a sauce handed round separately.

HERRINGS IN OATMEAL WITH SALAD LEAVES AND TOMATO

The essential ingredient for frying herrings in oatmeal is the fat in streaky bacon. You can adapt this recipe for other oily fish, too.

SERVES 4

4 herrings weighing about 225 g (8 oz) each
100 g (4 oz) oatmeal
25 ml (1 fl oz) vegetable oil
4 rashers streaky bacon, cut into thin strips
50 g (2 oz) salad leaves
2 tomatoes, seeded and chopped
50 ml (2 fl oz) *Mustard Dressing* (see p. 51)
Salt and freshly ground black pepper

Bone the herrings as on p. 21. Season and press with oatmeal until they are well covered. Heat the oil in a frying pan and fry the streaky bacon until crisp. Remove from the pan and keep warm. Fry the herrings in the same pan oil, flesh side first, until golden brown. Set the pan aside without washing it.

Divide the salad leaves between four warmed plates and sprinkle with the tomatoes and bacon. Place one herring on each plate, beside the salad. Pour the mustard dressing into the pan and heat through briefly before pouring over the salads. Serve immediately.

HERRING BEIGNETS WITH OLIVE OIL, MARJORAM AND CRACKED SPICES

I had always imagined that oily fish, like herring, deep-fried in batter would be too rich but I had some fritters like this in Corsica once and they were delightful.

SERVES 4

4 small herrings
25 g (1 oz) washed salad leaves
1 lemon cut into 4 wedges

FOR THE BATTER

100 g (4 oz) plain flour
½ teaspoon salt
2 tablespoons olive oil
160 ml (5½ fl oz) beer
1 egg white

FOR THE DRESSING

2 cardamon pods
12 coriander seeds

6 black peppercorns
½ teaspoon fresh marjoram chopped
big pinch of sea salt
85 ml (3 fl oz) virgin olive oil

To make the batter, whisk the flour, salt and olive oil and beer together until smooth. Leave for an hour. Just before deep frying, whisk the egg white to soft peaks and fold into the batter. Remove the seeds from the cardamom pods, crack the coriander and peppercorns with a rolling pin and place in a small bowl with the marjoram, sea salt and olive oil. Set your deep fryer to 185°C/360°F, or heat some vegetable oil in a large pan. Fillet the herrings (see p. 21), cut into finger-sized pieces, dip in the batter and fry for 2 minutes. Drain and arrange in four neat piles on four plates. Place the salad leaves next to the *beignets* and pour the dressing beside the salad leaves. Serve with lemon wedges.

PAN-FRIED HERRING MILT ON TOASTED BRIOCHE WITH NOISETTE BUTTER, CAPERS, SALAD LEAVES AND CHERVIL

I have always loved fried herring milt which is the roe of the male herring just fried and served on toast. My wife, Jill, suggested upgrading the idea by using brioche instead of toast and adding some salad leaves so that we could serve it as a first course at the restaurant. It has been a great success. But, if you don't want to make brioche, use toast instead.

SERVES 4

FOR THE BRIOCHE

15 g (½ oz) yeast
3 tablespoons warm water
2 tablespoons sugar
3 tablespoons tepid milk
450 g (1 lb) strong flour
1 tablespoon salt
4 eggs
100 g (4 oz) unsalted butter

FOR THE SALAD

50 g (2 oz) salad leaves
25 ml (1 fl oz) *Olive Oil Dressing* (see p. 51)
A small bunch of chervil, with the larger
    stalks removed

FOR THE HERRING ROE

350 g (12 oz) soft herring roe
25 g (1 oz) flour, seasoned with salt and
    pepper
75 g (3 oz) unsalted butter, softened
Juice of ½ lemon
1 tablespoon chopped fresh parsley
1 tablespoon capers
Salt and freshly ground black pepper

Pre-heat the oven to 200°C/400°F/Gas 6. To make the brioche, put the yeast, water, sugar, milk and one tablespoon of the flour in a bowl, whisk together then cover with a wet tea towel. Leave in a warm place until the mixture starts to froth. Put the rest of the flour and the salt in a large mixing bowl and add the eggs and yeast mixture. Mix thoroughly to form a soft dough. Turn out onto a floured surface and knead for 5 minutes. Add the butter and knead again to incorporate it into the dough. Cover with a clean tea towel and leave to prove in a warm place for 3 hours. Knock back to remove air bubbles and place in a 450 g (1 lb) bread tin. Bake for 35 minutes.

Mix the salad leaves with the olive oil dressing in a bowl then divide between four warmed plates. Scatter over the chervil. Cut four 1 cm (½ in) thick slices of brioche, toast lightly and place beside the salad.

Dust the roes in the seasoned flour then fry in 25 g (1 oz) of butter for about 2 minutes then place on top of the brioche.

Pour away the butter used to fry the roes and melt the remaining butter in the pan until it foams and starts to smell nutty. Pour over the herring roes, sprinkle with the lemon juice, scatter with a little salt and parsley and finish with a few capers. Serve immediately.

(LEFT) Fillets of Mackerel with Dill and New Potatoes (*see page 92*), (BELOW LEFT) Pan-fried Herring Milt on Toasted Brioche with Noisette Butter, Capers, Salad Leaves and Chervil (*see page 85*) and (BELOW) Grilled Herrings with Mustard and Onion Sauce and Fish Sausages (*see page 88*)

GRILLED HERRINGS WITH MUSTARD AND ONION SAUCE AND FISH SAUSAGES

This dish of herrings and fish sausages makes a pleasingly robust supper dish. The fish sausages are made with fish force meat and flavoured with lovage, a much under-used herb mainly, I suspect, because it is so strong and has such a singular flavour. But a little lovage in a fish sausage is a delight. Unfortunately, unless you are a keen herb gardener, or have a friend that is, you will probably find it hard to get hold of, which is a shame really because it

has long been used in English cookery. A suitable alternative to lovage is the tops of celery.

Ideally you should have some sort of sausage-making equipment to make these fish sausages but a piping bag and ½-inch plain nozzle will do equally well. It is quite easy to buy sausage casings from your local butcher – 100 g (4 oz) will be quite enough.

The best white fish fillets for the sausages are pollack, coley, plaice, flounder or whiting.

SERVES 4

4 herrings, each weighing about 225–275 g (8–10 oz)
A little melted butter, for brushing
1 large onion, finely chopped
50 ml (2 fl oz) balsamic vinegar
½ teaspoon salt
150 ml (5 fl oz) *Chicken Stock* (see p. 37)
100 g (4 oz) unsalted butter
1 tablespoon Dijon mustard

FOR THE SAUSAGES

250 g (9 oz) white fish fillet free of skin and bone
40 g (1½ oz) fresh white breadcrumbs
25 g (1 oz butter)
1 egg
½ teaspoon salt
A good pinch of white pepper
Juice of ½ lemon
½ teaspoon fresh lovage, finely chopped
2 tablespoons fresh parsley, chopped
15 g (½ oz) spring onion tops, sliced
120 ml (4 fl oz) cream

De-scale the herrings then slash them diagonally three times on each side, cutting right down to the bone. Season well inside and out with salt and pepper and brush with a little melted butter.

Before starting to make the sausages, make sure that all the ingredients are cold.

Put the fish, breadcrumbs, butter, egg, salt, white pepper and lemon juice into a food processor and blend until smooth. Add the lovage, parsley and spring onion tops and then quickly pour in the cream taking no more than 10 seconds. Fill the sausage skins with the force meat and twist into 9 cm (3½ in) long sausages.

Gently simmer the onion, balsamic vinegar, salt and chicken stock in a pan for 30–40

minutes. If the liquid boils away, add a little water. The aim is to cook the onions until they are extremely soft and to boil off all, or almost all, the liquid. Add the butter as if making *Beurre Blanc* (see p. 42). Remove from the heat and stir in the mustard. Set aside and keep warm.

Pre-heat the grill to high then grill the herrings for about 4 minutes on each side. Meanwhile, poach the sausages in lightly salted water for about 4 minutes. Drain then serve immediately, with the herrings and sauce, accompanied by mashed potatoes. *A good-quality farmhouse cider would be an ideal accompaniment for this dish.*

CHILLED FILLETS OF MACKEREL WITH CIDER AND AROMATIC HERBS

This recipe makes an excellent, cheap and simple first course. I think it is better than the similar dish, soused mackerel. Unlike soused mackerel, which is cooked for far too long, the mackerel fillets are poached briefly in a sharp *court-bouillon* then allowed to cool. It is at its best the day after it is made, so you need to plan in advance to make the most of this dish. For decoration, groove the whole carrot with an apple corer before slicing it for the *court-bouillon*.

600 ml (1 pint) cider
1 carrot, thinly sliced
3 shallots, thinly sliced
½ teaspoon black peppercorns
1 sprig of thyme
1 bay leaf
1 sprig of fennel
1 sprig of lovage or celery tops (optional)
½ teaspoon pickling spices
1 teaspoon salt
4 large mackerel fillets or 8 small ones

SERVES 4

Bring all the ingredients, except the mackerel, to the boil in a pan then simmer for 30 minutes.

Place the fish, skin side up, in a shallow pan. Pour over the hot *court-bouillon* and bring back to the boil. When it has bubbled once, remove it from the heat and leave to cool before chilling overnight. Remove the fillets from the *court-bouillon* and serve on individual plates and garnished with the sliced carrot and onions, and a few spoonfuls of sieved *court-bouillon*.

HOT MACKEREL SALAD WITH LETTUCE, LEMON GRASS AND CORIANDER

You really should try this recipe from Laos in South-east Asia. The traditional way to eat the grilled fish and dressing is with a pile of whole lettuce leaves. The fillet is removed from the mackerel, laid on a lettuce leaf, and some of the dressing is poured over. Coriander is sprinkled on top and the whole thing is wrapped up and eaten like a pancake.

Guests at the restaurant resisted eating it like this, so the whole fish is now served on the salad and the dressing is poured over the top. Eat it whichever way you like, but if you decide to use the 'lettuce pancakes', peel off whole leaves rather than slicing them.

SERVES 4

4 mackerel (small for a first course, large for a main course)
Vegetable oil, for brushing
Salt and freshly ground black pepper

FOR THE DRESSING

25 ml (1 fl oz) Thai fish sauce (*nam pla*)
150 ml (5 fl oz) water
1 green chilli, seeded and finely chopped
1 lemon grass stick, thinly sliced
Juice and zest of 1 lime, finely sliced
½ teaspoon sugar

FOR THE SALAD

> 1 tablespoon roughly chopped fresh
>   coriander and about 20 leaves
> ½ iceberg lettuce, thinly sliced or 1 whole
>   lettuce for 'lettuce pancakes'

Slash the fish diagonally three times on each side, cutting right through the bone. Brush with oil and season with salt and pepper. Grill the mackerel for 4 minutes on each side. Check to see if they are cooked by lifting up the gill covers. If there is no trace of pink left, then they are done.

Meanwhile, put the fish sauce, water, chilli, lemon grass, lime and sugar in a small pan. Warm the dressing through (don't boil) over a moderate heat. Add the chopped coriander just before taking the pan off the heat.

If serving the mackerel whole with the salad, divide the sliced lettuce between four plates and place the mackerel on top. Pour over the dressing and sprinkle with the coriander leaves.

If serving 'lettuce pancakes' serve the fish, sauce, whole coriander leaves and a pile of lettuce leaves separately.

MACKEREL ESCABÈCHE

This is a pleasant way of serving mackerel cold, as an *hors d'oeuvre*. The mackerel is fried in olive oil, then marinated with olive oil, wine vinegar, vegetables and herbs.

I made this dish one morning when Sandi Toksvig and John McCarthy arrived in Padstow by boat while making *Island Race*, a television series about their voyage around the coast of Britain. They had bought a string of mackerel in a shop on the quay. I knew I was going to be asked to cook some fish but I didn't know what. They asked me to do something quickly, so I filleted and fried the fish, sliced and cooked the vegetables and finished the dish all in, as they say in television, 'real time'. It took about 8 minutes.

SERVES 4

> 2 mackerel, each weighing about 225–275
>   g (8–10 oz)
> 175 ml (6 fl oz) olive oil
> Seasoned flour for dusting
> 50 g (2 oz) carrot, peeled and thinly sliced
> 50 g (2 oz) onion, thinly sliced
> 2 garlic cloves, sliced
> 4 tablespoons wine vinegar
> 4 tablespoons water
> 1 bay leaf
> 1 teaspoon chopped fresh thyme
> Salt and freshly ground black pepper

Either ask your fishmonger to fillet the mackerel for you or see p. 21 for instructions on filleting it yourself.

Heat half the oil in a large frying pan, dust the mackerel fillets with the seasoned flour, shake off any excess then fry the fillets on both sides until golden brown. Transfer to a shallow dish, which is just large enough to take the fillets side by side.

Pour the rest of the olive oil into the frying pan and fry the carrot, onion and garlic until they begin to colour. Add the wine vinegar, water, herbs and seasoning. Simmer until the vegetables are cooked then pour over the fish and leave to cool before serving.

MACKEREL RECHEADO

In this recipe from Goa in India, the head and bones are removed from a plump mackerel and the fish is stuffed with a 'masala' made with ginger, tamarind and chilli.

Traditionally the masala is made with a pestle and mortar and if you have one it is the easiest way to make this paste where dry and moist ingredients have to be ground together. If you don't have one, grind the dry ingredients in a spice mill or, at a pinch, a very clean coffee grinder and then combine with the chillies, garlic, tamarind, ginger and vinegar in a liquidizer. You can add a little water to the liquidizer to assist in the blending required but remember you need to end up with a paste not a liquid. The fish is pan-fried but the cooking is finished off in the oven. In Goa they serve the fish with freshly made naan bread which is so wonderful that you begin to think you could live forever after all!

SERVES 4

For the masala paste, grind together the cumin seeds, coriander seeds, peppercorns, cloves, turmeric, salt and sugar in a pestle and mortar, spice mill or very clean coffee grinder. If using a pestle and mortar, add the chillies, garlic, tamarind, ginger and wine vinegar and pound to a paste. Otherwise, combine the dry and wet ingredients in a liquidizer using a little water to loosen the paste but not turn it to liquid.

Remove the backbone from the mackerel following the instructions on p. 21.

4 large mackerel, each weighing about 275–350 g (10–12 oz)
Seasoned flour for dusting
Groundnut or vegetable oil for frying

FOR THE MASALA PASTE

½ teaspoon cumin seeds
2 teaspoons coriander seeds
1 teaspoon peppercorns
½ teaspoon cloves
¼ teaspoon turmeric
½ teaspoon salt
½ teaspoon sugar
5 red chillies
3 garlic cloves
A walnut-sized piece of tamarind, seeded
5 cm (2 in) piece of ginger
2 tablespoons red wine vinegar

Pre-heat the oven to its highest setting. Apply a generous layer of masala paste to the insides of the fish. Reassemble the fish and tie it in two places with string to secure. Dust the fish with the seasoned flour and shake off any excess. Heat the oil in a roasting tin and fry on one side until it turns deep brown. Turn the fish and cook in the oven for about 8 minutes then serve the fish tied, snipping the string at the last moment. The *Kachumber Salad* (see p. 52) and naan bread make good accompaniments.

FILLETS OF MACKEREL WITH DILL AND NEW POTATOES

This is one of my favourite dishes for early summer when I catch some mackerel, come back from sea, go straight into the kitchen and fillet them while they are still stiff. I don't even bother to wash them, just dust them with seasoned flour, fry them with a bit of oil and butter and sprinkle them with chopped fresh dill from my garden. I usually eat them with freshly dug new potatoes, boiled with dill, and served with lemon wedges. With a bottle of Muscadet to wash it all down, it's pure pleasure.

SERVES 4

- 4 mackerel, each weighing about 175–225 g (6–8 oz)
- 450 g (1 lb) new potatoes
- 1 small bunch of fresh dill, chopped, stalks reserved
- 50 g (2 oz) seasoned flour
- 25 ml (1 fl oz) vegetable oil
- 25 g (1 oz) unsalted butter
- 1 lemon
- Salt

Either ask your fishmonger to fillet the mackerel for you or see p. 21 for instructions on filleting it yourself.

Boil the new potatoes in a pan of well-salted water with the dill stalks.

Dust the fillets in the seasoned flour and shake off any excess. Heat the oil in a frying pan and add a knob of the butter. Fry the mackerel for 3 minutes on each side then remove from the pan and keep warm.

Pour away the fish-frying oil and butter. Add the rest of the butter to the pan and heat it until it smells nutty. Squeeze the juice of half the lemon into the pan then pour over the fillets. Season the mackerel with salt, sprinkle over the dill and serve with the remaining half of the lemon cut into wedges.

SALMON MARINATED IN DILL

The best cut of salmon for this dish known in Scandinavia as gravlax, is the middle of the fish. Ask your fishmonger to cut the salmon in half lengthways and remove the bones. Wash and scale it before beginning the marinating (see p. 20).

SERVES 6

- 1.25 kg (2½ lb) fresh salmon
- 1 large bunch of dill
- 100 g (4 oz) salt, preferably sea salt
- 75 g (3 oz) sugar
- 2 tablespoons white peppercorns, crushed

Place half the fish, skin side down, in a shallow dish. Roughly chop the dill and mix it with the salt, sugar and crushed peppercorns. Cover the salmon with this dry cure and place the other piece of salmon on top, skin side up. Cover the fish with aluminium foil or cling film and place a plate, slightly bigger than the salmon, on top. Place a weight on top of the plate to press the fish down. Refrigerate for two days, turning the fish about every 12 hours and spooning over the liquid from the salmon. Remember to replace the weight each time.

Remove the salmon from the brine and slice it thinly, like smoked salmon. You can scrape off the dill coating if you like but I think it looks rather nice to have a green line of dill on each slice. Serve with the *Horseradish and Mustard Sauce* (see opposite).

SALMON STEAKS WITH MUSCADET, WATERCRESS AND DILL POTATOES

In this recipe salmon steaks are fried briefly on both sides in clarified butter and then cooked in the oven until still slightly underdone. A sauce is made from the pan juices.

SERVES 4

    750 g (1½ lb) potatoes
    1 small bunch of dill
    75 g (3 oz) unsalted butter
    4 salmon steaks, each weighing about 200 g
        (7 oz)
    50 ml (2 fl oz) Muscadet or other dry white
        wine
    120 ml (4 fl oz) *Fish Stock* (see p. 36) or
        Chicken Stock (see p. 37)
    1 tablespoon fresh chopped parsley
    75 g (3 oz) watercress
    25 ml (1 fl oz) virgin olive oil
    1 teaspoon white wine vinegar
    Salt and freshly ground black pepper

Cut the potatoes into long, triangular finger-length pieces. Place in a pan with the dill (keeping back a few sprigs to garnish) and simmer gently in salted water.

Pre-heat the oven to 200°C/400°F/Gas 6. Clarify 25 g (1 oz) of the butter by melting it gently in a small pan then leaving it for 4–5 minutes until the solids fall to the bottom. Pour the clear butter off into a frying pan. Season the salmon steaks with salt and pepper. Heat the clarified butter, add the salmon and brown on both sides. Remove the pan from the heat and leave for 30 seconds. Pour over the wine, place the pan in the oven and cook for about 5 minutes.

Remove the salmon steaks from the pan and keep warm while you make the sauce. Pour the stock into the pan, bring to the boil and add the remaining butter. Boil rapidly to reduce the volume by half then add the parsley.

Arrange the salmon, watercress and the potatoes on four warmed plates. Mix together the olive oil, wine vinegar and ½ teaspoon of salt and spoon over the watercress. Pour the sauce over the fish and serve. *Serve a crisp Muscadet.*

HORSERADISH AND MUSTARD SAUCE

This is the perfect accompaniment to the *Salmon Marinated in Dill* opposite. It also goes well with smoked salmon.

    2 teaspoons grated horseradish
    2 teaspoons grated onion (grated on a
        cheese grater)
    1 teaspoon Dijon mustard
    1 teaspoon sugar
    25 ml (1 fl oz) white wine vinegar
    A good pinch of salt
    250 ml (8 fl oz) double cream

Mix together all the ingredients except the cream. Whip the cream to stiff peaks then fold in the rest of the ingredients and chill.

SALMON EN CROÛTE

No fish cookery book would be complete without a recipe for salmon cooked in puff pastry. I have always thought that tarragon has a great affinity with salmon and so I've put a lot of it in this recipe. This is quite a rich and filling dish so you don't need a tremendous amount of salmon per person. I've allowed just over 150 g (5 oz).

SERVES 6

100 g (4 oz) unsalted butter
1 carrot, cut into matchsticks
1 leek, cut into matchsticks
50 g (2 oz) button mushrooms, thinly sliced
50 ml (2 fl oz) white wine
2 teaspoons roughly chopped fresh tarragon leaves
1 teaspoon salt
Freshly ground white pepper
750 g (1½ lb) puff pastry, preferably made with butter
900 g (2 lb) salmon fillet, skinned and boned
1 egg, beaten
600 ml (1 pint) *Fish Stock* (see p. 36)
175 ml (6 fl oz) double cream
Juice of ¼ lemon

Put 25 g (1 oz) butter in a pan, add the vegetables, half the white wine and 1 teaspoon of the tarragon. Season with the salt and white pepper. Cover and cook very gently for about 5 minutes. Remove the lid and cook for another 2 minutes gently driving off the moisture. Remove from the heat and leave to go cool.

Pre-heat the oven to 230°C/450°F/Gas 8. Roll out the puff pastry to about 3 mm (⅛ in) in thickness. It should be the same shape and larger than your fillet of salmon so it can contain both the fish and vegetables. Trim the edges to neaten. Place half the cooked vegetables in the centre of one half of the pastry so that it covers an area the same size as the salmon. Lay the salmon on top, season and top with the remaining vegetables.

Brush the edges with some of the beaten egg and chill for 30 minutes. Lift up the other half of the pastry and fold it over the salmon and vegetables and pinch the two edges together to seal. Seal the two ends in the same way.

Place on a lightly greased baking tray and brush liberally with the beaten egg. You can decorate the top of the parcel with leaves cut from the left-over pastry and brush these with the egg. Bake for 20 minutes. Remove from the oven and leave to rest for at least 5 minutes before serving.

Meanwhile, make the sauce. Put the fish stock, the rest of the white wine, the cream and 25 g (1 oz) of the butter into a pan and boil to reduce it in volume by two-thirds. Make sure the sauce does not boil over when you begin the reduction. About 30 seconds before finishing the sauce, add the remaining tarragon, the lemon juice and a pinch of salt. Finally, cut the remaining butter into cubes and whisk into the sauce.

Slice the salmon at the table and serve the sauce separately.

A rich Chardonnay would go well with this – perhaps Rothbury Chardonnay from the Hunter Valley in Australia – or a Mâcon such as Mâcon Lugny.

ESCALOPES OF SALMON WITH A SORREL SAUCE

The thin escalopes of salmon are cooked so quickly that they are almost raw inside. I find salmon and salmon trout, which you can use equally well in this recipe, disappointing when cooked right through, as they become dry.

SERVES 4

- 750 g (1½ lb) salmon fillet, from a good-sized salmon
- 25 ml (1 fl oz) groundnut oil
- 600 ml (1 pint) *Fish Stock* (see p. 36)
- 175 ml (6 fl oz) double cream
- 50 ml (2 fl oz) vermouth (like Dry Martini or Noilly Prat)
- 25 g (1 oz) fresh sorrel leaves
- 75 g (3 oz) unsalted butter
- Juice of ¼ lemon
- Salt

Remove any bones from the fillet with tweezers, long-nosed pliers or by trapping them between the point of a small vegetable knife and your thumb.

With a sharp filleting knife or carving knife cut the salmon into 12 slices about 5 mm (¼ in) thick. Cut on the slant down to the skin angling your knife at about 45° so that you get wider slices. Brush a grilling tray with oil and put in the 12 escalopes of salmon. Brush lightly with oil and season with a little salt.

Pre-heat the grill to high and put four large plates in the oven to warm. Place the fish stock, half the cream and vermouth in a pan and boil rapidly to reduce by three-quarters. Meanwhile, wash and pick the stalks from the sorrel. Slice the leaves very thinly. When the fish stock has reduced, add the rest of the cream, the butter and the lemon juice. Reduce a little more then stir in all but a pinch of the sorrel.

Grill the escalopes for about 1 minute. Pour the sauce over the warm plates. Carefully lift the escalopes from the grilling tray with a palette knife and lay them on the plates, slightly overlapping. Sprinkle over a little chopped sorrel and serve.

A slightly off-dry white wine is excellent with this – perhaps a grassy New Zealand Sauvignon or a Chenin Blanc from the Loire, such as dry Vouvray.

SMOKED SALMON WITH SCRAMBLED EGGS

Smoked salmon with scrambled eggs is for the sort of breakfast at which you will also be drinking champagne with one of those euphoric hangovers after an evening which was quite special. On reflection, you'd better get somebody else to make it!

SERVES 4

    4 thin slices brown bread
    100 g (4 oz) unsalted butter
    12 eggs
    ½ teaspoon salt
    Freshly ground black pepper
    25 ml (1 fl oz) double cream
    100 g (4 oz) thinly sliced smoked salmon

Toast the four slices of brown bread, spread thinly with butter then cut off the crusts. Now cut each piece of buttered toast into six 'triangles' by cutting off each corner of the square midway between one corner and the next. Cut the small square of toast that remains in half. (Eating the scrambled egg is much easier when it's resting on neatly cut small pieces of toast.)

Break the eggs into a bowl and whisk together with the salt and pepper. Melt the butter in a pan and add the eggs. Stir with a wooden spoon scraping the cooked egg away from the bottom of the pan all the time until the degree of firmness that you like is achieved; I prefer the eggs to be a little runny.

Remove the pan from the heat and stir in the double cream. Fold the smoked salmon into the scrambled eggs and serve on the buttered toast.

PAN-FRIED TROUT WITH GARLIC AND BACON

This is one of the straight-out-of-the-river-into-the-pan recipes which reminds me of a passage from Mark Twain's *Tom Sawyer*:

'They fried the fish with bacon and were astonished; for no fish had ever seemed so delicious before. They did not know that the quicker a fresh fish is on the fire after he is caught, the better he is.'

SERVES 4

    4 trout or sea trout each weighing about
        225 g (8 oz)
    Flour, for dusting
    Small knob of butter
    25 ml (1 fl oz) vegetable oil
    6 rashers streaky bacon, cut into thin strips
    4 garlic cloves, chopped
    25 ml (1 fl oz) *Shallot Vinegar* (see p. 52)
    1 teaspoon fresh parsley, finely chopped
    Salt and freshly ground black pepper

Gut and scale the fish (see p. 20). Season inside and out then dust with flour shaking off any excess. Melt the butter with the oil in a frying pan. Add the bacon and then the trout and fry for about 5 minutes on each side. Remove the trout and bacon from the pan and keep warm.

Turn down the heat, add the garlic and cook gently until soft. Pour the vinegar into the pan and bring to the boil. Add the chopped parsley, stir and pour over the fish. Serve immediately.

POACHED SEA TROUT WITH MAYONNAISE, NEW POTATOES AND CUCUMBER SALAD

The sea trout in the recipe should be served warm, not hot.

SERVES 4

I sea trout, weighing about 1.5 kg (3–3½ lb)
750 g (1½ lb) new potatoes, preferably freshly dug
3 sprigs of mint
I cucumber
I tablespoon white wine vinegar
I quantity *Olive Oil Mayonnaise* (see p. 43)

FOR THE COURT-BOUILLON

½ lemon, thinly sliced
2 bay leaves
3.4 litres (6 pints) water
150 ml (5 fl oz) white wine vinegar
I carrot, thinly sliced
I onion, thinly sliced
12 peppercorns
5 tablespoons salt

Place all the *court-bouillon* ingredients in a fish kettle and bring to the boil. (See p. 35 for alternative ways of cooking if you don't have a fish kettle.) Simmer for 10 minutes. Add the sea trout, bring back to the boil and simmer very gently for 5 minutes. Remove the fish kettle from the heat and set aside to cool for about 20 minutes.

Boil the new potatoes with 1 sprig of mint in salted water until soft. Drain and keep warm.

Peel the cucumber and slice it as thinly as possible, preferably with a mandolin. (See p. 35). Chop the leaves of the remaining mint sprigs and mix them together with the sliced cucumber and white wine vinegar.

Remove the sea trout from the fish kettle and serve with a bowl of new potatoes, the mayonnaise and the cucumber salad.

Serve with a bottle of moderately priced white Burgundy like Rully, a Chardonnay from the Côtes Chalonnaise.

SEARED SMOKED SEA TROUT WITH CHIVE DRESSING

Smoked sea trout is cured in the same way as salmon: brined and then smoke-cured without heating. There is no need to cook the fillet through; it should be seared on the outside and just warm in the centre. Use a ribbed steak pan to get the sear marks. You can also use smoked salmon for this dish.

SERVES 4

350–450 g (12–16 oz) piece smoked sea trout, skinned and cut into 4
I small bunch of chives
I small shallot, finely chopped
85 ml (3 fl oz) extra virgin olive oil

I tablespoon white wine vinegar
½ teaspoon salt

Finely slice all but four chives. Mix the chives and shallot with the oil, vinegar and salt.

Heat the ribbed pan until smoking hot. Brush the fillets with olive oil and grill on each side for 30–60 seconds, depending on thickness. The centre should be just lukewarm.

Divide the dressing between four warmed plates and lay the fillets on top. Drape a chive over each fillet and serve.

(ABOVE) Escalopes of Salmon with
a Sorrel Sauce (*see page 95*), (TOP
RIGHT) Marinated Sea Trout with
Lime and Pink Peppercorns (*see
page 100*) and (RIGHT) Salmon
Marinated in Dill (*see page 92*)

BRAISED FILLET OF SEA TROUT WITH BASIL, CELERIAC AND CHAMBÉRY

Any dry white vermouth will do for this recipe if you can't get hold of Chambéry.

SERVES 4

100 g (4 oz) unsalted butter
175 g (6 oz) celeriac, cut into matchsticks
½ medium onion, finely chopped
120 ml (4 fl oz) white vermouth
600 ml (1 pint) *Chicken Stock* (see p. 37)
4 fillets of sea trout, each weighing about 200 g (7 oz)
6 fresh basil leaves, thinly sliced
Salt and freshly ground white pepper

Melt the butter in a heavy pan, big enough for the fillets to be cooked side by side without overlapping too much. Add the celeriac and onion and soften for 2 minutes. Add the vermouth and half the chicken stock and simmer gently, covered, for about 10 minutes, then remove the lid.

Season the fillets with the salt and white pepper and place them in the pan on top of the vegetables. Pour in the rest of the chicken stock and sprinkle all but a final pinch of the basil over the top of the fish. Cover and braise very gently until the fish has just cooked.

Remove the sea trout from the pan and keep warm on a serving dish. Concentrate the flavour of the braised vegetables by turning the heat to high and boiling rapidly to reduce the volume by about half. Pour the contents of the pan around the fillets and garnish with the remaining basil.

Accompany with some fine beans and boiled potatoes.

The best wine to accompany this rich and slightly sweet dish is a full-flavoured Chardonnay, maybe a New Zealand Chardonnay such as Wairau River or an Australian like Rothbury Estate.

MARINATED SEA TROUT WITH LIME AND PINK PEPPERCORNS

This is a wonderful way of serving sea trout. Pink peppercorns are available nowadays in good delicatessens.

SERVES 4

225 g (8 oz) sea trout fillet

FOR THE DRESSING

120 ml (4 fl oz) groundnut oil
10 g (¼ oz) fresh ginger, finely chopped
1 teaspoon pink peppercorns
Juice and zest of 1 lime
½ teaspoon salt

Place the fillet, skin side down, on a chopping board, take a very sharp, thin-bladed knife and cut thin slices on the slant towards the tail. Cut enough to cover four dinner plates. Flatten the fish by pressing a second plate briefly down on to the slices. Allow plenty of time to slice the fish as it is quite tricky.

Mix together all the dressing ingredients in a bowl or shake together in a screw-top jar. Five minutes before serving, pour the dressing over the fish, spreading it with the back of a teaspoon. Serve immediately.

DEVILLED SPRATS WITH RAVIGOTE SAUCE

In this dish of powerful flavours, sprats are brushed with mustard and coated with the breadcrumbs then grilled. You can make this dish with pilchards too.

SERVES 4

40 g (1½ oz) Dijon mustard
1 teaspoon dark soft brown sugar
75 g (3 oz) fresh breadcrumbs
¼ teaspoon cayenne pepper
½ teaspoon salt
16 whole, gutted sprats
Vegetable oil for brushing

FOR THE RAVIGOTE SAUCE

2 teaspoons Dijon mustard
1 tablespoon red wine vinegar
175 ml (6 fl oz) groundnut oil
1 tablespoon capers, coarsely chopped
2 sprigs of tarragon, finely chopped
1 tablespoon finely chopped flatleaf parsley
1 tablespoon finely chopped onion
Salt and freshly ground black pepper

Pre-heat the grill to high. Brush the sprats with some of the mustard. Mix together the rest of the mustard, sugar, breadcrumbs, cayenne pepper and salt in a wide flat dish. Roll the sprats in the coating, dab with vegetable oil and place on a grilling tray. Grill for about 2 minutes on each side. Mix together all the ingredients for the sauce. Serve with the fish accompanied by some boiled potatoes.

DEEP-FRIED WHITEBAIT WITH LEMON AND PERSILLADE

The action of chopping parsley with garlic to make *persillade* actually removes a lot of the hot taste of the garlic. The chlorophyll in the parsley neutralizes the powerful aroma in garlic which is why chewing parsley is good for getting rid of garlic on the breath. *Persillade* gives a very pleasant savoury herb taste which I use a great deal in my cooking. You can use sand eels instead of whitebait in this dish if you prefer them.

SERVES 4

2 garlic cloves
1 small bunch of parsley
75 g (3 oz) flour
½ teaspoon cayenne pepper
1 teaspoon salt
550 g (1¼ lb) whitebait or sand eels
Oil for deep-frying
1 lemon, cut into wedges

Peel the garlic and chop fairly finely. Remove the stalks from the parsley. Continue to chop the garlic, gradually chopping the parsley and incorporating with the garlic until you have a very fine mixture.

Put the flour, cayenne pepper and salt into a bowl and mix together. Wash the whitebait or sand eels under cold running water and shake them out vigorously in a colander.

Heat the oil to 190°C/375°F. Coat the whitebait with the seasoned flour, shaking off any excess. Deep-fry the fish in batches until they are crisp (about 3 minutes per batch). Remove from the fryer and drain on kitchen paper. Place in a large bowl and sprinkle with the *persillade*. Serve with lemon wedges.

MEDITERRANEAN FISH: BREAM, GURNARD, MULLET AND SEA BASS

This chapter is devoted to those fish that are neither oily nor non-oily. But another way of grouping them is to consider them as the sort of fish you might cook on a barbecue or with Mediterranean ingredients like olive oil, garlic, aromatic herbs, olives and anchovies.

BREAM

You can usually expect to find two types of bream in the waters around the British Isles: red bream or black. Occasionally, you will find the gilt-head bream or the ray's bream on sale too. The gilt head bream, or *daurade* as it is known in France, has the best flavour of them all, but all breams are well-flavoured.

GURNARD

Most fish is expensive if you consider the actual price per pound of fillet. So it is a great pleasure to find a fish of real quality which costs very little. But like travel writers who extol the virtues of some hitherto unknown paradise only to have it overrun, so I have a slight feeling of regret in telling you how wonderful gurnard is as it will inevitably push the price up. But it is good; the fillets are firm and sweet. So if you see one on a fishmonger's slab, go ahead and buy it. Not only is the fillet exceptional but the bones add an essential taste to Mediterranean fish soup.

MULLET

People often ask me 'What is your favourite fish?' Well it's a bit like being asked 'Which is your favourite child?' The obvious answer to both questions is 'I love them all'. But mullet has a special place in my affections, with its beautiful pink and yellow tinges and its firm flaky texture and taste somewhere between fish and shellfish. The smell of mullet cooking on a grill evokes memories of Greek tavernas at the beginning of the season, before the crowds have arrived.

Red mullet is a fairly common fish in the South West of England, particularly in October and November when they are caught off the North Cornish coast. I don't know why it is, but I have a real problem selling red mullet at the restaurant. Maybe it is because people have bought it in other restaurants and found it inferior. There is quite a trade in indifferent frozen red mullet but all I know is that I have to work extremely hard to persuade people to eat them by saying things like 'this utterly delicious fish' beside the description of the dish. To me it is incredibly good, full of flavour and aroma. The only problem with red mullet, though, is that in the South West of England it is usually only caught as a by-product of trawling for other fish; this means that only one or two will turn up in the nets at a time.

SEA BASS

It is generally true that mature, fully-grown fish taste better than immature undersized fish and this is particularly so with bass. A fillet from a large fish brushed with butter, seasoned with salt and pepper and roasted in the oven with maybe a simple *beurre blanc* or *Hollandaise* will be a revelation if you have never tried it before.

However, bass, even in its small form, is a delicious fish which easily justifies its high price. Soft in texture with a sweet delicate flavour, it never fails to delight people, particularly when it's cooked in a way that crisps up the skin.

The flesh of sea bass is moist and fresh with a soft texture which is slightly flaky. The skin, however, is quite oily and indeed bass is richer in oil than might be expected of a fish often described as delicate. But because of the balance between richness and delicacy, bass is a fish capable of being successfully cooked in a myriad of different ways.

What you're liable to see mostly in fishmongers these days is rather small bass because they are being successfully farmed.

No doubt, in time, fish farmers will grow their bass to much larger sizes. But at present, they're all coming out at about 550 g (1¼ lb). The quality of these farmed fish is perfectly acceptable, though I still have mixed feelings about fish farming. There is no doubt, if we wish to continue to be able to buy fish like bass, salmon and, probably, turbot, which is also being farmed, we will have to supplement the supply of wild fish with farmed. However, the wild fish will always taste better.

I never serve farmed fish at the restaurant because I feel that my reputation relies on serving seafood straight from the sea but it is perfectly acceptable at home.

BAKED RED BREAM AND FENNEL WITH ORANGE AND PROVENÇAL HERBS

In this dish, fennel and onions are cooked with olive oil, orange and herbs until soft. The fish is then baked with the fennel. The baking times are for bream weighing about 500 g (1 lb 2 oz) each. If using bigger ones bake for a little longer. This dish also works very well with snapper or parrot fish, red mullet, grey mullet and sea bass. Accompany with *Grilled Vegetables* (see p. 104). If making fresh *herbes de Provence* combine chopped thyme, fennel, savory, sage, hyssop and marjoram.

SERVES 4

1 teaspoon dried or 1 tablespoon fresh
   herbes de Provence
1 orange
3 anchovy fillets, chopped
2 tablespoons Pernod or Ricard
3 bulbs of fennel, outer leaves removed
1 teaspoon salt
1 large onion, chopped
2 fresh bay leaves, cut into thin strips or 2
   dried bay leaves, crushed
3 garlic cloves, thinly sliced
25 ml (1 fl oz) white wine vinegar
50 ml (2 fl oz) olive oil
1 teaspoon sugar
4 whole red bream weighing about 2 kg
   (4½ lb) in total
Salt and freshly ground black pepper

Pare the zest from half the orange with a potato peeler and cut into short, thin strips, like pine needles. Put all the ingredients (including the juice of the orange) except the fish, in a heavy-based pan and cook gently, covered, for about 15 minutes or until the fennel is soft.

Pre-heat the oven to 200°C/400°F/Gas 6. Remove any scales from the fish then wash and dry it thoroughly. Slash the fish three times diagonally on both sides cutting right down to the bone. Season generously with salt and pepper both inside and out.

Place half the fennel and onion mixture in the bottom of a shallow ovenproof dish, place the fish on top and spoon the rest of the fennel and onion over it. Cover with foil and bake for 20 minutes.

Remove the foil covering the fish and bake for a further 5 minutes.

GRILLED VEGETABLES

1 aubergine, sliced
2 courgettes, sliced
2 red onions, cut into quarters lengthways
1 bulb fennel, sliced lengthways
2 red peppers, seeded and cut into 8 pieces
25 ml (1 fl oz) olive oil
A pinch of marjoram
Salt and freshly ground black pepper

Pre-heat the grill, or a barbecue, to high.

Put all the ingredients in a bowl and stir to coat evenly with the oil, marjoram and seasoning. Grill or barbecue until cooked through.

POACHED QUENELLES OF GURNARD WITH PRAWN SAUCE

Gurnard makes a good *quenelle* because of its firm texture and positive flavour. *Quenelles* are a kind of fish forcemeat, moulded in dessert spoons and poached in water. Here, they are served with a prawn sauce. Reserve a few prawns removed from making the sauce to garnish.

SERVES 4

FOR THE QUENELLES

25 g (1 oz) butter
150 ml (5 fl oz) milk
50 g (2 oz) fresh white breadcrumbs
350 g (12 oz) gurnard, skinned and boned
1/8 teaspoon grated nutmeg
Juice of 1/4 lemon
1 egg
120 ml (4 fl oz) double cream
Freshly ground white pepper
1 teaspoon salt

FOR THE PRAWN SAUCE

1 quantity *Shellfish Reduction* made with prawns (see p. 37)
85 ml (3 fl oz) double cream
1 teaspoon unsalted butter mixed with flour (*beurre manié*)
1 egg yolk

To make the *quenelles*, melt the butter and add to the milk and breadcrumbs to form a coarse paste and chill. All the ingredients for the *quenelles* must be completely cold. Place the paste and all the ingredients except the cream in a food processor and blend until smooth. With the processor still running, pour in the cream taking no more than 10 seconds to add it.

To make the prawn sauce, heat the shellfish reduction then stir in half of the double cream and all of the *beurre manié*. Leave the sauce to thicken then remove from the heat, set aside and keep warm.

Fill a shallow pan of lightly salted water deep enough to immerse the *quenelles* (about 5 cm/2 in). Bring to the boil then reduce the heat until the water reaches a slow simmer.

Mould all the fish forcemeat into lozenge-shaped *quenelles* using 2 table- or dessert-spoons. Dip the spoons in a jug of hot water between making each *quenelle* to make it easier to achieve a smooth shape. As you form each *quenelle* drop it into the lightly simmering water. Leave to poach for about 5 minutes.

Remove from the water with a slotted spoon and dry on a clean tea towel or kitchen paper. This will prevent the excess water from weakening the sauce. Place the *quenelles* in a warm gratin dish. Pre-heat the grill to high.

Whisk together the egg yolk and the remaining cream and add to the prawn sauce. Re-heat the sauce over a low heat without boiling then pour over the *quenelles*. Place the dish under the grill to glaze until the surface starts to turn brown. Serve piping hot.

GURNARD WITH BOUILLABAISSE SAUCE AND HARISSA POTATOES

I have taken the flavours of the classic *bouillabaisse*: saffron, garlic, olive oil and *herbes de Provence* and reduced them to a sauce. It is served with grilled fillets of gurnard and boiled potatoes tossed in fiery *harissa*, a Moroccan blend of chilli and coriander.

SERVES 4

- 50 ml (2 fl oz) olive oil
- 50 g (2 oz) white of leek, finely chopped
- 50 g (2 oz) Florence fennel, finely chopped
- 3 garlic cloves, finely chopped
- 50 g (2 oz) onion, finely chopped
- 1 strip of orange peel
- A good pinch of saffron
- A pinch of cayenne pepper
- 600 ml (1 pint) *Fish Stock* (see p. 36)
- 50 ml (2 fl oz) dry white wine
- 1 tomato, chopped
- 50 g (2 oz) *Salt Cod* fillet, skinned and boned (see p. 53)
- 100 g (4 oz) potato
- 1 tablespoon *Harissa* (see p. 45)
- 900 g (2 lb) gurnard fillets, skin on
- 1 teaspoon green peppercorns, roughly chopped
- Salt

Heat the oil in a pan and add the leek, fennel, garlic, onion, orange peel, saffron and cayenne pepper. Fry for 2–3 minutes to soften then add the fish stock, white wine and tomato. Bring to the boil and boil rapidly to reduce the volume by three-quarters.

Cut the salt cod into tiny squares about 3 × 3 mm ($\frac{1}{8}$ × $\frac{1}{8}$ in). Add to the reduced stock and vegetables and simmer for another couple of minutes. Set the sauce aside and keep warm.

Peel the potato and cut it into pieces the size of matchsticks. Poach in salted water until just cooked. Drain thoroughly and mix with the *harissa*. Set aside and keep warm.

Pre-heat the grill to high. Brush the gurnard fillets with olive oil and sprinkle with salt and peppercorns. Grill, skin side up, for 4–5 minutes. Place the fillets on four warmed plates. Place a pile of potatoes on each plate and pour the *bouillabaisse* sauce beside each fillet.

Serve with a good robust Provençal white or rosé wine.

(BELOW) Baked Red Bream and Fennel with Orange and Provençal Herbs (*see page 103*), (TOP RIGHT) Roast Sea Bass with Braised Red Cabbage and Rösti Potatoes (*see page 115*) and (BELOW RIGHT) Grilled Red Mullet with an Aubergine and Pesto Salad (*see page 108*)

GRILLED RED MULLET WITH AN AUBERGINE AND PESTO SALAD

What could be better than fillets of red mullet with some grilled aubergines, *pesto* and salad? A perfect combination of flavours. This dish has its roots in the cooking of Simon Hopkinson, who used to be the chef at Bibendum restaurant in London. I'd rate him as about the best cook in the country.

SERVES 4

½ aubergine
Olive oil for brushing
4 fillets of red mullet each weighing about
   75–100 g (3–4 oz)

FOR THE PESTO

15 g (½ oz) fresh basil
2 large garlic cloves
175 ml (6 fl oz) olive oil
15 g (½ oz) Parmesan
15 g (½ oz) pine kernels

FOR THE SALAD

75 g (3 oz) mixed salad leaves
1 tomato, peeled, seeded and chopped
1 teaspoon *Lemon Olive Oil* (see p. 51)
Salt and freshly ground black pepper

Put all the *pesto* ingredients in a liquidizer, blend for about 10 seconds then remove half the mixture and set aside; it should be fairly coarse at this stage. Blend the remaining *pesto* until it is smooth.

Pre-heat the grill to high. Slice the aubergine into 4 × 1 cm (½ in) thick slices. Brush liberally with olive oil and season with salt. Grill until just cooked through.

Brush the red mullet fillets with olive oil and season with salt and pepper. Grill for about 4 minutes, 2 minutes on each side.

Meanwhile, spread the aubergine slices with the coarse *pesto* and place under the grill until the *pesto* has warmed through. Place an aubergine slice on each of four warmed plates and arrange the fish alongside them.

Toss the salad leaves with the tomato, lemon olive oil and salt and put a small pile on each plate. Pour the smooth *pesto* around each plate, making sure that some, but not all, trickles over the fillets, and serve.

DEEP-FRIED RED MULLET WITH LEMON GRASS, CHILLI, GARLIC AND GINGER

This dish is quite spicy and hot. The flavours are inspired by Thai cooking, making this a wonderfully aromatic way to cook fish. If you would prefer the dish to be a little less hot, remove the seeds from the chillies before chopping them.

Serve with the *Stir-fried Spinach with Garlic, Ginger and Chilli* on p. 112.

SERVES 4

Oil, for deep-frying
4 red mullet, each weighing about
    275–350 g (10–12 oz)
1 quantity *Tempura Batter* (see p. 53)

FOR THE MARINADE

2 teaspoons arrowroot
120 ml (4 fl oz) water
2 lemon grass sticks, outer leaves removed,
    finely sliced
3 small red chillies, finely chopped
4 cloves garlic, finely chopped
5 cm (2 in) piece fresh ginger, peeled and
    finely chopped
Juice and zest of 1 lime
3 tablespoons Thai fish sauce (*nam pla*)
15 g (½ oz) fresh coriander, roughly chopped

To make the marinade mix the arrowroot with the 120 ml (4 fl oz) of water in a small pan. Place over a moderate heat and bring to the boil until clear and thick. Remove from the heat and leave to cool before mixing with the rest of the marinade ingredients.

Heat the oil in a deep-fryer or large pan to 180°C/350°F.

De-scale and gut the fish and snip off the fins. Cut three 2.5 cm (1 in) pockets in each side of the red mullet. Insert ½ teaspoon of the marinade into each pocket and the gut cavity of the fish. Dip the red mullet in the batter and deep-fry in the hot oil for about 5 minutes. Remove and drain on kitchen paper. Place the fish on a serving dish and sprinkle over the rest of the marinade.

Serve the fish with the stir-fried spinach (see following recipe) and boiled rice, preferably jasmine which you can buy in most supermarkets now.

Serve with an Australian Chardonnay or Alsace Gewürztraminer or some chilled lager.

(ABOVE) Deep-fried Red Mullet with Lemon Grass, Chilli, Garlic and Ginger (*see page 109*), (TOP RIGHT) Grilled Sea Bass with Straw Potatoes and Salsa Verde (*see page 116*) and (RIGHT) Grilled Sea Bass with Beurre Blanc and Marsh Samphire (*see page 114*)

STIR-FRIED SPINACH WITH GARLIC, GINGER AND CHILLI

If you are lucky enough to be able to get fresh morning glory leaves from a Thai or Chinese supermarket, it is even better than the spinach.

SERVES 4

25 ml (1 fl oz) vegetable oil
1 teaspoon finely chopped garlic
1 teaspoon finely chopped fresh ginger
225 g (8 oz) spinach leaves

A pinch of chilli powder
1 teaspoon Thai fish sauce (*nam pla*) or anchovy paste

Heat the oil in a wok and add the garlic and ginger. Stir-fry quickly until they start to brown. Add the spinach and turn in the oil for about 30 seconds. Add the chilli powder and fish sauce or anchovy paste. Reduce the heat to low, cover and cook for about 1 minute, then serve.

GRILLED GREY MULLET WITH GARLIC, LEMON AND THYME

The grey mullets are slashed and marinated in olive oil, garlic and thyme. The marinade is made into a sauce with orange and anchovies.

SERVES 4

4 grey mullet each weighing about 350 g (12 oz)

FOR THE MARINADE

Juice of 1 lemon
150 ml (5 fl oz) olive oil
2 teaspoons very finely chopped fresh thyme
1 teaspoon sea salt
1 garlic clove, finely chopped
Freshly ground black pepper

FOR THE SAUCE

2 anchovy fillets, drained and finely chopped
1 orange
50 ml (2 fl oz) water

Slash the fish three times on each side cutting down to the bone. Place in a dish which is not much bigger than the fish itself. Mix together all the marinade ingredients and pour over the mullet. Leave to marinate for 1 hour, turning occasionally.

Pre-heat the grill to high and grill the mullet for 6 minutes on each side, baste with the marinade, twice on each side.

Transfer the fish to a warmed serving dish and add any cooking juices to the marinade. Pour the marinade into a small pan. Add the anchovy, grated rind of ½ orange and juice of the whole orange and the water. Bring to the boil, whisk a little and pour over the fish before serving.

STEAMED GREY MULLET WITH GARLIC, GINGER AND SPRING ONIONS

I consider this to be a perfect combination of flavours; it was the first Chinese fish dish that I really raved about. See pp. 35 and 205 for details on steamers and how to make them.

During the filming of the TV series we came up with the idea of a list of five or six fish recipes which have been the most influential in forming my style of seafood cooking, a sort of Desert Island Dishes. *Steamed Grey Mullet with Garlic, Ginger and Spring Onions* wasn't on it because we hadn't got any grey mullet on the day and with all the costs and shortage of time in filming we had to make a decision not to do it. However, this is one of those dishes.

SERVES 4

2.5 cm (1 in) piece fresh ginger, peeled and finely chopped
4 grey mullet about 350 g (12 oz) each
4 spring onions, finely sliced
2 tablespoons soy sauce
50 ml (2 fl oz) water
25 ml (1 fl oz) sesame oil
4 garlic cloves, finely chopped

Sprinkle the ginger over the fish. Bring the water in the steamer up to a fast boil, put the plate in and cover. Steam the fish for 15 minutes then transfer it to a warmed serving plate. Scatter the spring onions over the fish.

Pour the juice from the plate into a small shallow pan and add the soy sauce and water. Heat and pour over the fish and spring onions.

Heat the sesame oil in a small pan. When it is very hot, add the garlic and let it fry for 5 seconds. Pour the oil and garlic over the fish and serve.

CHAR-GRILLED GREY MULLET WITH SLIVERS OF GARLIC, CHILLI AND VIRGIN OLIVE OIL

This is such an amazingly simple dish that one is left wondering whether there is ever any point in doing anything more complicated with fish. It's a perfect dish for serving outside on a summer's evening.

You need either a barbecue grill or a heavy-ribbed grill pan (see p. 35) to make it.

The garlic in this dish must be cut into very thin slivers so that it loses its rawness when the sauce is warmed through. The easiest way to cut it is to slice it in half, place the cut edge on the chopping board, then cut it into long, thin slices.

SERVES 4

4 fillets of grey mullet, skin on, each weighing about 200–225 g (7–8 oz)
50 ml (2 fl oz) virgin olive oil
Salt
½ red chilli, seeded and very finely chopped
25 ml (1 fl oz) white wine vinegar
1 garlic clove, peeled and cut into very fine slivers
1 lemon, cut into wedges
1 teaspoon coarse sea salt

Brush the mullet with a little olive oil and sprinkle lightly with ordinary salt.

Soak the chilli in the vinegar for 20 minutes. Drain the chilli in a small sieve and discard the vinegar. The object of this is not only to make the chilli less hot than it would normally be but also provide a slight tartness to the sauce.

Pre-heat the barbecue or ribbed grill pan to hot and grill the fillets for 2–4 minutes each side depending on the thickness of the fillet. Cook them skin-side down first.

Meanwhile, gently warm the remaining olive oil, garlic and chopped red chilli in a small pan. Do not allow the sauce to heat too close to boiling point as this will destroy the flavour of the oil.

When the fish is cooked, pour the sauce onto four warmed plates. Place the fish on top with a wedge of lemon, sprinkle the sauce with the coarse sea salt and serve with a simple green salad and potatoes fried in their skins.

For the potatoes fried in their skins, wash, but don't peel, some new potatoes, then cut them into wedge shapes, lengthways, and deep-fry until tender.

GRILLED SEA BASS WITH BEURRE BLANC AND MARSH SAMPHIRE

First of all, don't put off cooking this dish if you can't get marsh samphire. Bass with *beurre blanc* is a classic. The samphire has been included because it is a highly fitting vegetable to serve with fish and is especially good with sea bass.

Marsh samphire grows on sandy mud in salt marshes and on muddy seashores all round the British Isles. It has a fresh, salty taste and a firm texture. Having unusual fleshy, light green joined branches rather than leaves and growing little more than 23 cm (9 in) high, it is easy to identify so, if you have the opportunity, try to find some to serve with the sea bass.

SERVES 4

| I sea bass, weighing about 1.5 kg (3½ lb)
| A little melted butter, for brushing
| 225 g (8 oz) fresh marsh samphire
| I quantity *Beurre Blanc* (see p. 42), made
| with fish stock
| Salt and freshly ground black pepper

Snip the fins off the bass, being careful to avoid spiking yourself, then scale the fish and remove the guts. Wash inside and out and slash the flesh of the fish two or three times on each side.

Pre-heat the grill to high. Brush the fish with some melted butter and season inside and out with salt and black pepper. Grill the bass for about 10 minutes on each side.

Wash the samphire thoroughly, then pull off the fleshy leaves and discard the thicker stalks with their woody centres. Bring a pan of unsalted water to the boil and boil the samphire for 2 minutes. Drain, set aside and keep warm.

Pass the *beurre blanc* through a sieve into a clean warm jug.

Serve the fish whole and fillet it at the table on to four warmed plates. Hand round the marsh samphire and *beurre blanc* separately.

ROAST SEA BASS WITH BRAISED RED CABBAGE AND RÖSTI POTATOES

An ideal dish for the cooler months where warming and comforting rösti pancakes are cooked with braised red cabbage sauce and a whole sea bass, which is roasted until the skin is crisp.

SERVES 4

I sea bass, about 1.5 kg (3½ lb)
A little melted butter, for brushing
½ teaspoon salt
Freshly ground black pepper

FOR THE RED CABBAGE

275 g (10 oz) red cabbage
175 g (6 oz) unsalted butter
150 ml (5 fl oz) *Fish Stock* (see p. 36) or
    Chicken Stock (see p. 37)
100 g (4 oz) onion, diced
150 ml (5 fl oz) red wine
25 ml (1 fl oz) wine vinegar
I teaspoon salt
I tablespoon sugar

FOR THE RÖSTI POTATOES

400 g (14 oz) potatoes
25 g (1 oz) smoked bacon or pancetta, cut
    into thin strips
50 ml (2 fl oz) clarified butter, for frying
Salt and freshly ground black pepper

Pre-heat the oven to 200°C/400°F/Gas 6.

To cook the braised red cabbage, remove the outer leaves of the red cabbage and cut out the thick white core. Slice the cabbage as thinly as possible then cut the slices into the smallest possible pieces. Place in an ovenproof dish with 50 g (2 oz) of the butter, half the stock and the remaining cabbage ingredients.

Cover and place in the oven for about 1¼ hours. Stir occasionally. Remove from the oven, add the remaining stock, bring to the boil and stir in the rest of the butter. Keep warm.

To make the rösti, peel the potatoes and shred them on the largest grid of a grater onto a clean tea towel. Gather the edges of the tea towel and squeeze as much moisture out of the potatoes as you can. Don't rinse the potatoes or you will remove the starch that binds the potatoes into a pancake. Season the potato with salt and pepper and add the bacon. Divide into four portions and mould into balls with your hands.

Pour the clarified butter into a small non-stick or well-tempered frying pan and add one ball of potato and bacon. Flatten it over the base of the pan to about 10 cm (4 in) in diameter using a fish slice. Fry over a gentle heat for about 5 minutes. Work the fish slice under the pancake to free it then turn it over to cook on the other side for 5 minutes. Towards the end of the cooking time press out then pour off the excess butter. Place the rösti on some absorbent paper to remove any remaining greasiness.

To cook the fish, pre-heat the oven to its highest setting. Brush the bass inside and out with the melted butter then season inside and out with the salt and pepper. Place in a roasting tin and roast in the oven for about 25 minutes basting a couple of times with the juices from the tray.

Place the fish on a large oval plate and pour over the juices from the pan. Serve at the table with the rösti potatoes and the braised red cabbage.

Serve with a fresh red wine such as an Australian Pinot Noir or a Merlot from the Pays d'Oc in France.

GRILLED SEA BASS WITH STRAW POTATOES AND SALSA VERDE

This is the sort of recipe that is very popular in restaurants in Sydney, Los Angeles and San Francisco. I have borrowed ideas from various cooking cultures, the grilled bass with the olive oil from the Mediterranean and the *Kachumber Salad* from India. Sometimes the result of this kind of mixing and matching leads only to pretentious rubbish. But here, the contrast of textures is very satisfying and the salad, with its chilli and coriander, seems to complement the flavour of the bass. For the best results, all the ingredients must be very fresh.

SERVES 4

750 g (1½ lb) sea bass fillet, skin on, divided
  into 4 equal portions
Olive oil for brushing
Salt and freshly ground black pepper

Kachumber Salad (see p. 52)
1 quantity *Salsa Verde* (see p. 48)

FOR THE STRAW POTATOES

175 g (6 oz) white potato, such as Maris
  Piper or Golden Wonder
Oil for deep-frying

To make the straw potatoes, cut the potato into tiny pieces the size of matchsticks. This is most easily done on a mandolin, if you have one (see p. 35). Wash in cold water.

Pre-heat the oil in the deep-fryer to 190°C/375°F. Fry the potatoes until crisp then drain, season with salt and set aside. Keep warm.

Pre-heat the grill. Brush the bass with olive oil and season with salt and pepper. Grill on both sides, taking care not to overcook. If cut from a small (450–900 g)/(1–2 lb) fish allow about 2 minutes on each side but up to 5 minutes on each side if the fillets are thick.

Place the bass on four warmed plates and serve with *Kachumber Salad*, a tablespoon of *Salsa Verde* and a pile of the straw potatoes.

GRILLED WHOLE SEA BASS WITH PERNOD AND FENNEL

The anise flavours of Pernod and fennel have an exceptional affinity with sea bass, especially when it is cooked over charcoal. The fennel-flavoured mayonnaise that the fish is served with has a pleasing, slightly bitter alcoholic bite. When the whole fish is served in this way with some freshly dug new potatoes it makes a tremendous combination.

You can either cook the fish on a barbecue or under the grill. If you cook the fish on a barbecue, make sure you light it at least 40 minutes before beginning to cook. It is important that all the flames have died away leaving hot ash because cooking a large fish or, indeed, a large piece of meat on a barbecue which is still flaming will result in a very burnt and charred exterior.

Ideally, some sort of grill wires should be used in-between which the fish can be sandwiched. This is because the best flavour is achieved when the fennel is laid along the outside of the fish so that it chars and flavours the fish. If you don't have grill wires, lay the fish on a bed of fennel sprigs over the barbecue.

SERVES 4

1 large sea bass, weighing about 1.5–1.75 kg (3½–4 lb)
25 ml (1 fl oz) olive oil
Salt and freshly ground black pepper
1 large bunch fennel sprigs
2 teaspoons Pernod, Pastis or Ricard
1 quantity *Fennel Mayonnaise* (see p. 44)

Trim and scale the bass then slash it three times on each side, cutting down to the bone. Brush the fish liberally with olive oil both inside and out then season with salt and pepper. Push several fennel sprigs into the gut cavity. Lay more sprigs on a grill wire and lay the fish on top, placing more on the other side of the fish before closing the grill wire. Grill carefully over charcoal for about 12 minutes each side, taking great care to avoid over-charring the fish. If it seems to be blistering too much move it to a cooler part of the barbecue. Just before turning the fish to cook the second side, sprinkle it liberally with Pernod. Repeat just before taking the cooked fish off the grill.

Serve the bass with the *Fennel Mayonnaise* and a large bowl of boiled new potatoes.
The ideal wine for this magnificent dish is a white Rhône such as Lirac or even a bottle of the Greek wine Retsina.

7

ROUND FISH: THE COD FAMILY, MONKFISH AND JOHN DORY

The great thing about members of the cod family is that they yield thick, succulent, relatively boneless fillets. What they lack a little in taste they more than make up for in texture, and lend themselves to baking and roasting with plenty of robust flavours. Like the cod family, monkfish and John Dory are both non-oily fish. Monkfish suits grilling and barbecuing very well, as does John Dory, which has the added bonus of being suitable for any flat fish recipes.

COD

It is a source of great satisfaction to me that we can now sell cod at the restaurant as easily as bass or salmon. I have always thought it a shame that such a beautiful fish was relegated as being suitable only for fish and chips (good though they are) or fishfingers. Cod doesn't have such a good flavour as other, more expensive, fish but there are some serious compensations for this. First, it has a satisfying chewy texture, second, it comes in enormous milky flakes and, third, with large cod, the bones are not a problem because they are too large and obvious to be eaten accidentally and to get stuck in your throat.

I like the occasional whole codling – a small cod weighing up to 750 g (1½ lb) – if they have jumped straight out of the sea on to the plate, but if they are not this fresh then they become dull. Fillets from large cod, cooked so that the skin is crisp and browned, are what delight me most about cod. I think the quotation on the first page of Keith Floyd's *Floyd on Fish* sums up the cod's superlative qualities.

> 'What on earth is this?'
> 'A piece of cod sir.'
> 'The piece of cod which passeth understanding.'
> (Attributed to Sir Edward Lutyens, speaking to a waiter at Brook's Club.)

A piece of perfectly fresh cod, chewy, flaky, moist and white – it's beyond description.

I was once asked by a leading supermarket chain to do a blind tasting of fish to prove how difficult it is to tell the difference between fresh and frozen fish. I, and the other tasters, sat in little booths bathed in eerie blue light and small lumps of fish on saucers were passed to us through hatches. Everything was deadly quiet, our total concentration was required. The fish had been carefully boiled in unseasoned water. By depriving us of any extraneous sensory influence (including taste, to my mind), we were expected to make a decision about the qualities of fresh over frozen fish. I was incapable of making any sensible critical judgement and concluded that all the fish tasted the same.

The judges were delighted, not only because my reaction was identical to everyone else's, but also because they thought it proved that frozen food is indistinguishable from fresh. That, I say, may well be true if you choose to boil your fish.

The staff running the test were quite well-informed about fish. They told me that, on death, a fish goes through the same sort of enzyme changes as meat, only much faster so the longer you keep fish the more tender it becomes. They actually aged cod before selling it. I remarked at the time that the piece of cod we had tried seemed to be extraordinarily soft. I was told that this was what customers wanted. Market research had shown that any suggestion of toughness in fish would not be tolerated. Interesting that what I consider to be one of the most glorious attributes of fresh cod, it's delightful chewiness, is the one thing that most people apparently don't like.

HADDOCK

'Faced with a fillet of haddock the heart doesn't sing.'

Jane Grigson

I know why. Haddock is one of the best-flavoured fish of all the cod family, but it doesn't look as exciting as cod. Cod has a gleaming steely-grey skin with flashes of yellow and green and sings loud. Haddock is a rather wan grey and black and is a bit limp looking. Don't be put off. Haddock has a sweet, soft flavour and it suits smoking better than all the other fish in the cod family.

Try and buy undyed smoked haddock because it indicates that the fish is of a higher quality. Finnan haddock has an incomparable flavour and is never dyed. But any haddock, if it comes undyed, is likely to have been well looked after.

Haddock can be easily identified because it has a black smudge, rather like a thumb print, near the head; a feature which it shares with John Dory. Both fish are said to have the thumbprint of St Peter on them.

HAKE

Hake fetches by far the best price of all the fish in the cod family at market. The reason for this is that the Spanish, who buy the majority of hake caught in the British Isles, are passionate about it and ensure that, because of great demand, the price is always high. I must say I share their enthusiasm and can't understand why we in Britain don't eat more of it. Hake has a fine flavour and a soft, milky texture. It is easy to buy steaks which are ideal for anyone who has a fear of fish bones because, like cod, the bones are large enough to be easily spotted. Like all the cod family hake also takes well to salting.

LING

Ling is one of those underrated fish which, in addition to being reasonably flavoured, is also firm in texture – a cheap version of monkfish, if you like. It is an extraordinary-looking fish which, though a member of the cod family, could easily be mistaken for an eel, so long and sinuous is it in appearance.

POLLACK

I used to think that pollack was just plain dull, it being about the least-flavoured of all the cod family. But all fish have their uses and pollack, being very cheap, and coming in large bone-free fillets, is excellent for fish pies (see p. 72).

WHITING

Whiting can be a bit on the bland side, but small fresh fish brushed with butter and grilled are very good, especially if accompanied by *Noisette Butter* (see p. 50) and capers.

When I was at cookery college we used to do an excellent deep-fried dish with small whiting called *Merlan en Colère* which means something like Whiting in a Temper. You bent the whiting round and inserted its tail into its mouth as if it were in such a state that it was trying to bite its tail off. The fish was dusted with flour, dipped in egg and breadcrumbs then deep-fried. We used to serve it with a tomato sauce like the one on p. 178.

JOHN DORY

An excellent fish, John Dory is firm-textured, well-flavoured and suited to any form of cooking. The only drawback is that they are expensive and you don't get a lot for your money; only about a third of the total weight of the John Dory is edible fillet.

John Dory has a massive head, impressive fins and a fine bone structure. The fillets come away from the fish bone-free and there are few greater pleasures than a really thick grilled fillet of John Dory. Because it's flat in appearance people tend to regard it as a flat fish but it's not. Flat fish live on the bottom of the sea but John Dory swims like a round fish. It is rather a slow swimmer but an inability to out-swim its prey is compensated by an almost invisible shape when viewed head on and an enormous mouth with which to gobble up smaller fish. With its long fins, great head and lugubrious eyes, it looks like something straight out of a nightmare!

John Dory is often named the St Peter fish in most other European languages because they have a round black mark on their side which looks like a thumbprint which is traditionally held to be that of St Peter.

MONKFISH

I find monkfish an interesting phenomenon. Fifteen years ago nobody had ever heard of it. When we sold monkfish in the restaurant then, often as not we'd call it 'other white fish' in some mixed fish dish. Now it is extraordinarily popular. Is this because of the lack of bones in the flesh, I wonder, and because of its texture which has more similarity to meat than fish? It is not, in fact, particularly well-flavoured but it does have the most marvellous texture, making it one of the best fish for barbecuing. It is excellent for a raw sashimi and very thinly sliced as in the *Carpaccio of Monkfish* recipe on p. 138. The larger tails fetch more money than the smaller ones. But the smaller tails make the best eating because they are sweeter.

A very fine purple membrane covers the fillet of monkfish and if your fishmonger has not removed it, you should take as much of it off the fillet as possible or it will cause the fillet to twist rather unattractively as it cooks.

ROAST COD WITH AÏOLI AND BUTTER BEANS

This is a hot version of the classic Provençal dish *Aïoli Garni*. Here, a fillet of cod is served roasted with sea salt and is accompanied by garlic mayonnaise, butter beans, eggs, fennel and a fish *fumet* flavoured with basil.

SERVES 4

50 g (2 oz) butter beans
2 eggs
1 bulb of Florence fennel
4 fillets of cod, skin on, each weighing about
  175–200 g (6–7 oz)
Melted butter, for brushing
6 basil leaves, thinly sliced
1 teaspoon sea salt
Freshly ground black pepper
1 quantity *Aïoli* (see p. 44)

FOR THE SAUCE

225 g (8 oz) chopped mixed carrot, leek,
  celery and onion
50 g (2 oz) unsalted butter
1 tablespoon cognac
10 g (¼ oz) dried mushrooms
1 tablespoon balsamic vinegar
¼ red chilli
2 tablespoons olive oil
1 teaspoon Thai fish sauce (*nam pla*)
600 ml (1 pint) *Fish Stock* (see p. 36)
½ teaspoon salt
4 fresh basil leaves, finely sliced

To make the sauce, sweat the mixture of carrot, leek, celery and onion in a large pan with half the butter, until soft. Add the cognac and let it boil, then add all the rest of the sauce ingredients, except the remaining butter and basil leaves. Simmer for 30 minutes then pass through a fine sieve. Bring the sauce back to the boil and simmer until it has reduced to about 150 ml (5 fl oz).

Bring the butter beans to the boil in a large pan of salted water. Simmer gently until very soft. Remove from the heat and keep warm in the cooking liquid.

Place the eggs in boiling water and boil for 8 minutes. Drain, remove the shells and keep warm.

Remove the outer leaves of the fennel but don't cut off the tops. Slice into thin sections then cook in salted water until just tender. Drain and keep warm.

Pre-heat the oven to 230°C/450°F/Gas 8. Roast the cod in the oven until just cooked through. This will take 10–15 minutes depending on the thickness of the fillets. Place the cod on four warmed plates. Drain the butter beans and divide between the plates. Add the fennel, then cut the eggs in half and put one half on each plate, then add a spoonful of *aïoli* to each serving.

Bring the sauce to the boil and whisk in the last 25 g (1 oz) of butter, then add the basil leaves. Pour the sauce over the butter beans, egg and fennel and serve.

I would suggest a Côtes de Provence rosé, a Portuguese white Dâo or a white Corbières from south-western France to go with this. All are what I would call gutsy, robust wines.

CLASSIC COD IN PARSLEY SAUCE

If you tried to think of one of the most mundane-sounding English dishes, it would probably be cod in parsley sauce. Most of us have childhood memories of cod with parsley sauce and it was with this in mind that I decided to make the dish to see if it really is as boring as it is made out to be. I took the trouble to make a good, but not complicated, parsley sauce to go with a very fresh piece of cod. It was like a sunny day proving that with English food, as long as the raw materials are the best, simplicity is everything.

SERVES 4

> 2.25 litres (4 pints) water
> 1 lemon, sliced
> 1 tablespoon salt
> 750–900 g (1½–2 lb) thick cod fillet, skin on
> 75 g (3 oz) unsalted butter
> 15 g (½ oz) flour
> 600 ml (1 pint) full-cream milk
> 25 g (1 oz) fresh parsley, stalks removed and chopped

Put the water, lemon and salt in a large pan. Bring to the boil then simmer for 5 minutes. Add the cod and simmer for 2 minutes. Remove the pan from heat and leave to finish cooking gently in the cooking liquid.

Melt 25 g (1 oz) butter in a heavy-based pan and sprinkle over the flour. Stir continuously with a wooden spoon to mix, then cook until the mixture smells nutty. Gradually pour in the milk, stirring all the time, to make a smooth sauce. Add 300 ml (10 fl oz) of the fish cooking liquid and leave to simmer for at least 20 minutes.

Drain the cod and cut into 4 portions. Place on 4 warmed plates. Stir the chopped parsley and the rest of the butter into the sauce and coat the fish liberally with it. Serve with some potatoes boiled in salted water and a sprig of mint.

KEDGEREE

There's a hint of Indian spice in my kedgeree; not enough to put you off your breakfast but just enough to serve as a faint reminder of where this dish came from.

SERVES 4

> 1 quantity *Court-bouillon for Poaching Smoked Fish* (see p. 38)
> 350 g (12 oz) smoked haddock fillet
> 2 tablespoons chopped fresh parsley
> 3 hard-boiled eggs, chopped into 4 rounds
> Salt

FOR THE RICE

> 40 g (1½ oz) butter
> A large pinch of turmeric
> 1 clove
> 1 cardamom
> 275 g (10 oz) long-grain rice
> 600 ml (1 pint) *Chicken Stock* (see p. 37) or *Fish Stock* (see p. 36)
> ½ teaspoon salt

Heat the *court-bouillon* to simmering point in a large pan. Add the haddock and cook for 8–12 minutes, depending on the thickness of the fillet. Remove from the pan and drain. Remove the skin and break up the fish into finger-sized pieces. Keep warm.

Pre-heat the oven to 200°C/400°F/Gas 6. Sweat the butter, turmeric, clove and cardamom together in a flameproof pan, stir in the rice and cook for 1 minute then pour in the stock. Add the salt and bring to the boil. Cover and cook in the oven for 17 minutes.

Remove the rice from the oven and gently fold in the fish, parsley and eggs to avoid breaking them up. Season with salt and serve immediately.

SMOKED HADDOCK WITH SAVOY CABBAGE, LEMON AND NOISETTE BUTTER

This recipe comes from one of my favourite cookery books, *Bistro Cookery* by Patricia Wells. It is full of the sort of French cooking that we all really love to eat as opposed to the three-star cuisine which is more a matter of impressing us than filling us with love and affection; I love this dish.

SERVES 4

| 1 savoy cabbage
| 750 g (1½ lb) smoked haddock fillets
| 1 quantity *Court-bouillon For Poaching Smoked Fish* (see p. 38)
| 175 g (6 oz) unsalted butter
| Juice of 1 lemon
| 2 tablespoons chopped fresh parsley
| Salt and freshly ground black pepper

Trim the outer leaves of the cabbage then quarter it and remove the thick central core. Thinly slice each quarter and cook in a large pan of boiling, salted water for 10 minutes. Drain and refresh in cold water. Drain again.

Heat the *court-bouillon* to simmering point in a large pan. Add the haddock and cook for 8–12 minutes, according to the thickness of the fillet. Remove from the heat and set aside without draining to keep the fish warm.

Melt half the butter in a large shallow pan over a medium heat. Add the cabbage and cook gently for about 2 minutes to drive off the excess water and concentrate the flavour. Season with salt and pepper. Transfer to a shallow serving dish.

Carefully drain the haddock and remove the skin. Place the fish on top of the cabbage and keep warm.

In a small pan melt the remaining butter over a medium heat until it turns a pale brown. Remove from the heat, stir in the lemon juice and season with salt and pepper. Spoon the sauce over the haddock, sprinkle on the parsley and serve immediately.

HADDOCK BOULANGÈRE

For this dish, you need a good thick chunk of haddock. This old French recipe, like all *boulangère* dishes, was made at home then taken down to the local bakery to be cooked. I have slightly altered the traditional method because the time taken to cook the potatoes is too long for the fish, so I cook them separately and only bring them together in the oven for 12 minutes.

SERVES 4

1.25 kg (2 ½ lb) potatoes, thinly sliced
225 g (8 oz) onion, thinly sliced
3 fresh bay leaves, finely chopped
1 sprig of thyme
600 ml (1 pint) *Chicken Stock* (see p. 37)
100 g (4 oz) unsalted butter
750 g (1 ½ lb) haddock fillet, skin on, or
   900 g (2 lb) haddock steaks
Freshly ground black pepper
2 teaspoons salt

Pre-heat the oven to 200°C/400°F/Gas 6.

Grease the base of a shallow baking dish with butter. Build up layers of potato, onion, bay leaf and thyme, seasoning each layer with the salt and ground black pepper as you go. Pour over the stock, dot with three-quarters of the butter and bake in the oven for 20 minutes.

While the potatoes and onions are baking, melt the rest of the butter in a frying pan, season the haddock and fry on both sides to brown the fish and to caramelize the outside.

Place the fish on top of the potato and onion. Cover and return to the oven for a further 12–15 minutes, depending on the thickness of the fish.

Serve with a green salad, tossed with the *Mustard Dressing* on p. 51.

BAKED HAKE WITH LEMON, BAY LEAF, ONION AND GARLIC

The original recipe for this dish came from a cook who influenced me a great deal in my early days of cooking, Sonia Stevenson who ran a restaurant at Gullworthy near Tavistock, Devon. I used to eat there a great deal and thought it the most civilized and exciting place in the world. It looked out over the Tamar valley and, as you sat in the light dining-room on a fine summer evening with a copy of the menu, it seemed to achieve an unattainably high style. Although the recipe has been altered over the years, the idea remains the same; a simple treatment of a great fish.

SERVES 4

225 g (8 oz) onions, chopped
4 garlic cloves, chopped
100 g (4 oz) unsalted butter
85 ml (3 fl oz) white wine
Juice of ½ lemon
½ teaspoon salt
Rind of 1 lemon, cut into long paper thin
   slices
2 bay leaves, very thinly sliced or 2 dried
   bay leaves, crushed
300 ml (10 fl oz) *Fish Stock* (see p. 36)
4 steaks of hake, each weighing about
   225 g (8 oz)
Salt and freshly ground black pepper

Gently fry the onions and garlic in half the butter until they are soft. Add the white wine, lemon juice, salt, half of the lemon rind and half the bay leaves. Cover and leave to cook gently for 40 minutes, until the onions are very tender. You can prepare this garlic and onion *confit* some time in advance.

Pre-heat the oven to 230°C/450°F/Gas 8. Take a flameproof casserole dish large enough to hold the fish in a single layer. Place the onion *confit* with half the fish stock in the bottom. Place the steaks of hake on top. Sprinkle the fish with salt and pepper, the rest of the bay leaves and the rest of the lemon rind. Cover with foil and bake for 13 minutes.

Remove the foil and bake for a further 4 minutes.

Remove the fish from the dish and place on four warmed plates. Sprinkle again with salt and black pepper. Add the rest of the fish stock to the casserole dish and bring to the boil on top of the oven, add the rest of the butter and reduce to a thick sauce.

Pour the sauce around the fish and serve. The best accompaniments are new potatoes sprinkled with chopped parsley and mint, and thinly sliced spring cabbage cooked in boiling salted water for just 3 minutes, then drained and tossed in a sauté pan with some butter.

HAKE WITH CLAMS IN GREEN SAUCE

This recipe comes from the Basque region of Spain. You will need a large frying pan so that all the fish can be cooked together.

SERVES 4

4 hake steaks, each weighing about 225 g (8 oz)
Flour, for dusting
4 tablespoons olive oil
4 garlic cloves, chopped
1 green chilli, seeded and finely chopped
4 tablespoons fresh parsley, roughly chopped
120 ml (4 fl oz) *Fish Stock* (see p. 36)
120 ml (4 fl oz) dry white wine
24 small live clams, in the shell
12 asparagus spears, blanched in salted water
50 g (2 oz) cooked green peas
Salt and freshly ground black pepper

Season the fish steaks with salt and freshly ground black pepper then dust with flour, shaking off any excess.

Heat the olive oil in a large frying pan then sauté the garlic and chilli until the garlic begins to colour. Remove the garlic and chilli from the pan and reserve. Return pan to the heat and sauté the hake in the oil for about 1 minute on each side. Add about one-third of the parsley and let it fry a little. Then add the fish stock, white wine and the reserved garlic and chilli. Simmer for about 4 minutes then add the clams and cook for a further 3 minutes, or until the fish is cooked and the clams have opened. Remove from the pan and keep warm.

Concentrate the stock and pan juices by rapid boiling then season with salt, if necessary. When you are happy that the sauce is strong and thickening add the asparagus, peas and the rest of the parsley. Pour the sauce over the fish and clams and serve with boiled potatoes and a salad.

(LEFT) Fillets of John Dory with Olives, Capers and Rosemary (*see page 132*), (BELOW LEFT) Baked Hake with Lemon, Bay Leaf, Onion and Garlic (*see page 124*) and (BELOW) Roast Cod with Aïoli and Butter Beans (*see page 121*)

GRILLED HAKE WITH SPRING ONIONS, MASHED POTATOES AND MORELS

The important ingredient in this dish is an Islay malt whisky like Laphroaig. The smoky flavours of the whisky blend subtly with the dried morel mushrooms to produce an unusual but exciting combination of flavours.

Finish the dish off with celery herb, which has a strong celery taste but if you can't find it, use celery tops instead.

Use either King Edward, Maris Piper or Wilja potatoes for the mash. Get thick hake fillets that have been cut from a large fish.

SERVES 4

4 hake fillets, each weighing about 225 g
   (8 oz)
Melted butter, for brushing
Coarse sea salt

FOR THE SAUCE

75 g (3 oz) unsalted butter
225 g (8 oz) chopped mixed onion, leek,
   carrot and celery
1 tablespoon Islay malt whisky
1 tablespoon balsamic vinegar
1.2 litres (2 pints) *Fish Stock* (see p. 36)
15 g (½ oz) dried mushrooms
10 g (¼ oz) dried morels
½ teaspoon celery herb, finely chopped (or
   celery tops)

FOR THE MASHED POTATOES

900 g (2 lb) potatoes
50 g (2 oz) butter
300 ml (10 fl oz) milk
6 spring onions
Salt and freshly ground black pepper

To make the sauce, melt half the butter in a shallow pan and add the chopped mixed onion, leek, carrot and celery. Cook hard until the vegetables start to caramelize (this gives the sauce an appetizing light brown colour), add the whisky and let the alcohol boil off. Then, add the vinegar and let it reduce. Finally, add all but a small cupful of the fish stock and the dried mushrooms. Bring to the boil and simmer for 30 minutes. Put the remaining fish stock in a small pan and add the dried morels, bring to the boil, remove from the heat and leave the morels to soften. When they are soft slice them into rounds. Strain and reserve the liquor.

To make the mash, scrub the potatoes but do not peel. Place in a large pan and cover with cold water. Bring to the boil and cook until very soft. Drain and leave to cool for 5 minutes. Peel off the skins with a small knife and mash with a fork or masher. Add the butter and milk and season with the salt and pepper. Keep warm. Cut the spring onions into thin rounds and add to the mashed potato just before serving.

Pre-heat the oven to 200°C/400°F/Gas 6.

Brush the hake with melted butter and season with ground black pepper and coarse sea salt. Brush the roasting dish with more melted butter and place the fillets in it. Roast in the oven for 12 minutes.

Meanwhile, pass the simmered stock through a sieve into a shallow pan and add the liquor from soaking the morels. Boil on a high heat and reduce to about 300 ml (10 fl oz). Cut the rest of the unsalted butter into a few pieces and whisk into the sauce. Remove from the heat and add the celery herb and the sliced morels.

Arrange the fish on four warmed plates. Pour over the sauce and divide the mashed potatoes between the plates. Serve immediately.

WHITE-COOKED LING WITH SPRING ONIONS, CHILLI AND SZECHUAN PEPPER

I have adapted this recipe from a Chinese chicken dish that we often cook at home. The fish is gently poached in water, flavoured with ginger, left to cool in the water and served with rice and a series of hot or salty dips. Both the fish and the rice are unsalted but the dips add plenty of seasoning. This is a simple dish that I hope you will want to cook often. Szechuan pepper is available from any good supermarket these days.

You will need three tiny bowls to hold the condiments that go with the ling and the rice.

SERVES 4

- 100 g (4 oz) long-grain rice
- 1.2 litres (2 pints) water
- 15 g (½ oz) fresh ginger, unpeeled and thinly sliced
- 750 g (1½ lb) ling fillet, skinned and boned
- 1 teaspoon black peppercorns
- 1 teaspoon Szechuan peppercorns
- 1 teaspoon sea salt
- 120 ml (4 fl oz) soy sauce
- 1 teaspoon fresh ginger, finely chopped
- 2 spring onions, finely sliced
- 1 red chilli, seeded and finely chopped
- 25 ml (1 fl oz) white wine vinegar
- 1 bunch of coriander, leaves picked from the stalks
- ½ iceberg lettuce, sliced

Place the rice in a large pan and pour in enough cold water to cover it by 2.5 cm (1 in). Bring to the boil then simmer gently until all the water has been absorbed by the rice. Remove from the heat and set aside, covered.

Bring the 1.2 litres (2 pints) of water to the boil with the sliced ginger and simmer for 10 minutes. Put the fish fillet into the water and simmer for exactly 2 minutes, then remove from the heat and leave to cool (this will take about 40 minutes). When cool, slice the fillet into 2.5 cm (1 in) wide pieces and arrange neatly on a serving dish.

Coarsely crush the black peppercorns, Szechuan peppercorns and sea salt together using a spice grinder or mortar and pestle, or by wrapping the spices in a tea towel and beating with a rolling pin.

Put the coarsely ground pepper and salt into one of the bowls and the soy sauce, chopped ginger and the spring onions in the second bowl. Finally, put the chopped chilli and the white wine vinegar in the third bowl. Pile the rice into a serving dish. Sprinkle the fish with some of the coriander and put the sliced iceberg lettuce and the rest of the coriander in a salad bowl (without any dressing).

To serve, each person takes a mound of rice, some of the fish and a pile of salad and dots the three condiments, i.e. the pepper and salt, the soy sauce and spring onion, and the vinegar and chilli, around their plate. The combination is totally satisfying.

SALT POLLACK WITH MAYONNAISE, CHILLI AND CANNELLINI BEANS

Cannellini beans take on flavours exceptionally well and are available in all large supermarkets these days. To make salt pollack use the recipe for salting cod on p. 53. Salting greatly improves the flavour of pollack.

SERVES 4

    350 g (12 oz) cannellini beans
    350 g (12 oz) salt pollack
    1.2 litres (2 pints) water
    1 teaspoon salt
    1 red chilli, seeded and chopped
    25 ml (1 fl oz) balsamic or sherry vinegar
    2 tomatoes, skinned, seeded and chopped
    2 garlic cloves, very finely chopped
    300 ml (10 fl oz) *Mustard Mayonnaise* (see
       p. 43)
    1 teaspoon fresh parsley, roughly chopped

Soak the cannellini beans for 8 hours in plenty of cold water. Soak the pollack in plenty of cold water for 2 hours.

Discard the water from soaking the cannellini beans. Put the beans in a large pan then add 1.2 litres (2 pints) of water, the salt, diced chilli and vinegar. Bring to the boil and simmer until the beans are very soft, like baked beans. Drain off the cooking liquor into a separate pan and reduce it down to about 2 tablespoons. Add to the beans and keep warm.

Poach the pollack in plain water for 10 minutes, strain, remove the skin and any bones, and add to the beans. Stir in the chopped tomato and the garlic. Finally, stir in the mayonnaise just before serving. Sprinkle with the parsley and serve.

WHITING AND POTATO BHAJI

This *bhaji* recipe comes from Goa and is completely different from the normal deep-fried *bhaji* we know in this country. Here finely diced potato is cooked with some oil, mustard seeds, onion, tomato and spices to produce a very mild vegetable curry. In Goa I am very fond of eating this *bhaji* with fried eggs but have discovered how well it also goes with a delicate fish like whiting. So here it is.

SERVES 4

    50 g (12 oz) potatoes
    25 ml (1 fl oz) vegetable oil
    ½ teaspoon mustard seeds
    A good pinch of turmeric
    100 g (4 oz) onion, finely chopped
    100 g (4 oz) tomato, peeled and chopped
    1 teaspoon coriander, roughly chopped

    450 g (1 lb) whiting fillet, skin on
    Melted butter, for brushing
    Salt and freshly ground black pepper
    1 lemon, sliced, to serve

Peel the potatoes and cut them into 1 cm (½ in) dice then boil in salted water. Heat the vegetable oil in a pan and fry the mustard seeds, turmeric and onions until the onions have softened. Drain the potatoes and add to the pan. Season and continue to cook gently. Add the tomato and simmer for a further minute, then add the chopped coriander.

Pre-heat the grill until hot. Brush the fillets with a little melted butter and season. Grill for 4–5 minutes then serve with the *bhaji* and slices of lemon.

CHAR-GRILLED JOHN DORY WITH CORIANDER, SAFFRON AND KUMQUATS

The char-grilled John Dory fillets are served on a citrus-dressed salad smelling of lemon and surrounded by a deeply-flavoured citrus dressing.

SERVES 4

- 1.75 g (4 lb) John Dory or 750 g (1½ lb) fillet, skin on
- Olive oil, for brushing
- Salt and freshly ground black pepper

FOR THE DRESSING

- 600 ml (1 pint) *Fish Stock* (see p. 36)
- 120 ml (4 fl oz) dry white wine
- A pinch of saffron
- 4 kumquats
- 50 ml (2 fl oz) extra virgin olive oil
- Juice of 1 orange
- ½ teaspoon salt
- 1 tablespoon balsamic vinegar
- 2 anchovy fillets, finely chopped
- 1 teaspoon chopped fresh coriander

FOR THE SALAD

- 1.2 litre (2 pint) measuring jug loosely filled with washed and dried salad leaves
- ¼ *Preserved Lemons*, cut into small pieces (see p. 52)
- 1 large tomato, skinned, seeded and cut into dice
- 1 tablespoon *Lemon Olive Oil* (see p. 51)
- Salt

Light the charcoal grill at least 45 minutes before cooking the fish (gas grills take about 20 minutes to heat or you can use a ribbed grill pan instead).

If using a whole fish, fillet the John Dory (see p. 24) but leave the skin on then cut the fillets into four equal portions. Brush with a little olive oil and season with salt and black pepper.

To make the dressing, put the fish stock, white wine and saffron in a small, wide pan and bring to the boil. Simmer to reduce the volume by half.

Thinly slice the kumquats and remove the seeds. Assemble and prepare all the other dressing ingredients so that you can make the hot dressing at the last minute.

Grill the fillets of John Dory, skin side first for 3 minutes on each side. When the fish is cooked, keep warm while you make the dressing and toss the salad.

Place the salad leaves in a mixing bowl and add the chopped preserved lemon, the tomato, the lemon olive oil and a pinch of salt. Mix carefully with your hands, taking care not to bruise the leaves, then arrange in the centre of warmed plates.

Bring the reduced saffron stock to the boil then add all the remaining dressing ingredients, except the coriander. Boil rapidly for 2 minutes then add the coriander.

Place the fish fillets on top of the salad, spoon some of the hot dressing over the fish and drizzle the rest around the plates.

FILLETS OF JOHN DORY WITH OLIVES, CAPERS AND ROSEMARY

This dish is very much in the light Mediterranean style. The fish is filleted but the skin left on. Once grilled, it is served with olives, capers, tomato, flatleaf parsley, waxy potatoes and rosemary; all carefully warmed through in the very best olive oil. It makes a perfect first course.

SERVES 4

1 John Dory fillet, weighing about 450 g (1 lb), skin on
50 ml (2 fl oz) extra virgin olive oil
4 small waxy new potatoes, such as Wilja
2 anchovy fillets
2 medium-sized tomatoes
3 pieces sun-dried tomato
4 black olives
A small bunch of flatleaf parsley
12 capers, preferably the tiny non pareil
10 rosemary needles
Salt and freshly ground black pepper

If you have small fillets of John Dory cut each in half lengthways. If they are from a larger fish, cut each fillet into three, again lengthways. Brush each piece of fillet with olive oil then place on a baking tray and season with salt and black pepper.

Cut each new potato into four long pieces. Simmer in salted water until just cooked then drain and keep warm.

Cut each anchovy fillet in half lengthways then in half again to make thin slithers. Remove the skin from the tomatoes by either spearing the tomato on a fork and turning it around over a gas flame (you will hear the skin pop as it splits which takes about 10 seconds) or by briefly immersing in boiling water until the skin splits. Cut the tomatoes into quarters and remove the seeds. Slice each of the quarters into three long segments.

Cut the segments of sun-dried tomato into long thin strips. Remove the stones from the olives and slice them. Take the stalks off the parsley and cut up very roughly so that the leaves are still almost intact.

Pre-heat the grill to high. Grill the John Dory until only just cooked. Put the extra virgin olive oil, new potatoes, anchovy fillets, tomatoes, sun-dried tomato, olives, capers and rosemary into a shallow pan and warm through gently, but don't overheat the oil. Very gently, mix the ingredients around so that they are all coated with the oil then add the parsley. Avoid losing the shape of any of the ingredients.

Divide the fish between four warmed plates and arrange the contents of the pan over, under and around the fillets. Try to make the ingredients look as attractive as possible, making sure that each plate has roughly the same quantity of all the ingredients.

PAN-FRIED FILLET OF MONKFISH WITH THE NEW SEASON'S GARLIC AND FENNEL

I thought up this dish to make use of the very tender-skinned fresh garlic which arrives in May and June and, if you can get hold of some of this, you don't have to actually peel the garlic. However, the dish is very good made with any garlic.

SERVES 4

  100 g (4 oz) semolina
  16 large garlic cloves
  15 g (½ oz) fennel sprigs
  100 g (4 oz) unsalted butter
  450 g (1 lb) Florence fennel, thinly sliced
  600 ml (1 pint) *Fish Stock* (see p. 36)
  900 g (2 lb) monkfish fillet, cut into 4 equal
    pieces
  50 ml (2 fl oz) groundnut oil
  Juice of ¼ lemon
  Splash of pastis, such as Ricard or Pernod
  Salt and freshly ground black pepper

Put the semolina and two of the cloves of garlic and all but one sprig of the fennel in a food processor or blender. Blend until the garlic and fennel have all amalgamated with the semolina to produce a pale-green aromatic powder. It is a good idea to slice the cloves of garlic a little to make it easier for them to be blended.

Cut the remaining cloves of garlic lengthways then place in a pan with half the butter and the Florence fennel. Fry the garlic and fennel until both start to brown, then add half the fish stock, salt and black pepper. Cover the pan and leave to simmer until the garlic and fennel are soft. This will take about 15 minutes.

Pre-heat the oven to 200°C/400°F/Gas 6. Coat the fillets generously with the semolina, fennel and garlic mixture. Heat the groundnut oil in a flameproof dish or casserole with a small knob of butter. Add the fish and fry over a moderate heat until golden brown then turn and transfer the pan to the oven. Cook for 10 minutes.

Remove the monkfish fillets from the pan, place them on a chopping board and slice them carefully on the diagonal so that each slice rests pleasingly against the next. Transfer to a warmed dish and keep warm.

Finish the sauce by adding the garlic, fennel and butter, lemon juice, pastis and the remaining sprig of fennel, finely chopped.

Reduce the sauce a little by rapid boiling. Add the rest of the butter. Lay the sliced fish on four warmed plates and surround them with the sauce.

(BELOW) Monkfish with Saffron and Roasted Red Pepper Dressing (*see page 136*), (TOP RIGHT) Salt Pollack with Mayonnaise, Chilli and Cannellini Beans (*see page 130*) and (BELOW RIGHT) White-cooked Ling with Spring Onions, Chilli and Szechuan Pepper (*see page 129*)

MONKFISH WITH SAFFRON AND ROASTED RED PEPPER DRESSING

Like many of my recipes there's not a lot to this dish really, but that is all to the good, providing you have the very freshest of fish.

SERVES 4

> 4 fillets of monkfish, each weighing about
>   200 g (7 oz)
> 25 ml (1 fl oz) olive oil
> 1 tablespoon finely chopped fresh thyme
> ½ teaspoon salt
> Freshly ground black pepper

FOR THE ROASTED RED PEPPER SAUCE

> 600 ml (1 pint) *Fish Stock* (see p. 36)
> 85 ml (3 fl oz) dry vermouth
> A large pinch of saffron
> 2 red peppers
> 85 ml (3 fl oz) virgin olive oil
> 15 ml (½ fl oz) balsamic vinegar or sherry
>   vinegar
> Salt and freshly ground pepper
> 1 teaspoon unsalted butter
> 1.2 litre (2 pint) measuring jug loosely filled
>   with salad leaves
> 15 ml (½ fl oz) *Lemon Olive Oil* (see p. 51)
> A good pinch of sea salt, preferably coarse

To make the roasted pepper sauce, put the fish stock, vermouth and saffron in a small pan and simmer to reduce the volume by three-quarters. Roast the red peppers by putting them on a tray (you don't need to coat them with any oil) and charring them under the grill, or in a hot oven, until the skins are blistered. Leave to cool, cut in half, remove the seeds, take off the skins and finely chop the flesh. Mix together the virgin olive oil, vinegar, salt and pepper.

Light the barbecue 30–40 minutes before you intend to grill the monkfish. (You can, as with all my char-grilled recipes, use a ribbed steak pan instead.)

Brush the fillets of monkfish with a mixture made up of the olive oil, thyme, salt and pepper. They will take about 10 minutes to cook. Turn them over frequently to prevent burning.

Return the fish stock and saffron back to the heat, add the chopped red peppers and the olive oil dressing and bring to a brisk boil. Check that the sauce is pleasantly strong; it should taste tart but not too tart, salty but not too salty and generally round and pleasing. If it has not reached this stage, continue to reduce by rapid boiling to concentrate the flavour. Once you are satisfied that a suitably concentrated taste has been achieved, whisk in the teaspoon of butter to give the sauce a light amalgamation and remove from the heat.

Mix the salad leaves with the lemon olive oil and sea salt. Place the salad leaves on four plates. Slice the 4 monkfish fillets into four thick pieces on the slant so that the slices fall together against each other pleasingly. Place each sliced fillet on top of a pile of lettuce and pour the sauce around it. Serve immediately.

TANDOORIED MONKFISH WITH TOMATO AND CORIANDER SALAD

For this dish you need small monkfish tails which have a sweet and delightful flavour and are ideally suited to cooking in a tandoori style.

We can never quite capture the taste of tandooried food because we don't possess, most of us anyway, such a spectacular piece of equipment as a tandoor. But fairly convincing results can be achieved using a barbecue grill. Alternatively use your overhead grill or oven.

You need to be a bit careful when chargrilling fish or meat marinated in tandoori spices. While you do need the barbecued flavour, you don't want to burn the marinade too much otherwise it tastes bitter. This is an occasion to use one of those hinged grill wires. Cooking in tandoori ovens is done using long spears on which the food is impaled so that it doesn't touch anything in the oven.

I'm afraid this is one of those rare occasions when food colour has to be used. You can make tandoori without, but it just doesn't look right.

4 small monkfish tails, each weighing about 275–350 g (10–12 oz)
I quantity *Kachumber Salad* (see p. 52)
Lemon wedges to serve

FOR THE LEMON CHILLI MARINADE

I teaspoon chilli powder or cayenne pepper
I teaspoon salt
Juice of I large lemon

FOR THE TANDOORI MARINADE

50 g (2 oz) natural yoghurt
50 ml (2 fl oz) double cream
I tablespoon finely chopped fresh ginger
I tablespoon finely chopped garlic
I teaspoon garam masala
¾ teaspoon cumin powder
I teaspoon red food colour

FOR THE RAITA SALAD

85 ml (3 fl oz) natural yoghurt
½ cucumber, thinly sliced
I teaspoon chopped fresh mint
A pinch of salt

Slash the monkfish tails 3–4 times right down to the central bone on either side to allow the marinade to permeate right into the fish. Place in a small dish with the lemon chilli marinade ingredients and leave to marinate for 1 hour, turning occasionally and rubbing more marinade into the cuts. Make the tandoori marinade, add to the dish, and leave for a further hour.

Light the barbecue 30–40 minutes before you start cooking. Cook the monkfish over the coals, turning frequently to prevent burning. They will take about 10–12 minutes to cook.

While the fish is cooking, prepare the two salads. For the raita simply mix all the ingredients together. Serve the tandooried monkfish with the two salads, some wedges of lemon and some fresh naan bread.

CARPACCIO OF MONKFISH WITH LEMON OLIVE OIL

This recipe was given to me by our sous chef, Paul Ripley. He has taken the idea of thinly sliced raw fillet of beef and transferred it to fish; in this case monkfish, which is excellent for such treatment. Being very firm in texture, monkfish slices thinly very easily, so it is perfect as *carpaccio*. You can make your own lemon olive oil (see p. 51) but it's quite easy to buy in good delicatessens.

SERVES 4

225 g (8 oz) monkfish fillet
50 ml (2 fl oz) *Lemon Olive Oil* (see p. 51)
Salt and freshly ground white pepper
50 g (2 oz) rocket leaves
15 g (½ oz) Parmesan

The best *carpaccios* are made from very thin slices of meat or, in this case, fish. To slice the monkfish very thinly you will need to part-freeze it. Freeze the fillet for about 1 hour, then thinly slice with your sharpest, thinnest knife. Lay the slices neatly onto four cold plates. Pour over the lemon olive oil and dust lightly with salt and a little freshly ground white pepper.

Lay the rocket leaves on top. Make shavings of the Parmesan from a block of cheese by using a potato peeler. Lay about 6–8 shavings of Parmesan over the rocket. Serve at once.

FLAT FISH: BRILL, HALIBUT, PLAICE, SOLE AND TURBOT

The recipes in this chapter include some of my all-time favourites. They are ideal for anyone who doesn't like bones in fish. We have, in our waters, the greatest range of flat fish anywhere in the world. From the regal turbot down to the humble dab, the recipes here reflect that range and are a mixture of quick and easy and more elaborate dishes.

BRILL

Whenever you read about brill it is always classed as being a second-division turbot, a sort of brother of the more famous turbot! It is not quite so sweetly flavoured as turbot but brill is still extremely good and quite often can be half the price. Large brill cut into small steaks and served with Hollandaise sauce in the same way as the roast turbot on p. 157, are stupendous. As with all flat fish, if you're going for fillets, go for the larger fish. In the case of brill these should be about 1.5–3.5 kg (3–8 lb).

It is quite difficult to distinguish large brill from large turbot, but brill are more oval in shape and turbot have little lumps on their skin. Running your finger over the skin of either the brill or the turbot will soon tell you which is which.

HALIBUT

Sadly, halibut is not a fish caught off the South West of England so we only occasionally get one but it is a marvellous fish. The fillet is firm and white and well-flavoured but prone to dryness if at all overcooked. It is one of the most spectacular-looking fish because it can come as large as 2 metres long and 1 metre wide. A dark browny-green in colour, it is by far the largest of the flat fish and tremendously speedy looking.

PLAICE

Of all sea fish plaice has the closest flavour to freshwater fish, a taste I find irresistible. For this reason I normally cook my *meurette* of sea fish with plaice (see p. 66). This fish stew, made with a good Beaujolais or Burgundy, was originally created for fish caught in the Rhône and the Loire rivers. Plaice is a most attractive fish with almost fluorescent orange and red spots.

DOVER SOLE

Some of the world's best fish are caught off Padstow between February and April in a rich fishing ground off Trevose Head about twelve miles out to sea called the Trevose Bank. For those three months, not only Dover sole, but superb large cod, brill, haddock, turbot, monkfish, hake, pollack and coley, ray and pout are caught in great abundance. But the prize catch is Dover sole – from large 1.5–1.75 kg (3–4 lb) fish the fishermen call tombstones down to the little tiny soles, no more than 15–20 cm (6–8 in) long, that they call tongues.

The great attraction of this bounty from the sea is that the weather is so appalling at that time of year with gales coming from every direction, that the price of fish everywhere in the British Isles is high. Dover sole will fetch high prices. Fishing for sole is extremely uncomfortable; I know, I've been there. I was sick most of the time. I stood there on a pitching deck in the freezing cold with green mountains of sea powering over me and tons of rusty iron chains and beams crashing against the metal sides of the trawler, a point of impact where most fishermen lose their fingers. All around me was the howl of wire hawsers hauling a bulging bag of net over onto the deck with fish heads poking through it grotesquely. Then one of the crew pulled open the cod end and everything flopped down into a stainless steel trough and I was amazed by the freshness of it all: the ozone smell, the brightness of all those different fish and the lumps of coal in amongst them. There was an old fisherman's glove, star fish, some crabs, whelks, scallops, the dark fearful mouth of a large monkfish, a couple of enormous cod, a coley, an octopus, a beautiful pink gurnard, a large brill, some little chicken turbot, the fluorescent orange and red spots of plaice and flounder and, above all, everywhere the brown flatness of Dover sole. The crew looked after its fish, everything was hand-washed after being gutted and placed carefully in ice, but none more carefully than the Dover sole; the prize catch. In spite of constant nausea and a feeling of anxiety about the howling wind and the enormous seas, I was filled with a cook's enthusiasm for the beautiful raw material of those Dover soles. I wanted to take them home and simply grill them knowing nothing on this planet could taste better.

LEMON SOLE

I'm particularly fond of the skin of lemon sole and never serve it without, even though people may fastidiously set it aside. It has a very soft but well flavoured flesh. A lemon sole brushed with plenty of butter, sprinkled with salt and freshly ground black pepper and cooked under a grill is a delight, but it is also well-suited to serving with sauces. It seems to have a particularly sweet affinity with cream, fish stock and white wine.

As with all flat fish, go for the bigger ones. For serving whole lemon sole, I would suggest a weight of around 400–450 g (14 oz–1 lb).

TURBOT

To me turbot is in the same class as lobster and inevitably, I'm afraid, very expensive. It has firm, sweet flesh, white and moist. Of all fish it is the densest and therefore loses least of its precious liquor when resting particularly when cooked on the bone. There is an added advantage in that the flesh near the bone is imbued with a sort of gelatinous moistness after having been cooked which is lost when the fish is filleted.

Turbot served simply with Hollandaise sauce is always a great success. Large turbot about 4.5–6.75 kg (10–15 lb) in weight make much better eating than small ones but, if you can get hold of a perfectly fresh small turbot that is up to about 550 g (1¼ lb) in weight (called a chicken turbot) and grill it, you'll have a splendid meal, though it won't quite aspire to the luxury of a *tronçon* (steak) cut from a big fish.

A Casserole of Brill with Shallots and Wild Mushrooms

You can use either brill, turbot or large plaice for this dish if your budget won't run to the pricier fish. But this recipe is definitely only for large fish so you need a good thick fillet for its success. Some people feel that partnering fish with rich dark sauces like this one is a mistake. I disagree. You don't lose the taste of the fish as long as it's good and fresh. Also, flat fish and wild mushrooms go very well together. If you can't get wild mushrooms go for ordinary field mushrooms and maybe some shiitake and oyster mushrooms to provide variety. You can get these in any supermarket these days. Dried ceps, on the other hand, are usually only available from good delicatessens.

SERVES 4

15 g (½ oz) dried ceps
90 g (3½ oz) unsalted butter
½ teaspoon sugar
12 small shallots
8 garlic cloves
900 ml (1½ pints) *Chicken Stock* (see p. 37)
¼ teaspoon salt
Freshly ground black pepper
1 slice cooked ham, cut into fine dice
1 carrot, chopped
1 leek, chopped
1 celery stick, chopped
½ medium onion, chopped
2 teaspoons balsamic vinegar
2 sprigs of thyme
50 ml (2 fl oz) red wine
750 g (1½ lb) brill fillets, divided into 4 equal portions
100 g (4 oz) sliced wild mushrooms

Soak the ceps for 30 minutes in 150 ml (5 fl oz) of warm water.

Use a shallow pan large enough to take the fillets of brill side by side. Melt 25 g (1 oz) of the butter with the sugar, then add the shallots and garlic and cook until lightly browned. Barely cover them with some of the chicken stock and add ¼ teaspoon salt and the black pepper. Add the diced ham and simmer gently until both shallots and garlic are tender. Turn up the heat and reduce the stock to a thick syrupy glaze so that both the onions and garlic are coated with it and become dark. Remove from the pan and keep warm. (Use the same pan, unwashed, to finish the dish so the syrupy juices combine with the rest of the sauce.)

To make the stock fry the carrot, leek, celery and onion in 25 g (1 oz) of the butter. Allow the vegetables to catch a little to create a rich brown finish to the sauce. Strain the soaking water from the ceps and add it to the rest of the chicken stock, the balsamic vinegar, 1 sprig of thyme and the red wine. Simmer for 20–30 minutes then pass through a conical strainer into another pan.

To cook the brill, heat a frying pan then melt a small piece of butter. Quickly brown the skin side of the brill, season with salt and pepper and remove. Place the fillets side by side, in the pan used to cook the shallots and garlic, and pour on the rest of the stock. Add the second sprig of thyme. Cover the pan and braise until the brill is just cooked.

While the fish is braising, take the frying pan in which you browned the skin of the fish, add 15 g (½ oz) butter and fry the mushrooms, seasoning with a little salt and pepper.

Remove the brill from the pan and keep warm. Reduce the cooking liquor a little then add the final 25 g (1 oz) of unsalted butter. Add the mushrooms to the sauce, place the pieces of fish on four warmed plates, add the glazed shallots and garlic and pour over the sauce and mushrooms.

(LEFT) Grilled Scored Plaice with
Garlic, Oregano and Lemon Juice
(*see page 148*), (BELOW LEFT)
Escalopes of Halibut with Dill,
Carrots and Celery (*see page 147*)
and (BELOW) A Casserole of Brill
with Shallots and Wild
Mushrooms (*see page 141*)

FILLETS OF BRILL WITH STIR-FRIED SPINACH AND CORIANDER

The sauce which accompanies this is rather an interesting combination of West and East. Fish stock, butter and tomato on one side and soy sauce and coriander on the other.

SERVES 4

4 fillets of brill, each weighing about 200–225 g (7–8 oz)

FOR THE STIR-FRIED SPINACH

100 g (4 oz) spinach
25 g (1 oz) mangetout
½ bulb of fennel
6 basil leaves, thinly sliced
A splash of Thai fish sauce (*nam pla*)
Juice of ¼ lemon

FOR THE SAUCE

600 ml (1 pint) *Fish Stock* (see p. 36)
2 tablespoons soy sauce
1 tablespoon virgin olive oil
50 g (2 oz) unsalted butter
2 tablespoons tomato, skinned, seeded and diced
1 teaspoon chopped fresh coriander

Wash the spinach in plenty of cold water and remove the stalks. Tear into small pieces if the leaves are big. Thinly slice the mangetout. Remove the outer leaves of the fennel bulb and thinly slice. Cut the fennel slices into thin strips.

Pour the fish stock and soy sauce into a small pan and bring to the boil. Reduce the volume by half by rapid boiling.

Pre-heat the grill to high. Brush the brill with olive oil and season with salt then cook under the grill for 5–8 minutes, depending on the thickness of the fillets.

Heat a wok and pour in the olive oil.

Add the mangetout and fennel and turn in the hot oil. Add the spinach, basil, fish sauce and lemon juice and stir briefly. Cook long enough to allow the spinach to wilt, then divide the contents of the pan between four warmed plates.

Add the butter to the boiling stock and soy sauce and as soon as it has blended in, add the tomato and coriander. Remove from the heat.

Place the fish on top of the stir-fry vegetables and pour over the sauce. Serve.

FILLETS OF BRILL IN MADIRAN WITH YOUNG BROAD BEANS

The title of this recipe was partly chosen because I love the name Madiran. It's a little-known red wine from an adventurous wine maker in South-west France called Alain Burmont, who is responsible for a collection of unusual and delicious wines including the sweet and dry Pachérenc du Vic-Bilh whites and the dark rich red Madiran. I don't expect you to go to the expense of buying a bottle just to cook with so use a good deep Côtes du Rhône instead; the results will be quite similar. This is a seasonal dish using young fresh broad beans. You can, of course, use frozen beans, but if you wait till June and make the dish once a year only, you'll enjoy it much more.

SERVES 4

4 fillets of brill, each weighing about 100 g (4 oz), skinned
Salt
900 g (2 lb) broad beans, weighed in the pod
300 ml (10 fl oz) *Chicken Stock* (see p. 37)
300 ml (10 fl oz) Madiran or Côtes du Rhône
½ teaspoon sugar
100 g (4 oz) unsalted butter
½ teaspoon chopped fresh mint

Prepare a steamer (see pp. 35 and 205) for cooking the brill. Season the skinned fish fillets lightly with salt.

Shell the broad beans and bring a pan of salted water to the boil. Cook the beans for 4–5 minutes. Drain, remove the grey skins and discard.

Bring the stock to the boil, together with all but a tablespoon or so of the red wine and the sugar and simmer until the volume has reduced by three-quarters.

Arrange the fish fillets in the steamer and steam until just cooked – there should be a slight suggestion of translucency right in the centre of the fillet when you part it with a small knife.

Arrange the fish on four warmed plates. Bring the reduced red wine and stock to a final boil. Add the rest of the red wine and whisk in the butter. Pour the red wine sauce over the four fillets of fish. Mix the finely chopped mint with the beans and place in neat piles beside the fish.

CEVICHE OF BRILL

In this South American dish, fillets of fish are cured in fresh lime juice. I like the fish a little undercured; most recipes call for the fish to be left for some hours. I think 2 hours quite enough when the fillets are cut into finger-sized slices. It tastes much fresher this way. The accompanying salsa is extremely hot as it contains lots of chilli.

SERVES 4

450 g (1 lb) brill
Juice of 2 limes
1 teaspoon finely chopped fresh fennel
A good pinch of sea salt
1 avocado

FOR THE SALSA

225 g (8 oz) tomato, skinned, seeded and chopped
½ green pepper, diced
2 spring onions
2 garlic cloves, finely chopped
2 chillies seeded and finely chopped
1 tablespoon roughly chopped fresh coriander
1 tablespoon virgin olive oil
½ teaspoon sea salt

Cut the fish into strips the length of your finger but half as thick. Cover with lime juice. Turn over and marinate for 2 hours. Drain and sprinkle with the fennel and salt.

Cut the avocado into quarters, remove the skin and thinly slice lengthways. Sprinkle the avocado with some lime juice and a little sea salt and arrange on four plates.

Mix all the salsa ingredients just before you serve the dish then put a pile on each plate with the fish. Serve immediately.

SPINACH WITH BUTTER

The standard way of cooking spinach is to just wash it and then let it cook gently in its own juices adding plenty of butter. It is then left to stew for some time producing a rich, satisfying and smooth green flavour. However, much as I love this way of cooking it, I think this recipe is ideal for partnering fish.

SERVES 4

FOR THE SPINACH

225 g (8 oz) spinach leaves
25 g (1 oz) unsalted butter
Salt and freshly ground black pepper

Pick over the spinach leaves and wash in at least two changes of water. Bring a pan of salted water to the boil, drop in the spinach leaves, bring back to the boil and strain. Give the colander you strain the leaves through a good shake to get as much moisture out of the spinach as possible, then return the leaves to a clean pan with the butter. Cook very gently for about 2 minutes driving off the steam and concentrating the flavour slightly. Season with salt and pepper.

ESCALOPES OF HALIBUT WITH DILL, CARROTS AND CELERY

These are thin slices of the fish which are cooked very quickly in a little vegetable oil, so quickly, in fact, that they are still very underdone in the middle when they're served and therefore moist.

SERVES 4

> 750 g (1½ lb) halibut fillet, preferably a single
>   piece cut from a large fish
> 2 carrots
> 2 tender celery sticks
> 175 g (6 oz) unsalted butter
> 50 ml (2 fl oz) white wine
> 1 tablespoon finely chopped fresh dill
> 600 ml (1 pint) *Fish Stock* (see p. 36)
> Juice of ¼ lemon
> 15 ml (½ fl oz) groundnut oil
> Salt and freshly ground black pepper

Cut the halibut into thin escalopes with a sharp, thin-bladed knife. Cut the fish on the slant so that you get a few, wide pieces. It doesn't really matter if you don't do it neatly, providing the pieces are no more than about 5 mm (¼ in) thick.

Peel the carrots and cut into fine neat dice by first slicing the carrot lengthways into 3 mm (⅛ in) slices, then cutting into 3 mm (⅛ in) sticks and finally cutting into 3 mm (⅛ in) dice. Repeat with the celery.

Melt 25 g (1 oz) of the butter in a pan and start to fry the carrot and celery over a gentle heat. Just as they are beginning to soften add the white wine and all but a generous pinch of the dill (keep some back to garnish the dish). Cook gently with a lid on the pan for a further 5 minutes. Season with salt.

In a separate pan, boil the fish stock until the volume has reduced by three-quarters then pour into the carrot and celery. Whisk in the remaining butter and lemon juice.

Heat the groundnut oil in a frying pan. When the oil is hot, add only enough escalopes to cover the base of the pan. Sprinkle with salt and pepper and turn over almost immediately then remove from the pan to a warm plate after only 20 seconds of cooking. Cook the rest of the escalopes.

Take a long, elegant serving dish and pour all the sauce onto it. Layer the escalopes of halibut down the middle and sprinkle with the pinch of dill. Serve with a few potatoes cut into triangular, finger-length pieces and boiled with dill (see p. 93).

GRILLED SCORED PLAICE WITH GARLIC, OREGANO AND LEMON JUICE

The fish, scored and marinated with olive oil, garlic, oregano, chilli and sea salt, is good served with a bowl of chips and a soft lettuce salad with mustard and chive dressing. I have never forgotten the wonderful earthy flavour of some chips eaten in a taverna in Paxos, Greece, caused by not being too fastidious with the peeling. Just roughly peel some potatoes (such as Maris Piper) leaving on some of the peel, then cut into large, irregular chips and deep-fry in hot oil.

SERVES 4

4 whole plaice, each weighing about 450 g
　(1 lb)
1 small red pepper
½ mild red chilli, seeded and finely chopped
50 ml (2 fl oz) virgin olive oil
1 large garlic clove, finely chopped
1 teaspoon chopped fresh oregano or ½
　teaspoon dried
1 teaspoon salt
A pinch of freshly ground black pepper
Juice of ¼ lemon

Cut off the fins with a pair of scissors and trim the tail. Make a deep cut down the back of each fish from head to tail. Then make a series of diagonal cuts across from this cut to the sides so that the slashes look like the veins of a leaf. Turn the fish over and do the same on the other side.

Roast the red pepper by placing it in a hot oven for 10 minutes or by putting it under a hot grill and turning it as it blackens. Cut in half, remove the seeds and skin and chop the flesh very finely, into 3 mm (⅛ in) dice. Put in a bowl with the olive oil, garlic, oregano, salt, black pepper and lemon juice to make the marinade.

One hour before cooking, coat both sides of the fish with the marinade, making sure that it spreads right into the slashes.

Turn on the grill and heat it until it's very hot. Grill the fish for 5 minutes on each side starting with the light side. Serve with chips and a salad of soft green leaves with its *Mustard Dressing* made with chives (see p. 51).

CHAR-GRILLED WHOLE DOVER SOLE WITH SEA SALT AND LIME

The skin of the sole is very pleasant to eat when crisply cooked, as it is here. The fish can be cooked either on a barbecue or under a very hot grill.

SERVES 4

- 4 Dover soles, each weighing about 400–450 g (14 oz–1 lb), skin on
- Vegetable oil, for brushing
- Sea salt

FOR THE SAUCE

- 300 ml (10 fl oz) *Fish Stock* (see p. 36)
- 1½ teaspoons Thai fish sauce (*nam pla*)
- 3 limes
- 15 g (½ oz) unsalted butter
- ¼ small red onion, finely diced
- 1 bunch fresh flatleaf parsley, roughly chopped, a few sprigs reserved for a garnish

De-scale the soles and cut off the fins. Dry the fish with kitchen paper.

To make the sauce put the fish stock and fish sauce in a small pan. Grate the rind of 1 lime and add to the pan with its juice.

Pre-heat the grill until it's very hot.

Just before cooking the fish, dry them one more time, then brush with vegetable oil and sprinkle the dark side with sea salt. Brush the grill bars with oil and immediately put the fish on, dark (top) side down. Cook for about 5 minutes then sprinkle the light side with sea salt, turn and cook for 5 minutes on the other side. Remove the fish from the grill and sprinkle with more sea salt. You may find that, in spite of all you've done, the fish will stick a bit. Don't worry, they will still taste wonderful and they don't look bad with some of the top skin pulled off.

Place each fish on a warmed plate then finish the sauce.

Bring the ingredients in the pan to the boil and add the butter. Whisk until it has all melted then add the chopped red onion and the parsley. Pour the sauce around the fish immediately and garnish with the remaining limes cut into wedges and sprigs of parsley.

DOVER SOLE À LA MEUNIÈRE

Dover sole *à la Meunière* or 'miller's wife style' gets it name from the light dusting of flour it is given before frying. The flour should be just a dusting and not a thick layer. I don't actually fry the fish in a pan on top of the cooker because I never have enough stove-top space. Instead, I paint the fish liberally with melted butter and put it under the grill. I think it works better this way and is equally helpful in the domestic situation as well. Frying large fish at home is a near impossibility. The same dish done in an oven grill becomes easy and something you will probably want to do at least once a week – if you can afford the fish, that is!

The success of this dish lies in making sure there is ample *noisette* butter and plenty of lemon juice. How often have I had soles cooked like this in restaurants where, by the time I've got in the second two fillets, I've run out of the delicious butter and wedges of lemon. So make sure you serve plenty of butter and plenty of lemon juice and, if you can be troubled, some preserved lemon as well to add little bites of piquancy as you eat the fish. Serve with *Grilled Potatoes* (see below) and a salad of soft green leaves tossed with *Mustard Dressing* (see p. 51).

SERVES 4

50 g (2 oz) flour seasoned with 1 teaspoon salt
4 Dover soles, each weighing about 400–450 g (14 oz–1 lb), skinned
40 g (1½ oz) unsalted butter
2 lemons
1 tablespoon finely chopped fresh parsley
¼ of a *Preserved Lemon* (see p. 52) (optional)
1 quantity *Noisette Butter* (see p. 50)
Salt and freshly ground white pepper

Pre-heat the grill to high. Put the seasoned flour in a tray and drop the fish into it, one side at a time, then smack them sharply to remove all the excess flour. Melt the butter in a small pan and use it to brush the soles, then season them on both sides with salt and freshly ground white pepper.

Grill the fish for 5 minutes on each side.

Place the soles on four large warm plates. Season again with salt then sprinkle with the juice of one of the lemons, the parsley and the finely chopped preserved lemon (if using). Pour over the *noisette* butter and serve with the other lemon cut into wedges.

For this dish, you need to splash out on an expensive Loire like a top-notch Pouilly Fumé or Sancerre.

GRILLED POTATOES

SERVES 4

450 g (1 lb) large potatoes
50 ml (2 fl oz) virgin olive oil
Salt and freshly ground black pepper

Pre-heat the grill to high.

Peel the potatoes and cut them lengthways into 5 mm (¼ in) slices. Boil in salted water until tender then drain. Lay on a grill tray and brush liberally on both sides with olive oil. Season with black pepper and grill until beginning to turn brown.

CHAR-GRILLED FILLETS OF DOVER SOLE WITH CORIANDER, CUMIN AND CHILLI

This is a dish which makes the most of Moroccan flavours. I first went to Morocco on my honeymoon and I recall it as not being a total success in culinary terms because we arrived during Ramadan, a time of fasting in the Muslim calendar and so we couldn't get anything to eat between sunrise and sunset, or not much anyway.

But, despite this drawback, I began to become aware of the richness and variety of the cuisines of North Africa, especially the clean, fresh-tasting mix of strong herbs and spices – very exciting. I wouldn't like to suggest that this dish is authentically Moroccan, but I don't think a Moroccan would disapprove of it. I've tried various combinations for the marinade, *charmoula*, but this one from Robert Carrier is, I think, the best. The sole fillets don't need to be marinated for very long because they're so thin. They should, ideally, be cooked in a ribbed steak pan (see p. 35).

SERVES 4

550 g (1¼ lb) Dover sole fillets
1 quantity *Charmoula* (see p. 45)

FOR THE COUSCOUS

100 g (4 oz) couscous
85 ml (3 fl oz) boiling water
25 ml (1 fl oz) virgin olive oil
25 g (1 oz) unsalted butter
A good pinch of salt
1 tablespoon fresh mint, chopped

FOR THE SALAD

¼ of a *Preserved Lemon*, finely chopped (see p. 52)
25 g (1 oz) rocket leaves or mixed salad leaves
15 ml (½ fl oz) virgin olive oil
Salt

Put the couscous in a bowl and pour over 85 ml (3 fl oz) of boiling water and add a good pinch of salt. Stir a little then leave for a couple of minutes so the grains can absorb the water. Heat the olive oil and butter in a frying pan, add the couscous and cook gently for 4 minutes then add the mint, set aside and keep warm.

Mix the preserved lemon with the rocket or salad leaves, 15 ml (½ fl oz) of virgin olive oil and a little salt.

Heat the ribbed pan until very hot. Brush the sole fillets with some of the *charmoula* and cook for about 2 minutes on each side. Arrange a pile of rocket, the sole fillets, couscous and a tablespoon of *charmoula* on each of four warmed plates. Serve immediately.

(TOP LEFT) Char-grilled Whole Dover Sole with Sea Salt and Lime (*see page 149*), (ABOVE) Roast Tronçon of Turbot with Hollandaise Sauce (*see page 157*) and (LEFT) A Ragout of Turbot and Scallops with Chicory, French Tarragon and Noilly Prat (*see page 158*)

DEEP-FRIED GOUJONS OF LEMON SOLE WITH TARTARE SAUCE

Goujons are small pieces of fish fillet, cut to about the size of your little finger, coated in breadcrumbs then deep-fried. We use a Japanese breadcrumb called *panko*, they fry much crisper than any other coating. At the time of writing, I am fairly certain that you cannot get *panko* in shops or supermarkets. But when writing a cookery book, one has to look into the future slightly as far as new products are concerned, and I am certain that within a short time *panko* breadcrumbs will be available because they are so extremely good. However, you can still get perfectly acceptable results making *goujons* with ordinary fresh bread-crumbs; they make a perfect first course and are universally popular.

SERVES 4

350 g (12 oz) lemon sole fillet, skinned
25 g (1 oz) seasoned flour
2 eggs
50 g (2 oz) *panko* or fresh breadcrumbs
1 lemon
1 quantity *Tartare Sauce* (see p. 44)

To cut the lemon sole into *goujons*, slice the fillet diagonally to make long pieces of about the size of your little finger. Put the flour in a small shallow dish or tray. Beat the eggs together and put in a second dish or tray and put the breadcrumbs in a third. Set the deep-fryer to 190°C/375°F, or heat some oil in a large pan to the same temperature or until a cube of bread browns in about 30 seconds.

Dip the *goujons* first in the seasoned flour, then the egg and finally the breadcrumbs and deep-fry until golden brown. Drain on kitchen paper and serve with the lemon cut into wedges and the tartare sauce.

FILLETS OF LEMON SOLE WITH A VERMOUTH SAUCE AND WHOLEGRAIN MUSTARD

The fillets of lemon sole are accompanied by a variation of the classic sauce *beurre blanc* (made with dry Vermouth instead of white wine) and thinly sliced cucumber flavoured with Thai fish sauce (*nam pla*), which I use as a subtly-flavoured substitute for salt, so if you can't get it use plain salt instead.

SERVES 4

½ cucumber
1 quantity *Beurre Blanc* (see p. 42) made with 50 ml (2 fl oz) dry vermouth
1 teaspoon wholegrain mustard
750 g (1½ lb) lemon sole fillets, skin on
1 tablespoon Thai fish sauce (*nam pla*)
1 teaspoon roughly chopped fresh coriander
Salt and freshly ground white pepper

First, prepare the cucumber by cutting into sections about 5 cm (2 in) long, then slice into matchsticks.

Pass the *Beurre Blanc* through a sieve into a clean pan. Add the mustard grains and a small pinch of salt. Keep warm.

Pre-heat the grill to high. Brush the fillets with butter then season with salt and freshly ground white pepper. Cook under the grill for 4 minutes.

Put the cucumber in a small pan and add a tablespoon of fish sauce (or a good pinch of salt) and the coriander. Cover and cook gently for 2 minutes. Stir then divide between 4 warmed plates. Arrange the lemon sole fillets neatly beside the cucumber so they overlap each other on the plates and pour the vermouth sauce all around. Serve immediately.

ROAST TRONÇON OF TURBOT WITH HOLLANDAISE SAUCE

The *tronçon*, a steak cut from a big fish, is accompanied by not only the Hollandaise but also a thin, very well-seasoned liquor which is flavoured with chopped fresh parsley, tarragon, chervil and chives.

SERVES 4

| 25 g (1 oz) unsalted butter |
| 4 steaks or *tronçons* of turbot, each weighing about 225–275 g (8–10 oz) |
| 85 ml (3 fl oz) *Fish Stock* (see p. 36) |
| 1 teaspoon chopped fresh *fines herbes*: parsley, French tarragon, chives, chervil |
| ¼ teaspoon Thai fish sauce (*nam pla*) or a pinch of salt |
| Juice of ½ lemon |
| Salt and freshly ground black pepper |
| 1 quantity *Hollandaise Sauce* (see p. 40) |

Pre-heat the oven to 230°C/450°F/Gas 8. Heat a frying pan and melt a small piece of butter. Add the *tronçons* and quickly brown them before transferring to a roasting tray. Season with salt and pepper then roast in the oven for about 15 minutes.

To make the sauce, combine the fish stock, the *fines herbes*, the Thai fish sauce or salt, the lemon juice and the remaining butter in a small pan and bring to the boil.

Arrange the *tronçons* on four warmed plates and just cover the top of each *tronçon* with the *fines herbes* sauce. Spoon the Hollandaise sauce onto the plate against one side of each *tronçon*. Serve with some plainly boiled new potatoes and a simple green vegetable such as spinach, French beans or mangetout.

I would suggest a South African Chardonnay to go with this. They seem to me to fall between the full roundness of Australian Chardonnay and the elusive subtlety of Burgundies, having a little of each. I particularly like those from Stellenbosch.

A Ragout of Turbot and Scallops with Chicory, French Tarragon and Noilly Prat

The turbot and scallops are braised on top of some sliced vegetables with white vermouth and a splash of fish stock. It is important not to overcook the scallops which is easily done given the difference in size between the turbot and the scallops.

SERVES 4

350 g (12 oz) turbot fillet
25 g (1 oz) French tarragon, weight including stalks
12 scallops
6 fl oz (175 ml) double cream
1.2 litres (2 pints) *Fish Stock* (see p. 36)
75 g (3 oz) unsalted butter
50 ml (2 fl oz) Noilly Prat or other vermouth
1 head of chicory, thinly sliced
100 g (4 oz) white of leek, thinly sliced
100 g (4 oz) fresh button mushrooms, thinly sliced
1 tablespoon fresh chervil, roughly chopped
Juice ¼ lemon
Salt and freshly ground white pepper

Slice the turbot into 2 cm (¾ in) slices across the fillet. Strip off enough tarragon leaves to make about a teaspoonful of roughly chopped tarragon. Cut each scallop into three rounds. Put half the cream and all of the fish stock in a pan with the remaining tarragon. Bring gently to the boil to avoid boiling over and simmer until the volume has reduced by three-quarters.

While the sauce is simmering, place the butter and the Noilly Prat in a wide shallow, heavy-based pan. Add the chicory and leeks, cover and cook gently for about 5 minutes. Add the sliced mushrooms and cook for a further 1 minute. Place the turbot and scallops on top of the vegetables, add half a teacup or so of the reduced fish stock and cream, lightly season and simmer, covered, for 3 minutes when the fish will be just cooked. Carefully lift out the fish and vegetables with a fish slice and keep warm. Add the rest of the cream and the chopped tarragon to the pan and boil vigorously for 3–4 minutes to concentrate the flavour.

Return the fish and vegetables to the pan, sprinkle with the chopped chervil, add a little lemon juice to taste and serve on four warmed plates.

LARGE FISH: SKATE, SHARK, SWORDFISH, TUNA AND CONGER EEL

Most of the recipes in this chapter are fairly exotic, reflecting the fact that these fish also swim in warmer waters – except the conger eel which is a cold water fish. It can grow up to six metres in length, though, so I've included it among the large fish here.

SKATE

Lots of people and lots of cookery books say that the smell of ammonia in skate is perfectly acceptable and that it is driven off by cooking. If you are offered a piece of skate that smells strongly of ammonia do not buy it. You will never get rid of the taste, and even if you can't smell it when you eat it, it will come back into your mouth as an aftertaste and haunt you for at least the rest of that day, if not the next.

Skate, when it is very fresh, is inedible because it's so tough and after about a week it is inedible because of its taste of ammonia. The gradual build up of ammonia in the flesh is also the process by which the fish is tenderized. You have a window of about five days to buy the fish when it will be both tender and delicious. Fortunately, it freezes very well and you can extend its shelf-life in this way. To all intents and purposes, although they are different species, skate, thornback ray, starry ray and spotted ray are normally sold at a fishmonger's

as skate. The wings of skate are the only parts sold and are normally skinned before sale. I would suggest that if possible you should go for skate wings weighing about 450–900 g (1–2 lb). Larger than that the skate becomes rather coarse; smaller and they can be a bit fiddly to eat. Skate has no bones, just cartilage, and it is not necessary to fillet it. The best eating of all the skate or rays is the thornback ray. Be a bit careful if you happen to get hold of a whole fish, though, because they're called thornback rays for a reason.

SHARK

All sharks are good for eating – well flavoured, lemony, slightly sweet and oily. But some are better than others. The porbeagle, closely related to the great white, is the best. Would a large porbeagle ever turn nasty I wonder? The mako also makes good eating and is very similar in flavour to the porbeagle and probably, though I have never tasted it, the great white. Some have likened porbeagle to veal. It has a similar pink colour and is meaty in texture. Try dusting with flour, egg and breadcrumbs and frying it like a veal escalope.

The blue shark is less good but still worth char-grilling or making into curry (see p. 163) as are most of the dogfish. The angel shark tastes more like skate than anything else. The other name for angel shark is monkfish, which is rather confusing as it in no way resembles the more common monkfish in flavour or, apart from a passing similarity in shape, in appearance. The monkfish or angler fish, with its enormous teeth, looks like something out of hell; the monkfish or angel shark looks like a benign Labrador.

Like skate, other members of the shark family also smell of ammonia after death as they use urea in their bloodstreams to counteract the salinity of the sea. Without it, they would dehydrate through osmosis. The urea breaks down after death and is responsible for tenderizing the flesh but after a week it becomes too powerful. Give a fillet of shark a good sniff before you buy.

DOGFISH AND TOPE

Dogfish and tope are both members of the shark family. The best dogfish to eat is the spurdog. That's the one with a sort of thin spike or spur just in front of the dorsal fins. Next, in order of good eating, comes the lesser-spotted dogfish and lastly the starry smooth hound and the smooth hound. I'm not passionate about dogfish; maybe if they had always been known by their popular names of huss, flake and rigg it would have been different. I do think a certain amount as a fillet with other seafood makes a good contrast – you can use it in the seafood salad on p. 163. It smokes extremely well though. If you ever have a chance to smoke fish or meat, make a brine of 65 g (2½ oz) salt to 600 ml (1 pint) of water, soak a fillet for a couple of hours, then cold smoke it for 4–5 hours. Serve it sliced with the horseradish and mustard sauce on page 93. Like all the sharks, dogfish suits cooking on a barbecue very well. I would combine it with some other fillets of fish, perhaps sea bass, John

Dory or red mullet and serve say three grilled fillets with a *sauce vierge* (Virgin olive oil sauce) of tomato, garlic, shallot, lemon juice, salt and basil. Tope, on the other hand, should be kept only for soup in my opinion.

SWORDFISH AND TUNA

Elsewhere in the book I have purposefully confined the fish used in the recipes to those which can be bought fresh and, in particular, those landed in Cornish fishing ports, because they are familiar to me. This is now the case with swordfish and tuna; they are both caught out in the bay of Biscay and landed at Newlyn and are delicious.

The flesh of both fish is compact and swordfish is ideal for cutting into thin steaks and grilling. Tuna is better when cut into thicker steaks and left a little underdone in the centre. If you don't want to go to the (not enormous) trouble of making *Char-grilled Swordfish Steaks with Salsa Fresca* on p. 164, just grill some steaks of swordfish or tuna and serve them with a pool of extra virgin olive oil.

CONGER EEL

There are some signs today that conger eel is not going to remain the abundant cheap fish that it always has been. The price is beginning to edge up, a fact that I regard with some consternation. Conger eel is one of the main constituents of our fish soup but large eels also provide beautiful, firm, bone-free fillets. I have put conger eel in this chapter because they can be enormous – the largest I've had delivered was 3½ metres (12 ft) long – quite fearsome at that size.

SKATE WITH BLACK BUTTER

This is one of my favourite dishes. I'll never drop it from my repertoire at the restaurant. It's always popular. One of those perfect combinations that I'm always looking for when producing recipes myself. Skate, being one of the shark family, has a flavour that is what I would call insistent. The first few mouthfuls are delicious but after a while you sort of feel

1 quantity *Court-bouillon* (see p. 38)
900 g (2 lb) skate wings
15 g (½ oz) capers

Bring all the *Court-bouillon* ingredients to the boil in a large pan. Remove from the heat and leave to cool before using to complete the infusion of flavours.

Cut the skate into four portions and place in a wide shallow pan. Pour the *court-bouillon* over the fish, bring to the boil and simmer very gently for 15–20 minutes, depending on the thickness of the skate. Drain the fish and keep it warm on a serving dish. Sprinkle with the capers.

that maybe you've had enough unless, that is, you partner the fish with some strong and sharp sauce like black butter where lots of red wine vinegar is used. For the same reason, the Indians tend to use shark for their most aromatic fish curries. (See the recipe for shark curry on p. 163.)

SERVES 4

FOR THE BLACK BUTTER

175 g (6 oz) salted butter
50 ml (2 fl oz) red wine vinegar
1 tablespoon finely chopped fresh parsley

Melt the butter in a frying pan. When it foams, begins to go really dark and smells nutty, pour in the vinegar. Add the parsley, and let it boil down for a minute or so then pour over the fish. Serve at once with plainly boiled potatoes.
Serve with a bottle of young Chilean Sauvignon or a Sauvignon from one of the lesser-known, and therefore better-value, wine areas of the Loire, such as Quincy, Reuilly, Ménétou-Salon or Haut Poitou.

SKATE, LEEKS AND WILTED LETTUCE WITH A CIDER VINEGAR AND BUTTER SAUCE

I based this recipe around an old Cornish farmhouse cider that a friend gave me. It had an unusual nutty flavour, in some ways similar to, but then again quite unlike, a good sherry vinegar.

SERVES 4

4 skinned skate wings, each weighing about
   275–350 g (10–12 oz)
175 g (6 oz) unsalted butter
2 leeks
100 g (4 oz) mangetout
1 soft-leaf lettuce
600 ml (1 pint) *Fish Stock* (see p. 36)
120 ml (4 fl oz) good quality cider vinegar
1 tablespoon roughly chopped fresh parsley
Salt and freshly ground black pepper

Pre-heat the oven to 200°C/400°F/Gas 6. Brush the skate wings with a little melted butter, season with salt and roast in the oven for 15 minutes. Remove and keep warm.

Remove the outer leaves from the leeks, thinly slice and wash carefully in a colander. Top and tail the mangetout and cut into long thin strips. Put 50 g (2 oz) of the butter in a pan, then cover and soften the leeks and the mangetout over a gentle heat for 3–4 minutes.

Remove and discard the outer leaves from the lettuce then wash, dry and slice the rest.

Add the lettuce to the leeks and mangetout and cook for a further 4–5 minutes. Season with salt and pepper.

Put the vinegar and fish stock in a small pan and boil rapidly to reduce the volume by three quarters. Add the rest of the butter and simmer until it coats the back of a spoon.

To serve, divide the leek and lettuce mixture between four warmed plates and place a skate wing on top of each. Pour the vinegar and butter sauce over the fish and scatter with parsley. Serve with boiled potatoes.

SKATE MAYONNAISE WITH A VEGETABLE SALAD

Having no bones and a firm texture, skate is an ideal fish for poaching and serving cold in a salad.

SERVES 4

1 quantity *Court-bouillon* (see p. 38)
750 g (1½ lb) skate

FOR THE VEGETABLE SALAD

50 g (2 oz) celery
50 g (2 oz) carrot
50 g (2 oz) leek
25 ml (1 fl oz) groundnut oil
25 ml (1 fl oz) white wine
Salt and freshly ground black pepper
50 g (2 oz) French beans
50 g (2 oz) mangetout
8 lettuce leaves and the heart of a lettuce

FOR THE MAYONNAISE

100 g (4 oz) *Olive Oil Mayonnaise* (see p. 43)
75 g (3 oz) tomato, peeled, seeded and roughly chopped
1 avocado pear, chopped
100 g (4 oz) cooked peeled potato, diced

Bring the *court-bouillon* to a gentle simmer, add the skate and poach for 15–20 minutes. Leave to cool in the liquid.

Cut the celery, carrot and leek into 5 cm (2 in) matchsticks. Heat the oil in a shallow pan and gently cook the vegetables for 1 minute. Add the white wine, salt and pepper and cook until the wine has boiled off completely. Turn out on to a plate and chill.

Top and tail the beans and mangetout. Cut the beans into lengths of about the same size as the rest of the vegetables; the mangetout can be left whole. Bring a pan of salted water to the boil and blanch the beans and mangetout for 30 seconds, then plunge them into the cold water. Drain through a colander and mix with the rest of the vegetables. Season with salt and black pepper.

Remove the skin and cartilage from the skate and mix with the olive oil mayonnaise, tomato, avocado and potato. Check and adjust the seasoning as necessary. Serve garnished with a couple of leaves from the heart of the lettuce and the vegetable salad.

GOAN SHARK CURRY

This curry is known in Goa as *amo-tik* which means sour-hot. The sourness comes from the tamarind and vinegar. It is particularly suited to any of the shark family, all of which have a rather sweet, oily flavour. I would suggest using porbeagle shark for the best flavour but any of the following would produce a good dish: blue shark, ray, angel shark or dogfish. These are all sharks native to the UK but shark or dogfish from other countries will work very well too.

SERVES 4

550 g (1¼ lb) shark or dogfish fillet cut into 2.5 cm (1 in) pieces

FOR THE MASALA

2 garlic cloves
2.5 cm (1 in) piece fresh ginger
A walnut-sized piece of tamarind, seeded
½ teaspoon black peppercorns
½ teaspoon turmeric
6 red chillies

2 onions, chopped
25 ml (1 fl oz) vegetable oil
½ teaspoon cumin seeds
2 tomatoes, chopped
2 tablespoons wine vinegar
300 ml (10 fl oz) water
1 teaspoon salt
1 teaspoon chopped fresh coriander

Sprinkle the shark with some of the salt and leave for 20 minutes before cooking.

Grind the garlic, ginger, tamarind, peppercorns, turmeric and chillies in a mortar and pestle or food blender. If using the latter grind the peppercorns in a pepper mill first.

Fry the onions in the oil until transparent. Add the cumin seeds and fry for another minute then add the dry masala ingredients. Cook for 2–3 minutes then add the chopped tomatoes, wine vinegar, water and the rest of the salt. Bring to the boil and simmer for 2–3 minutes. Add the shark and simmer gently for 5 minutes. Sprinkle with the chopped coriander and serve with boiled rice.

SHARK, WHELK AND OCTOPUS SALAD WITH LEMON, GARLIC AND OLIVE OIL

This Italian salad has a simple dressing so that the flavours of the fish and shellfish are not smothered. I have purposely chosen cheap but unusual seafood for this dish because it is just as good using shark and whelks as the expensive monkfish, langoustine and Mediterranean prawns.

SERVES 4

1 octopus, prepared for cooking (see p. 28)
350 g (12 oz) shark fillet
4 cooked or uncooked whelks
Juice of ½ lemon
85 ml (3 fl oz) extra virgin olive oil
2 garlic cloves, finely chopped
1 tablespoon roughly chopped fresh parsley
1 tablespoon white wine vinegar
100 g (4 oz) button mushrooms, thinly sliced
1 teaspoon salt
½ iceberg lettuce

Simmer the octopus in lightly salted water for 1 hour. Cool, remove the dark brown skin, and thinly slice.

Cook the shark by poaching it in salted water for about 5 minutes. Leave to cool in the water, then remove and slice into 1 cm (½ in) pieces.

If you need to cook the whelks bring them to the boil in sea water or water salted at the rate of 20 g (¾ oz) of salt to 600 ml (1 pint) for 5 minutes. Remove the meat from the whelk shells taking care to cut away the little round 'door' at the front of the shell. Cut off and discard the brown end then thinly slice the meat.

Mix all the ingredients together in a large bowl and serve.

CHAR-GRILLED SWORDFISH STEAKS WITH SALSA FRESCA

You can just as successfully use tuna or sea bass for this dish. The grilled fish steaks are served with a chilli hot sauce and an ice-cold *salsa* with avocado, cucumber, tomato and spring onions. It is dressed with a thin mayonnaise-based sauce from Mexico. Try to keep all the avocado, cucumber, tomatoes and spring onion roughly the same size when chopping them. If the spring onions are large cut them into quarters lengthways before thinly slicing.

SERVES 4

4 swordfish steaks, each weighing about
   175 g (6 oz)
Olive oil, for brushing
Salt and freshly ground black pepper

FOR THE SALSA

1 green chilli, seeded and finely chopped
1 avocado, cut into 5 mm (¼ in) dice
2 garlic cloves, finely chopped
3 spring onions, thinly sliced
½ cucumber, cut into 5 mm (¼ in) dice
Juice of 2 limes
2 under-ripe tomatoes, skinned, seeded and
   cut into 5 mm (¼ in) dice
1 tablespoon fresh coriander, roughly
   chopped

FOR THE SAUCE

4 green olives
4 heaped tablespoons *Olive Oil Mayonnaise*
   (see p. 43)
50 ml (2 fl oz) double cream
120 ml (4 fl oz) water

Keep all the prepared *salsa* ingredients cold, and separate until just before serving, then quickly mix them together in a bowl and divide between 4 plates.

Cut the olive flesh from the stone in strips then cut these strips into thin pine needle sized shards. In a small pan, mix the mayonnaise, cream and warm water with the olive shards then warm through – the sauce should be served warm not hot.

Light the barbecue or heat a ribbed grill pan. Season the swordfish steaks with salt and pepper and brush with olive oil. Grill for about 3 minutes on each side.

Serve with a portion of salsa and some of the sauce spread over the steaks and around the plates.

Serve with the Mexican beer, Sol, which is very light in alcohol, so you can drink lots of it to combat the heat of the chilli.

SASHIMI WITH SOYA AND JAPANESE HORSERADISH

Sashimi is raw, sliced fish served here with a Japanese horseradish called *wasabi*, a green, fiery horseradish which is mixed with soy sauce and lime juice to make a hot dressing. If you can't get hold of any *wasabi* use hot English horseradish sauce instead. Even if this recipe does not appeal to you at first, try it. You'll be amazed how full of flavour raw fish, particularly tuna, is.

Buy the fillets of three or four different types of fish for this dish. The Japanese insist on absolute freshness – so fresh that the fish is still jumping around just before being cut up. But, as long as you can trust your fishmonger, the best fillets that he has will be perfectly adequate. All you need to do is just say to him that you don't mind what fish it is as long as it's the freshest that he's got. At the restaurant we tend to go for fish with differing textures and shades so, for example, there will normally be an oily fish like salmon or tuna for its colour and two other oily fish, such as mackerel or herring which are both excellent for sashimi. There may also be a fish like turbot, brill or plaice, which slice very satisfactorily and are always free from bones and perhaps, finally, a sliced scallop or some bass or red mullet. Raw lobster is a particular delicacy for sashimi.

You need to buy about 350 g (12 oz) of fillet as a first course for four people. If you are not too adept at skinning fillet then ask your fishmonger to do it for you.

To make the slicing of the fish easier, make sure it is well chilled. Cut the fillet slightly on the diagonal so that the slices lie against each other in an attractive way. The presentation of a dish like *Sashimi* is very important and no one does it better than the Japanese. The great thing with delicate presentation is not to fiddle around with things. It is far better to slice the fillets on a cutting board, pick them up on a palette knife and put them confidently on the plate. Don't attempt to neaten them up. I find that it doesn't really matter if the slices are not totally neat as long as they're natural.

SERVES 4

350 g (12 oz) skinned fish fillet
1 tablespoon green *wasabi* powder mixed to a stiff paste with water or English horseradish sauce
A few chives
A few sprigs of coriander

FOR THE LIME AND SOY SAUCE

15 g (½ oz) fresh ginger, finely chopped
85 ml (3 fl oz) soy sauce
85 ml (3 fl oz) water
2 spring onions, finely chopped
Zest and juice of 1 lime

First, cut the fish fillets into four equal portions, then slice each portion of each fish as thinly as possible, slightly on the diagonal. Lay the fish around four cold plates. Place a teaspoon of the *wasabi* (or horseradish) on each plate. Lay a couple of chives and some sprigs of coriander across the plates to garnish.

Mix together the ingredients for the lime and soy sauce and hand round separately.

(ABOVE) Shark, Whelk and Octopus
Salad with Lemon, Garlic and
Olive Oil (*see page 163*), (TOP RIGHT)
Skate with Black Butter (*see page
161*) and (RIGHT) Char-grilled
Swordfish Steaks with Salsa Fresca
(*see page 164*)

CHAR-GRILLED TUNA WITH OLIVES, LEMON AND SORREL

This recipe comes from Gay Bilson, an inspired cook from Sydney. Her restaurant, The Berowra Waters Inn, produced one of the most memorable meals of my life. She has now moved on to running a restaurant in the Opera House.

The tuna fish steak is seared on the outside but left underdone inside; this is by far the best way to eat it. A cast-iron ribbed steak pan is the ideal utensil for cooking this dish, though a real barbecue imparts a superior flavour. The quantities are for a first course.

SERVES 4

12 green olives
50 g (2 oz) sorrel
450 g (1 lb) skinned tuna fillet
50 ml (2 fl oz) virgin olive oil
25 ml (1 fl oz) water
½ teaspoon Thai fish sauce (*nam pla*)
Juice of ¼ lemon
Salt and freshly ground black pepper

Remove the stones from the olives and cut into thin slivers. Wash the sorrel, remove the stalks and cut into long, fine strips.

Put the grill pan on the heat to get really hot. Cut the tuna fillet into four pieces and brush with a little olive oil and season well with salt and black pepper. Grill for 1 minute only on each side.

Put the fish sauce, lemon juice, 2½ teaspoons of the olive oil and water into a small pan. Bring to the boil then remove from the heat immediately and keep warm.

Warm the remaining olive oil in another small pan, add the olives and about three-quarters of the sorrel. Allow the sorrel to wilt but don't cook it any further or it will brown.

Divide the olive and sorrel sauce between four warmed plates, place the tuna on top and pour the other sauce over the fish. Sprinkle with the remaining sorrel and serve.

GRILLED TUNA SALAD WITH GUACAMOLE

This dish comes from the Fifth Floor Restaurant in Harvey Nichols Department Store in London. The idea that raw tuna is cooked on a charcoal grill so briefly that only the outside is coloured and caramelized and the inside practically raw has been much copied and adapted, especially to meat like fillet steak. But I know from talking to the chef, Henry Harris, at the Fifth Floor, that he was the one that brought the dish to England from California, and jolly good for him. This is not his exact recipe. I much prefer to get enthusiastic about a dish in someone else's restaurant than attempt to copy it. By doing this, two surprisingly different versions of the same dish emerge; two for the price of one, if you like.

SERVES 4

450 g (1 lb) tuna fillet
Oil, for brushing
Sea salt and freshly ground black pepper
4 sprigs of coriander, to garnish

FOR THE GUACAMOLE

1 large avocado
1 green chilli, seeded
Juice of 1 lime
2 spring onions, chopped
1 tablespoon chopped fresh coriander plus
  4 sprigs
3 tablespoons vegetable oil
½ teaspoon salt

FOR THE SOY SAUCE DRESSING

50 ml (2 fl oz) water
1 tablespoon soy sauce
1 spring onion, finely chopped
¼ green chilli, seeded and chopped
Juice and zest of ½ lime
½ stick lemon grass, finely sliced
1 teaspoon chopped fresh ginger

Heat a charcoal grill or ribbed grill pan until it is very hot. Brush the tuna with oil and sprinkle liberally with salt and freshly ground black pepper. Blacken the fillet on the grill for 2–3 minutes, turning to colour it all over. Remember the centre of the tuna should remain raw. Remove from the grill and season again. Leave to cool completely.

Blend all the *guacamole* ingredients in a food processor until smooth then mix all the dressing ingredients together.

Slice the tuna into 5 mm (¼ in) slices and arrange on four cold plates. The slices should slightly overlap and be to the side of the plates. Put a spoonful of the *guacamole* on each plate, again slightly to the side (offsetting food on plates makes it look more natural). Add a generous pool of dressing and decorate the *guacamole* with a sprig of coriander.

(BELOW) Skate Mayonnaise with
a Vegetable Salad (*see page 162*),
(RIGHT) Grilled Tuna Salad with
Guacamole (*see page 169*) and
(BELOW RIGHT) Goan Shark Curry
(*see page 163*)

CONGER EEL WITH HARICOT BEANS, SMOKED HAM AND GARLIC

One of my themes in fish cookery is to break down the barriers between fish and meat. You may think that the idea of fish in a sort of cassoulet is in poor taste, but the cubes of conger eel with smoked ham, Toulouse sausage, tomato and garlic with plenty of haricot beans works very well here. Try to use cold smoked ham in this recipe, something like Black Forest or any air-dried smoked ham.

SERVES 4

450 g (1 lb) dried haricot beans
1 teaspoon salt
2 tablespoons roughly chopped parsley
4 slices of fresh white bread
6 cloves garlic, chopped
50 g (2 oz) smoked ham, sliced and cut into
   1 cm (½ in) strips
3 Toulouse sausages, cut into slices
200 g (7 oz) tin chopped tomatoes
600 ml (1 pint) *Chicken Stock* (see p. 37)
½ red chilli, seeded and chopped
450 g (1 lb) conger eel fillet, skinned, boned
   and cut into 2.5 cm (1 in) cubes
150 ml (5 fl oz) extra virgin olive oil
Salt and freshly ground black pepper

Soak the beans for 8 hours and drain. Put them in a pan, add enough water to cover them generously and simmer for 25 minutes. Add the salt and simmer for a further 25–30 minutes until nearly tender.

Pre-heat the oven to 180°C/350°F/Gas 4. Place the parsley, white bread and half the garlic in a food processor and process until you have a breadcrumb mixture. Season with salt and pepper. Add the remaining ingredients, except 65 ml (2½ fl oz) of the oil and the salt and pepper to the pan. Simmer for 20 minutes then season with ground black pepper. Transfer the contents of the pan to a deep ovenproof pot, preferably earthenware. Pour over the rest of the olive oil and sprinkle with the breadcrumb mixture. Bake in the oven for about 1 hour pushing the breadcrumbs down into the *cassoulet* three or four times during the baking to build up a crust.

Serve with a lightly dressed green salad. *I would suggest a young, fresh Cabernet Sauvignon from the Languedoc in South-West France – a Vin de Pays d'Oc – to go with this.*

10

CRUSTACEANS: CRAB, LANGOUSTINE, LOBSTER, PRAWNS AND SHRIMPS

Crustaceans are some of the most highly prized species of the sea, and lobsters, langoustines, prawns, etc. often represent the ultimate treat for seafood lovers. The best way to appreciate their delicate, salty-sweet flavour is to serve them very simply, with just mayonnaise or salad. However, they are also the ideal choice for spectacular dishes such as *Lobster Ravioli with Basil and Spinach* (p. 189) and *Crab in Filo Pastry with a Rich Tomato Sauce and Basil* (p. 178).

CRAB

If the meat of crab came out of the shell in the same solid chunks as lobster it would, without doubt, fetch the same sort of price. Crab is as sweet and full of flavour as lobster, but it comes out in small flakes. Even when lobster meat is taken from the shell it looks presentable but crab, on the other hand, is just a pile. Many of my recipes for crab, therefore, include some sort of container to improve the appearance of the dish. Thus, the recipes in this chapter include crab quiche, crab in filo pastry and crab fish cakes.

Crab is delicate and a common error is to partner it with overpowering flavours so the taste is lost completely. When writing my own recipes I have kept that thought in mind.

GREEN SHORE CRABS

'Where the hell am I supposed to get shore crabs from?' I hear you say. Well, you could go down to a nearby beach and turn over a lot of large stones, which is what I would do or, if you were in France, you could nip down the road to your local supermarket and buy a kilo or two. That is because in France they are aware of the great value of these tiny green crabs both for making *bisques* and for making shellfish *fumets*. Just as important, though, is the fact that the back shell supplies a neat little container for crab meat dishes.

One of the problems in writing a fish cookery book for the British market is that the supply of raw materials is limited to the more popular species. One feels a certain guilt in including recipes for things like fresh whelks, velvet crabs, razor-shell clams, trigger fish, and garfish (a sleek silver fish with a small sword like beak and green bones with oily firm flesh) and even such very common species as spider crabs, because one knows that they are not going to be easily available all over the country. But one of my main reasons for taking up seafood cookery in the first place was to show everyone in Britain that seafood is rich and varied. Just because you can't readily get hold of a raw material, I still feel that you should share my enthusiasm for some dishes which require it because it may just make you go and demand them from your fishmonger – and it is customer demand which will, in the end, improve the variety available.

In the meantime, however, as far as green shore crabs are concerned, go and pick your own. Simply turn over rocks on a rocky beach and you will find plenty, or else dangle a net with a couple of fish heads inside it and a length of twine over any harbour quay side and the green crabs will jump onto the net trying to get at the fish heads and you haul them up. Why not get your children to do it! Velvet crabs can be bought anywhere near the sea where there is also lobster fishing because they get caught in the same pots as lobsters. Most lobster fishermen now are aware of their value, having got good prices for them in France and Spain, and will gladly sell them to you.

days. They are much more akin to lobsters than prawns and look more like lobsters. Also, like lobsters their flesh deteriorates very quickly after death. Again, like lobsters, this is not due to any poisonous organism in them but because of a chemical change. The flesh becomes soft like cotton wool. It is easy to tell if they are fresh – pull back their tails, if they have a good degree of spring in them the meat inside will be firm. If the tail stays spread out when you pull it, the meat will be soft. Be governed by your sense of smell with langoustine, they should smell sweet and appetizing. If there is any suggestion of sourness or, worse still, ammonia, don't buy them.

Apart from serving them hot with a cream and garlic sauce (see p. 182) or with *Garlic Butter* (see p. 49) they are best served simply with a good mayonnaise such as the *Mustard Mayonnaise* on p. 43.

LANGOUSTINE

Of all the raw materials that are used at our restaurant, langoustine causes the most trouble. Although they are in great abundance in the Irish Sea 100 miles north-west of the restaurant, no one in Britain seems inclined to go fishing for them. The French, on the other hand, are there in force. Consequently we have to get our langoustine from Scotland and suffer the same sort of problems of varying quality that everyone else in Britain seems to have to put up with as far as fish and shellfish are concerned if they can't buy fish straight from the quayside. We have to have langoustine because they are what any self-respecting fish restaurant sells. One day the fishing industry in the South-west may find a market for them but, meanwhile, we have to buy them from Scotland.

A couple of tips about the quality of langoustine that you get in fishmongers these

LOBSTER

Every country with a coastline thinks that their seafood is the best. We say that fish and shellfish from our colder waters have a finer flavour. Australians say theirs is best because the warmer waters of the Pacific produce abundant and therefore cheap seafood from unpolluted waters. They cite the Pacific prawn as the best large prawn in the world and I would not disagree. But our lobsters are the best in the world. I have tried spiny lobsters in the Mediterranean, South-east Asia and Australia and I have tried lobsters from the Eastern seaboard of the United States and Canada and I now know, without doubt, that ours are the sweetest and richest of all seafood.

I regard lobster as the same calibre of delicacy as caviar or truffles. For the amount of work that goes into catching them, I think they are astonishingly good value for money. Canadian or American lobsters, which are now available live and air-freighted into the UK are, however, a good buy for dishes where the meat is taken out of the shell and served with other ingredients like the *Special Salad of Lobster, Avocado, Green Beans and Duck Livers* on p. 185. But if it's a straight grilled lobster or a lobster with mayonnaise it has to be one from the western seas of Britain and Ireland.

It is easy for me to tell the difference between our own lobsters and those from Canada and America. The New World lobster is a deep green when live and a fairly uniform orange red when cooked. The European lobster is blue when live and more of a pinky red with a lot of white mottling when cooked. The lobster from America has rounder claws than those from Europe. I must try eating Maine lobsters in Maine. It may be that they lose something in the journey, I suspect thay will taste much better eaten right by the sea where they came from just as the only place to eat Cornish lobster is Cornwall.

CRAWFISH OR SPINY LOBSTER

We are lucky in the South West of Britain to be one of the only places in the world where both the blue cold-water lobster and the browny-red spiny lobster abound. Any further north and the water is too cold for the spiny lobster, and the blue lobster becomes rarer further south as the water becomes warmer. From a chef's point of view the spiny lobster is not as prized as the common lobster because it grows to a much larger size and is therefore difficult to get hold of in 1–2 portion sizes, i.e. weighing between 450 g–1.25 kg (1 lb–2½ lb).

Serving slices from a bigger fish just doesn't have the same impact as giving someone half or a whole lobster. However, for cooking at home they are ideal because of the impact achieved by bringing such stunning-looking seafood to the table. All recipes for lobster suit the spiny lobster as well. I don't, myself, think they have such a good flavour as ordinary lobster but others disagree. To me spiny lobster should only be eaten freshly boiled because their flavour is more ephemeral than ordinary lobsters and disappears when they are left, particularly if they are chilled. No fresh seafood is as good as when served recently boiled and left to cool at ambient temperatures. Chilling removes some of that fragrant iodine flavour.

PRAWNS

Apart from langoustine, or Dublin Bay prawns as they are also known, it is almost impossible to get fresh prawns in Britain. We get small quantities from time to time, a by-product of lobster fishing and caught up, unbelievably, in lobster pots. I have tried to persuade local lobster fishermen to have a go at using some creel pots and even offered to pay for the gear but so far I have achieved nothing. The prawns you are likely to see everywhere at fishmongers and fish counters are not fresh but have been caught out in the North Atlantic and boiled at sea in sea water and then deep frozen. Fortunately the quality is excellent and while no one would mistake the fragrance of fresh prawns for the rather obvious salty sweet and savoury taste of frozen ones, they have an undeniably good flavour.

The situation as far as imported large prawns is concerned seems to be getting better and better. Frozen raw prawn tails can be very good and fresh whole prawns from South-east Asia and best of all Australia are now quite common. In fact the supply of raw materials from all over the world is becoming ever more varied, thanks to air freight. A fishmonger I know from Sydney who runs a very up-market business called the Flying Squid Brothers has his seafood store not by the sea but by the airport as most of the best fish from around Australia arrives in Sydney by plane.

SHRIMPS

Why can't we get plenty of fresh shrimps? Occasionally someone comes to the back door with a bag of them. Once in a while we find a new supplier who produces a couple of 10 lb bags boiled in sea water. I try to tempt my children to nip out with a net and catch a few but only occasionally does it work. In Brittany, there they are, in Britain there they aren't. One day we may find someone enterprising enough to maintain a supply. It isn't from any unwillingness on my part to pay good money for them. I love fresh shrimps, their taste reminds me of long-gone holidays as a child with a shrimping net bringing them back in buckets of sea water and having them for tea with thinly sliced bread and butter. I'd love to have the time to sail up the estuary in a small boat, fish for some myself and then bring them back to boil up and serve to the customers; that would be ideal.

The only drawback to the sweet, salty taste of shrimps is that there is such a lot of labour involved in peeling them. They are really of the same order of food as sunflower seeds: something to pick at. In Brittany they may give you a small bowl as an appetizer with your Muscadet and that's what I do when I can get them. If you do want to go to the trouble of picking them out to make a recipe, may I suggest mixing fresh shrimps with peeled langoustine tails, salad leaves and a simple dressing of olive oil, peeled, seeded and chopped tomato, lemon juice and basil.

Alternatively, fresh shrimps make an exquisite *bisque*. Follow the same recipe as for the *Shore-crab Bisque* on p. 57 but use shrimps instead of crabs. Don't bother to buy frozen shrimps; they taste of bits of string.

FRESHLY BOILED CRAB

This needs to be served as a whole crab, straight from the pot, which means it is a dish for those who like eating with their fingers. It is not so much a recipe – since all it includes is the crab, some mayonnaise, new potatoes and a salad – as a set of instructions on the best way to cook and serve up whole crabs to make them easy to eat. I've also included some instructions for dressing crabs, removing the meat from a whole crab, if you prefer to serve it like this.

Crabs should be boiled in plenty of water, salted at the rate of 150 g (5 oz) to 4.5 litres (1 gallon) of water. This is about the same salinity as sea water. Unlike lobsters, crabs can be killed by skewering (see the instructions on p. 25) or by immersing them in cold, salted water and gradually bringing them to the boil until they drown. It is never a good idea to drop live crabs into rapidly boiling water because they shed claws and legs in the process.

I believe in serving a big crab, say 900 g (2 lb) for one person, or an even larger crab, 1.5–1.75 kg (3–4 lb) in weight, for two to three people. A 900 g (2 lb) crab should be boiled for 15 minutes while a 1.75 kg (4 lb) crab will take up to 20 minutes.

When they are cooked, take the crabs out of the water and run them under the cold tap to make them easier to handle. Remove the tail flap from underneath the crab and the two flaps which cover the mouth on the undershell beneath the eyes. Once you have removed these two flaps you can separate the body from the main shell section (carapace). Place the crab face down on a chopping board and give its rear end a sharp thump with the heel of your hand. This will split the body from the back shell. Alternatively, you can do this with the point of a large knife inserted between the body and the back shell and twisted. Once you have removed the body from the carapace, pull off the gills, known as Dead Man's Fingers, which are popularly held to be poisonous but are just inedible, like feathers. If you look in the cavity of the carapace right in the centre behind the eyes you will see the stomach sac. Push the little piece of shell behind the eyes and you will hear a click. The piece of shell and the stomach sac can then be removed. Empty any excess water from the back of the shell.

Now cut the body section in half from front to back and then in half from side to side. Crack each of the claw sections with the back of a large knife. Try to do this without completely shattering the claws so that you can reassemble the crab to look much as it was. Take a large plate for each person, put the four sections of body back together, put the carapace on top, rearrange any legs that have fallen off so they are the right way round and put the claws back at the front of the crab as they were.

If you prefer to remove all the meat you will need a lobster pick or a teaspoon. Remove the white meat from the cracked claws. Pull off the legs, crack open the top joints and remove the meat from them. It is not normally worth removing the meat from the other leg joints unless the crabs are large. Push the thin end of the pick or the handle of the spoon into the knuckle-like joints on to which the claws and legs were attached and twist them off. Remove all the meat from the cavities behind.

Remove any brown meat from the body which you cut into four sections and the back shell. Chop the brown meat. Pick out the white meat from the body sections, taking care not to remove the wafer-thin pieces of shell. Serve the dressed crab in the back shells. The traditional accompaniments are chopped hard-boiled egg yolks and whites and chopped parsley. These are placed in the back shell in lines separating the brown meat from the white. I always like to fold a little mayonnaise and some black pepper into the brown meat.

Serve with boiled, minted new potatoes, a mixed leaf salad and *Mustard Mayonnaise* (see p. 43).

CRAB NEWBURG

I found this recipe in the *Faber Book of Food* edited by Colin Spencer and Clare Clifton, a marvellous anthology of eating. The recipe appealed to me as a period piece from the 30s and 40s; the sort of dish that may well have appeared on the menu at dinner on the *Queen Mary* or the *Mauretania*. We tried it out in the kitchen and it was delicious, but go easy on the sherry.

We boil the crabs immediately, 20 minutes in salted water. We like best to eat them just so, with home-made mayonnaise and Cuban bread and cold bitter ale. The meat comes from the shells in enormous flakes, snow-white and incredibly sweet and flavoursome...

When we have crab meat to spare, I make a crab Newburg so superlative that I myself taste it in wonder, thinking 'Can it be I who has brought this noble thing into the world?'

It is impossible to give proportions, for I never twice have the same amount of crab meat to work with, and here indeed I have no mother, but only instinct, to guide me. In an iron skillet over a low fire I place a certain amount of Dora's butter. As it melts, I stir in the flaked crab meat, lightly, tenderly. The flakes must not become disintegrated; they must not brown. I add lemon juice, possibly a tablespoonful for each cup of crab meat. I add salt and pepper frugally, paprika more generously, and a dash of powdered clove so temporal that the flavour in the finished Newburg is only as though the mixture had been whisked through a spice grove. I add Dora's golden cream. I do not know the exact quantity. It must be generous, but the delicate crab meat must never become deluged with any other element. The mixture bubbles for a few moments. I stir in dry sherry, the quantity again unestimable. Something must be left to genius. I stir in well beaten eggs, perhaps an egg, perhaps two, for every cup of flakes. The mixture must now no more than be turned over on itself and removed in a great sweep from the fire. I stir in a tablespoon, or two,

of the finest brandy, and turn the Newburg into a piping hot covered serving dish. I serve it on toast points and garnish superfluously with parsley, and a Chablis or white Rhine wine is recommended as an accompaniment. Angels sing softly in the distance.

We do not desecrate the dish by serving any other, neither salad nor dessert. We just eat crab Newburg. My friends rise from the table, wring my hand with deep feeling, and slip quietly and reverently away. I sit alone and weep for the misery of a world that does not have blue crabs and a Jersey cow.

CRAB IN FILO PASTRY WITH A RICH TOMATO SAUCE AND BASIL

I have added a rich tomato sauce containing one of those secret ingredients beloved by chefs: a *gastrique*. It is simple, you boil vinegar and sugar together until very rich and concentrated and add a teaspoon or so to a tomato sauce to give it real muscle.

SERVES 4

4 sheets filo pastry 30 × 40 cm
  (12 × 16 in) each
25 g (1 oz) butter, melted

FOR THE TOMATO SAUCE

1 medium onion, finely chopped
1 garlic clove, finely chopped
25 ml (1 fl oz) olive oil
400 g (14 oz) tin chopped tomatoes
50 ml (2 fl oz) red wine vinegar
2 teaspoons sugar
225 g (8 oz) white crab meat, preferably fresh
10 basil leaves, thinly sliced
15 ml (½ fl oz) extra virgin olive oil
Juice of ¼ lemon
Salt and freshly ground white pepper

Pre-heat the oven to 180°C/375°F/Gas 5. Brush 1 side of 2 of the sheets of filo pastry with melted butter. Lay the other sheets on top to form 2 pairs. Cut each into 6 rectangles giving you 12 pieces in all. Place on a baking sheet and bake for about 5 minutes until crisp.

Fry the onion and garlic in the olive oil until translucent. Add the chopped tomatoes and simmer for 30 minutes. Meanwhile put the vinegar and sugar in a small pan and boil down to about 1 teaspoon. Add to the tomato sauce then pass through a conical strainer pushing as much of the debris through with the back of a ladle as you can. Return the sauce to the heat in the small pan, and simmer until the sauce coats the back of a spoon. Season with salt and white pepper.

Mix the crab meat, the basil, the virgin olive oil and the lemon juice in a pan. Carefully warm through over a low heat. Put 1 piece of filo on each of the 4 plates, a tablespoon or so of crab meat and basil on top and add another layer of filo. On top of that add another tablespoon or so of crab meat and basil and then the final layer of filo. Spoon the sauce around and serve.

CRAB FISH CAKES WITH A TOMATO, CRAB AND BASIL DRESSING

This dish is designed to reinforce the delicate flavour of crab so, as well as there being a lot of crab in the crab cakes, there is also some crab oil. The oil is made by very gently cooking fresh crab debris with a light olive, not virgin, oil over a long period of time.

Use potatoes that are good for mashing, such as Golden Wonder, King Edward, Wilja or Maris Piper.

SERVES 4

1 cooked brown crab, weighing about
    1.25 kg (2½ lb)
300 ml (10 fl oz) olive oil
1 large carrot, chopped
1 leek, chopped
1 medium onion, chopped
900 g (2 lb) potatoes
Flour, for dusting
2 eggs, beaten
100 g (4 oz) breadcrumbs
2 tomatoes, skinned, seeded and chopped
10 fresh basil leaves, 6 thinly sliced and 4 left
    whole
Juice of ¼ lemon
Salt and freshly ground black pepper

Pre-heat the oven to 150°C/300°F/Gas 2.

Extract all the meat from the crab but reserve all the shells. Place the shells with the olive oil in a shallow roasting pan with the carrot, leek and onion. Bake in the oven for 2 hours to gently extract the flavour. Leave to cool then strain the oil and discard the debris.

Cook the potatoes in lightly salted boiling water until soft. Mash with a fork and mix in three-quarters of the white crab meat, half the brown crab meat and one third of the crab oil. Correct the seasoning with salt. Divide the mixture into balls each weighing about 50 g (2 oz). On a floured surface, shape into round flat patties with a palette knife. Pass the cakes first through the flour, then the egg and then the breadcrumbs.

Put the remaining crab oil, the tomatoes, sliced basil, lemon juice and the rest of the crab meat in a pan and warm through but do not boil.

Set the deep-fryer to 160°C/320°F or heat some oil to the same temperature in a large pan. Add the cakes and fry for 3 minutes. Remove and drain on kitchen paper.

Divide the crab cakes between four warmed plates. Pour the dressing around the crab cakes. Garnish with a whole basil leaf placed on top of the dressing. Serve immediately.

FRESH CRAB SALAD WITH TARRAGON MAYONNAISE, CUCUMBER AND ENDIVE

This is based on a similar salad I ate in a restaurant in Dartmouth and is typical of the innovative cooking of the owner, Joyce Molyneux. The crab meat is best picked from a freshly boiled crab (see instructions on p. 176).

SERVES 4

225 g (8 oz) white crab meat
100 g (4 oz) brown crab meat

FOR THE TARRAGON MAYONNAISE

1 teaspoon finely chopped fresh parsley
1 teaspoon finely chopped fresh tarragon
½ teaspoon ground star anise
½ quantity *Olive Oil Mayonnaise* (see p. 43)

FOR THE CUCUMBER SALAD

½ cucumber
1 teaspoon fresh chopped parsley
1 teaspoon Thai fish sauce (*nam pla*)
Juice and zest of 1 lime
50 ml (2 fl oz) water

FOR THE ENDIVE SALAD

50 ml (2 fl oz) groundnut oil
1 tablespoon white wine vinegar
½ teaspoon English mustard
½ small garlic clove, finely chopped
½ shallot, finely chopped
1 teaspoon *Quatre Épices* (see p. 54)
½ teaspoon salt
2 handfuls endive leaves

For the tarragon mayonnaise, add the parsley, tarragon and star anise to the *Olive Oil Mayonnaise*.

To make the cucumber salad, peel the cucumber, cut it into segments lengthways, remove the seeds and slice thinly. Mix the parsley, fish sauce, lime juice and zest, and water together in a small bowl. Pour over and mix with the cucumber.

To make the endive salad, put the oil, vinegar, mustard, garlic, shallot, *quatre épices* and salt in a bowl. Whisk together and use to dress the endive leaves.

To serve, place a pile of crab meat on each plate with a dollop of mayonnaise, and a portion each of the cucumber and endive salads.

SPIDER CRAB WITH PASTA, PARSLEY AND CHILLI

Spider crab meat takes more time to pick out than plain brown crab. It doesn't come out so easily and the claws are smaller so you get less meat for your labour, but the flavour is so good, fragrant and sweet that it's worth the extra trouble. I would suggest using *trenette, linguine*, pasta or spaghetti. *Trenette* and *linguine* are long pastas, like spaghetti but flat rather than round. Buy only 100% durum wheat pasta for this, the best you can afford.

If the crab has red roe in it, use equal quantities of brown and white meat. (The red roe of the spider crab is excellent.)

SERVES 4

350 g (12 oz) trenette, linguine or spaghetti
3 medium tomatoes, skinned, seeded and
   chopped
225 g (8 oz) white crab meat, cooked
50 g (2 oz) brown spider crab meat, cooked
1 tablespoon roughly chopped fresh parsley

Juice of ½ lemon
50 ml (2 fl oz) extra virgin olive oil
1 good pinch of dried, crushed chilli
1 garlic clove, very finely chopped

Boil the pasta in plenty of well salted water, until tender but still firm with some bite to it. The best way to cook pasta until it is *al dente* is to keep biting until it feels right.

Warm the tomato, crab meat, parsley, lemon juice, olive oil, chilli and garlic over a low heat. Let the mixture warm through but don't let it boil or you will alter the flavours. Spoon the pasta onto four warmed plates and spoon over the sauce.

I would drink Soave with this dish, which is now a very much more acceptable Italian white than the rather tasteless, always cheap wine it was in the 70s and 80s. Pleasantly soft and fruity, it would match the sweet garlicky flavours of this dish to perfection.

CRAB, SAFFRON AND LEEK QUICHE

Crab meat and creamed leeks are cooked here in a light savoury custard flavoured with Noilly Prat and saffron. You will need a deep 20 cm (8 in) flan ring or flan case for this dish.

SERVES 4

225 g (8 oz) shortcrust pastry
100 g (4 oz) leeks, outer leaves and top removed
A pinch of saffron strands soaked in 1 tablespoon warm water
15 g (½ oz) unsalted butter
300 ml (10 fl oz) *Fish Stock* (see p. 36)
25 ml (1 fl oz) Noilly Prat or other dry vermouth
A little lemon juice and salt
Salt
A pinch of cayenne pepper
3 eggs
120 ml (4 fl oz) double cream
175 g (6 oz) white crab meat

Pre-heat the oven to 190°C/375°F/Gas 5.

Roll out the pastry and line a 20 cm (8 in) flan ring. Prick the pastry, cover it with greaseproof paper and fill with baking beans. Bake for 10 minutes then remove the beans and paper and leave to cool.

Slice the leeks and boil them in lightly salted water for 10 minutes until really soft. Drain and place in a pan. Add the soaked saffron with the butter and drive off the excess moisture by stirring over a high heat.

Boil the fish stock and Noilly Prat together to reduce it to about 25 ml (1 fl oz). Add the lemon juice, salt and cayenne pepper then beat into the eggs and cream. Line the pastry case with the leeks and sprinkle the crab meat over the top. Pour over the eggs and cream and bake in the oven for 20 minutes. You can serve this either hot or cold.

DEEP-FRIED SOFT-SHELL CRABS WITH CHILLI SAUCE

This recipe came about after I read a Pulitzer prize-winning book called *Beautiful Swimmers* by William Warner about 'the pugnacious, succulent, Atlantic blue crab in its home waters, the salt water marshes and shoals on the Chesapeake Bay'. It is a most unlikely book to win a major prize but has so much information about crab fishing that it is enthralling.

The prize of the Chesapeake blue crab fishing industry is the soft-shell crab. The fishing of it is a real art. It is only for a few days, while changing from one shell to another slightly bigger one, that these crabs have soft shells and only then can the whole crab be eaten.

It occurred to me that the green shore crab, like all crustaceans, goes through a phase of

being soft-shelled and so might also be good when deep-fried. I found a bait fisherman who said that he could get good quantities of these at low tide, because, and this is rather a sad part of the story, at night the soft-shell crabs move about from one hiding place to another under the body of a hard-shell crab for protection. It is easy, with a strong torch, to see them scuttling about and pick off the soft-shell crabs. So I tried them and they were very good.

You could use frozen blue soft-shell crabs instead. You will need about 12–16 for four people.

SERVES 4

20 soft-shell crabs
1 quantity *Tempura Batter* (see p. 53)

FOR THE CHILLI SAUCE

120 ml (4 fl oz) water
1 teaspoon arrowroot
25 ml (1 fl oz) Thai fish sauce (*nam pla*)
½ lemon grass stick, thinly sliced
½ red chilli, seeded and finely chopped
1 teaspoon sugar
Juice and zest of 1 lime
1 spring onion, chopped
1 tablespoon fresh coriander, roughly
   chopped

To make the chilli sauce, bring the water to the boil in a small pan and add the arrowroot then remove from the heat and add the fish sauce, lemon grass, chilli, sugar, lime zest and juice, spring onions and half the coriander. Pour into a small serving bowl.

Set the deep-fryer to 190°C/375°F or heat some oil in a large pan.

Drop the crabs into the tempura batter and turn over to coat them well. Transfer to the fryer and fry for 4 minutes if they're small crabs, 6 minutes if they are larger. Remove from the fryer and drain on kitchen paper.

Arrange the crabs in one large pile on a serving plate. Sprinkle with the coriander. Hand round the chilli sauce separately.

GRILLED LANGOUSTINE WITH CREAMED GARLIC AND CHIVES

I got this recipe from a restaurant in La Baule in Brittany. The restaurant was dreadful, damp and cheaply done out like lots of places by the sea in both Britain and France trying to make a quick buck in the summer. But this dish caught my imagination. It seemed a delightful way of grilling fresh langoustine with lots of cream and garlic. The langoustine can either be raw or cooked.

SERVES 4

FOR THE SAUCE

1 large bulb of garlic
150 ml (5 fl oz) water
150 ml (5 fl oz) cream
1 tablespoon Thai fish sauce (*nam pla*)
Juice of ½ lemon
24 good-sized langoustine
25 ml (1 fl oz) oil infused with 1 garlic clove,
   for grilling
1 tablespoon chopped chives

Remove the cloves of garlic from the bulb but don't peel them. Put them and the water in a small pan and cook very gently on a low heat until soft. Squeeze the flesh out of the skins into a liquidizer, add the cooking water and blend until smooth. Add this, the cream, fish sauce and lemon juice back to the pan, and warm through over a gentle heat.

Turn on your grill.

Pre-heat the grill to hot. Brush the langoustine with the garlic oil and grill until the shells begin to char. This will be long enough to heat the prawns through, if you are using cooked ones. Raw langoustine will need a little longer, about 5 minutes in total.

When ready to serve, add the chives to the warm garlic sauce, arrange the langoustine on four plates, pour over the sauce and serve. *Serve with an ice-cold bottle of Greek Retsina.*

LOBSTER WITH MAYONNAISE

In the end I regard this and the recipe for grilled lobster below as the best ways of eating lobster. This is the first way I ever tried it and it just has the edge over the grilled lobster in my estimation. My wife, Jill, prefers them grilled. When eating whole lobster, remember that the body section contains plenty of meat, particularly in the joints where the claws and legs join the body. You remove the meat with a lobster pick in exactly the same way as picking out crab meat.

Serve the lobsters with the mayonnaise, a salad of mixed leaves dressed with a little *Lemon Olive Oil* (see p. 51), salt and some minted new potatoes

SERVES 4

    5.5 litres (10 pints) water
    200 g (7 oz) salt
    2 live lobsters, each weighing about 700–
        800 g (1½–1¾ lb)
    1 quantity *Olive Oil Mayonnaise* (see p. 43)

Pour the water into a large pan and bring to the boil. Add the salt. When the water is boiling fiercely, put in one lobster. Wait until the water comes back to the boil, then add the second one. Boil for 15 minutes. If you don't have a pan big enough, boil the lobsters one at a time as they must be fully immersed to cook properly.

Remove the lobsters from the water and leave to cool. To cut the lobster in half, place on a chopping board and drive a large knife through the middle of the carapace (the body section) and cut down towards and between the eyes, then, turn the knife around, place it in the original cut and bring the knife down right through the tail to split it in half. Pull off the claws and cut off the rubber bands binding them together. Crack open each of the three claw sections with a short sharp chop from the thickest part of your knife blade. Remove the stomach sac behind the mouth and the intestine which runs down the tail.

For a wine accompaniment it's got to be a bottle of good Australian or Californian Chardonnay or, if you can afford it, a Burgundy from the Côte d'Or such as Montrachet or Meursault. Two other wines from this area, St Aubin and Auxey-Duresses, are nearly as good and far less expensive.

GRILLED LOBSTER WITH FINES HERBES

This is the way we have cooked lobster at my restaurant ever since we opened: very simple and perfect. The herbs should be fresh and only cut up at the last minute. Par-boil the lobsters as described below or simply split them in half while still alive and grill them. This is not as barbaric as you might think, since as long as you cleave them in two efficiently, they are quickly killed. For more general notes on killing lobsters see p. 25.

SERVES 4

    5.5 litres (10 pints) water
    2 live lobsters, each weighing about 700
        800 g (1½–1¾ lb)
    A little melted butter, for brushing
    175 ml (6 fl oz) *Fish Stock* (see p. 36)
    ½ teaspoon Thai fish sauce (*nam pla*)
    Juice of ¼ lemon
    50 g (2 oz) unsalted butter
    1 teaspoon chopped fresh parsley
    1 teaspoon chopped fresh chervil
    1 teaspoon chopped fresh tarragon
    1 teaspoon chopped fresh chives

Bring the water to the boil in a large pan. When it is boiling fiercely, put in one lobster, wait until the water comes back to the boil, then add the second one. Boil for 5 minutes.

Pre-heat the grill to high. Remove the lobsters from the water. To cut in half, refer to the instructions in *Lobster with Mayonnaise* on p. 183.

Place the lobster, flesh side up, on a grill tray, brush with melted butter and grill for about 10 minutes.

In a small pan, bring the fish stock, fish sauce and lemon juice to the boil and whisk in the butter. Add the herbs and pour over the lobster.

SAUTÉD LOBSTER WITH SAFFRON AND CHAMBÉRY

This dish is far easier to make than you might think. The flavour of the saffron, a little butter and a sweetish, spicy vermouth like Chambéry are very well suited to the lobster.

SERVES 2

  5.5 litres (10 pints) water
  1 live lobster, weighing about 750 g (1¾ lb)

FOR THE SAUCE

  65 g (2½ oz) unsalted butter
  50 ml (2 fl oz) Chambéry
  300 ml (10 fl oz) *Fish Stock* (see p. 36)
  ½ teaspoon saffron strands
  A few drops of lemon juice

Bring the water to the boil in a large pan. Add the lobster, cover and cook for 5 minutes. Remove from the pan and leave until cool enough to handle. Place the lobster on a chopping board and refer to the instructions for cutting up lobsters in *Lobster with Mayonnaise* on p. 183.

Put 50 g (2 oz) of the butter in a large shallow pan and melt quickly over a fierce heat. Place all the lobster pieces in the pan and cook until they start to turn red. Pour in the Chambéry and three-quarters of the stock and add the saffron. Cover and leave to simmer gently for 10 minutes.

Remove from the heat and take out the lobster pieces. Leave until cool enough to handle then crack the claws and carefully extract the meat with a lobster pick. Remove the meat from the tail sections. Keep warm and slice into pieces 2.5 cm (1 in) thick.

Add the remaining stock to the pan. Reduce the sauce a little then whisk in the rest of the butter and finish with lemon juice to taste.

Arrange the lobster pieces on two warmed plates. Through a strainer, pour over the sauce and serve.

SPECIAL SALAD OF LOBSTER, AVOCADO, GREEN BEANS AND DUCK LIVERS

Salads like this appear on the menu of virtually every three-star restaurant in France, but there the duck livers would be *foie gras*. By cooking a simple duck liver terrine you can produce something surprisingly similar.

SERVES 4

- 75 g (3 oz) fine green beans, topped and tailed
- 1 ripe avocado
- 750 g (1½ lb) lobster, cooked
- 50 ml (2 fl oz) extra virgin olive oil
- 1 tablespoon balsamic vinegar
- ½ teaspoon salt
- A small bunch of fresh chervil, leaves only

FOR THE DUCK LIVER TERRINE

- 100 g (4 oz) duck liver
- ¼ teaspoon salt
- A pinch of white pepper
- ½ small garlic clove
- 1 tablespoon port
- 2 teaspoons brandy
- 50 g (2 oz) unsalted butter

Make the terrine the day before you want to eat the salad and keep it chilled. You will need some sort of mould. I would suggest using a mug if you have nothing better. Line the mould with well-buttered paper or greaseproof paper.

Pre-heat the oven to 150°C/300°F/Gas 2. Place all the terrine ingredients, except the butter, in a liquidizer and blend for 1 minute. Melt the butter in a pan then pour into the liquidizer and blend in thoroughly. Pour the mixture into the lined terrine, cover with buttered paper and some sort of lid. Stand the mould on a cloth in the bottom of a roasting tin and pour in enough warm water to come about half-way up the terrine mould. Bring the water to the boil on the top of the cooker, then transfer to the oven and cook for about 25 minutes. Remove and chill.

Slice each bean in half lengthways. Blanch in boiling salted water for 30 seconds only, strain and refresh in very cold water. Drain well.

Cut the lobster in half and remove the meat from the tail. Crack open the claws and remove the meat. Slice the lobster tail into 1 cm (½ in) slices. If you have a hen lobster with the bright red coral, add the coral to the lobster meat, cut into thin slices.

Cut the avocado in half, remove the stone then cut in half again, lengthways. Peel and thinly slice.

Make little lozenge shapes out of the terrine using two teaspoons.

Put the beans, avocado, olive oil, balsamic vinegar and salt in a bowl and toss gently. Divide between four plates, add the lobster but do not put it all on top. Finally, place the lozenges of duck liver in the salad, again not all on top. The salad should be a contrast in flavour between the oily salad ingredients and the lobster and duck liver terrine. Garnish with a few leaves of chervil.

Serve with an Alsace Muscat or Pinot Gris. Both wines are slightly spicy with round, full flavours. I would also suggest a New Zealand Sauvignon Blanc.

(BELOW) Grilled Lobster with Fines Herbes (*see page 183*), (RIGHT) Fresh Crab Salad with Tarragon Mayonnaise, Cucumber and Endive (*see page 179*) and (BELOW RIGHT) Sautéd Lobster with Saffron and Chambéry (*see page 184*)

LOBSTER À L'AMÉRICAINE

There has always been some doubt as to where this excellent lobster dish came from. Some say it should be Lobster Armoricaine, the old name for Brittany, others say it couldn't possibly have come from Brittany because most of the ingredients would suggest the Mediterranean and not Brittany. One thing is for certain, the dish came from France not America. I am a little wary of lobster served in sauces because I believe that fresh lobster needs very little accompaniment except some butter or mayonnaise and a few herbs, it having such a wonderful taste in its own right. However, I make an exception of this dish because the sauce, when made properly, is so fresh tasting.

It is traditionally made with live lobsters, but if you do not like the idea of cutting up lobsters alive, bring a large pan of boiling water to the boil and plunge the lobsters into it. Bring back to the boil and boil for 5 minutes to kill them.

Make sure the tomatoes you use in this recipe are good, sun-ripened, sweet ones.

SERVES 4

2 live lobsters, each weighing about 750–900 g (1½–2 lb)
85 ml (3 fl oz) olive oil
50 g (2 oz) onion, finely chopped
1 tablespoon cognac
2 garlic cloves, finely chopped
750 g (1½ lb) fresh tomatoes, skinned, seeded and chopped
1 tablespoon roughly chopped tarragon
85 ml (3 fl oz) dry white wine
1 teaspoon sugar
600 ml (1 pint) *Fish Stock* (see p. 36)

Cut the live lobsters in half lengthways; refer to the instructions on p. 183 in *Lobster with Mayonnaise*. Pull each tail section away from the head section and cut each section of tail into 4–5 pieces. Break the claw sections apart and crack each section so that the meat can be extracted easily later. The easiest way to do this is with the thickest part of a large knife.

Put the olive oil into a heavy-based pan, big enough to hold all the pieces of lobster. Sweat the onion and garlic in the olive oil until they are beginning to soften then add all the pieces of lobster. Turn up the heat a little and turn the lobster pieces over until they are beginning to colour red. Add the cognac and let the alcohol boil off. Add the tomatoes, chopped tarragon, white wine, sugar and fish stock. Cover. Leave the lobsters to cook through for about 8 minutes.

Remove the lobster pieces and keep warm. Return the pan to the heat and reduce the sauce by half.

When the sauce has reduced return the lobster pieces to the sauce, heat through, transfer to an attractive serving dish and serve with grilled potatoes as in the recipe for *Dover Sole à la Meunière* on page 152.

LOBSTER RAVIOLI WITH BASIL AND SPINACH

This is a dish where the use of North American lobsters is perfectly acceptable. Most of the cooked lobster that you see in supermarkets and fishmongers in this country is from North America. This dish is designed to make a small amount of lobster go a long way but it is still very much a luxury first course.

SERVES 4

FOR THE RAVIOLI

I quantity *Egg Pasta Dough* (see p. 54)
550 g (1¼ lb) cooked lobster
350 g (12 oz) skinned fillets of cheap flat
   fish such as plaice, flounder or dabs
I egg
Juice of ¼ lemon
1½ teaspoons salt
600 ml (1 pint) double cream
5 basil leaves, thinly sliced

FOR THE SAUCE

600 ml (1 pint) *Fish Stock* (see p. 36)
85 ml (3 fl oz) double cream
50 g (2 oz) unsalted butter
85 ml (3 fl oz) dry white wine
5 basil leaves, thinly sliced
12 spinach leaves, preferably small ones

If you have a pasta machine, roll the dough to setting number 6. If you don't, roll out to no more than 3 mm (⅛ inch) thick. The ravioli are single large ones. Using a 10 cm (4 in) round pastry cutter or a plate or bowl, cut out 8 discs. Allow the pasta to rest for 10–15 minutes.

Remove the meat from the lobster. Slice the lobster meat into 5 mm (¼ in) slices.

If there is any coral in the lobster or berries under the lobster's tail, cut the coral up and remove the berries and add with all the brown meat from the lobster's head.

Put the fish fillet, the egg, the lemon juice and salt and 150 ml (5 fl oz) of the double cream in a food processor. Blend until smooth then pour in the rest of cream in a steady stream taking only about 10 seconds; any longer and the mixture will curdle. Transfer to a bowl and fold in the lobster meat and the basil. Remember to remove the stomach sac.

Put a pile of filling in the centre of each of four of the pasta discs, leaving a 1 cm (½ in) border. You should be able to get most of the mixture into the ravioli. Moisten the outer edge of each disc with water, including the discs you will put on top. Put the four remaining discs on top, slide a palette knife under the ravioli and place on the palm of your hand. Gently crimp the edges together with your fingers, pulling the ravioli round as you do.

Drop each ravioli into a large pan of boiling salted water for about 40 seconds. Remove and drop into a bowl of cold water for 5 seconds before placing on a tray. You can make these ravioli a day in advance. Cover with cling film and store in the fridge.

To serve, rapidly boil the fish stock, cream, butter and white wine together until the sauce has reduced to the point where it will coat the back of a spoon. Stir in five sliced basil leaves and keep warm.

Bring a pan of salted water to the boil, drop in the spinach leaves and blanch briefly for about 20 seconds. Remove and keep warm. Put the ravioli in the same water, reduce the heat and poach for 4–5 minutes. Take four warm plates and lay the spinach leaves out in the centre of them. Put the raviolis on top and cover with the sauce. Serve immediately. *Serve with a good-quality Australian or New Zealand Chardonnay.*

(LEFT) Prawn Cocktail with Malt Whisky (*see page 192*), (BELOW LEFT) Lobster Ravioli with Basil and Spinach (*see page 189*) and (BELOW) Special Salad of Lobster, Avocado, Green Beans and Duck Livers (*see page 185*)

STIR-FRIED PRAWNS

This is a Szechuan recipe often characterized by plenty of chilli. The chilli bean sauce in the recipe can be easily bought at Chinese super-markets but, if you can't get hold of it, mix together yellow bean sauce and chilli sauce. If you want to make the dish even hotter put in a few finely chopped red chillies as well.

SERVES 4

1 teaspoon Szechuan peppercorns
½ teaspoon black peppercorns
1 tablespoon groundnut oil
3 spring onions, white and green separated, finely sliced
2.5 cm (1 in) fresh ginger, finely chopped
4 garlic cloves, finely chopped

450 g (1 lb) raw prawns, peeled
1 teaspoon dry sherry
1 tablespoon soy sauce
2 tablespoons chilli bean sauce
225 g (8 oz) tomatoes, skinned and sliced
½ teaspoon sugar

Grind together the Szechuan and black peppercorns. Put the groundnut oil in a wok and stir-fry the white part of the spring onions, the ginger and the garlic for 1 minute. Add the prawns and stir-fry for another 1 minute, then add the sherry, soy sauce, chilli bean sauce, tomatoes and sugar. Cover and cook for 3 minutes. Sprinkle with the green part of the onions and serve.

PRAWN COCKTAIL WITH MALT WHISKY

There is no substitute for tomato ketchup for a prawn cocktail, no fresh tomato sauce ever tastes so good. However, the other ingredients can make all the difference. The difference here is malt whisky which gives the prawn cocktail a subtle aftertaste of open log fires: just the thing for Christmas.

In this recipe I have included a small amount of natural yoghurt which gives the sauce a subtle extra tartness. If, as I do, you love prawn cocktails, make them big, particularly for a special occasion. Go to a glassware shop and buy some really voluminous glasses. The glasses we use are large and no attempt is made to fill them although the portions in this recipe are generous.

SERVES 4

225 g (8 oz) large peeled frozen North Atlantic prawns

FOR THE MARIE ROSE SAUCE

2 egg yolks
2 teaspoons white wine vinegar
A pinch of ground white pepper
¼ teaspoon salt
250 ml (8 fl oz) vegetable oil
5 tablespoons tomato ketchup
2 tablespoons single malt whisky
4 tablespoons natural, unsweetened yoghurt

FOR THE SALAD

90 g (3½ oz) mixed salad leaves, including, if possible, some radicchio
4 basil leaves, thinly sliced

Defrost the prawns overnight in the refrigerator and chill four large glasses.

Take a small bowl and whisk together the egg yolks, vinegar, pepper and salt. Continuing to whisk, gradually drizzle in the oil to make a mayonnaise. Add the tomato ketchup, malt whisky and yoghurt.

Tear the salad leaves into pieces no more than 5 cm (2 in) across and divide between the chilled glasses. Place the prawns gently on top so that they cover the salad but leave a gap around the circumference of the glass.

Pour the sauce over the prawns without totally covering all of either them or the salad. The dish looks much more appetizing if you can see a few pink pieces of uncovered prawn and some uncoated leaves. Finally put a little pile of the sliced basil leaves in the centre of each glass.

SALAD OF PRAWNS, ROCKET AND PARMA HAM

The supreme strength of Italian cuisine is that the unique flavours of the ingredients are presented in such a way that they enhance but do not smother each other. All the flavours in this salad are interesting on their own, but drawn together with some good olive oil they produce an effect greater than the sum of their parts.

SERVES 4

100 g (4 oz) large peeled prawns, defrosted if frozen
6 very thin slices of Parma ham
50 g (2 oz) rocket leaves
4 tablespoons extra virgin olive oil
Freshly ground black pepper

Tear the Parma ham into pieces about 5 cm (2 in) across. Divide the rocket leaves between four cold plates and arrange the Parma ham among the leaves. Scatter over the prawns then drizzle 1 tablespoon of olive oil over each salad. Finally, grind over some black pepper and serve.

Serve with a bottle of chilled white Pinot Grigio.

PRAWN TERRINE WITH COURGETTE SALAD

This terrine, which sells well in our deli-catessen in Padstow, uses the North Atlantic prawns in the shell which have a far better flavour than the same type of prawn sold out of the shell. Use any white fish such as cod, whiting, lemon sole or plaice. It makes a light first course. You will need a terrine mould about 15 × 7 × 7 cm (6 × 3 × 3 in) in size.

SERVES 6–8

350 g (12 oz) prawns in the shell
15 g (½ oz) unsalted butter
1 small carrot, chopped
1 small onion, chopped
½ tablespoon brandy
½ teaspoon tomato purée
150 ml (5 fl oz) *Fish Stock* (see p. 36) or
    Chicken Stock (see p. 37)
225 g (8 oz) white fish fillet, skinned
1 small egg
Juice of ½ lemon
1 teaspoon salt
300 ml (10 fl oz) double cream, chilled
4 courgettes
1 quantity *Olive Oil Dressing* (see page 51)

Pre-heat the oven to 150°C/300°F/Gas 2. Peel the prawns and reserve the shells. Melt the butter in a pan, add the carrot, onion and prawn shells and cook gently for 5 minutes. Pour in the brandy and add the tomato purée. Cook for a few minutes longer then add the stock and simmer for 20 minutes. Pour into a liquidizer or food processor and blend for about 30 seconds.

Pass through a fine sieve into another pan, pushing against the debris with the back of a ladle to extract as much flavour as possible. Bring the sieved liquid back to the boil and simmer until there is only about 1 tablespoon of strong shellfish reduction.

Cool the concentrated stock then place in a food processor with the fish fillet. Add the egg, lemon juice, salt and one third of the cream. Blend together until smooth then pour in the remaining cream taking no more than 10 seconds or the mousse will curdle.

Brush the terrine mould with melted butter then fill with the fish mousseline adding the peeled prawns as you fill the mould. Place some butter papers over the top and cover. Stand the terrine on a cloth in the bottom of a roasting tin and pour in enough warm water to come about half-way up the sides. Bring to the boil on the top of the cooker, then transfer to the oven and cook for about 40 minutes.

Leave to cool then refrigerate for at least 3 hours before attempting to remove the terrine from the mould. Slip a thin-bladed knife around the sides of the terrine and turn out onto a flat dish. Slice carefully with a serrated knife, holding each slice of terrine in place until it is cut right through.

Slice the courgettes into thin strips. Dress with *Olive Oil Dressing* and serve each slice of terrine with a little pile of courgettes.
A perfect wine for this rich and sweetly flavoured dish would be a New Zealand Sauvignon Blanc.

PRAWN JAMBALAYA

Jambalaya comes from New Orleans and is based on paella but not being able to get saffron and olive oil the Spanish settlers used what was available locally and in using the combination of green peppers, celery and onions they produced what is now known as the 'holy trinity', the flavour that most typifies Creole cookery.

Raw prawn tails are now available in most supermarkets. For extra flavour in the Jambalaya, fry the shells in about 50 ml (2 fl oz) of vegetable oil then pass the oil through a sieve into the dish just before adding the rice.

SERVES 6

50 ml (2 fl oz) vegetable oil
100 g (4 oz) *cabanos*, smoked Spanish
   sausage, sliced
2 teaspoons paprika
8 garlic cloves, chopped
1 medium onion, chopped
2 green peppers, seeded and chopped
4 celery sticks, sliced
2 red chillies, seeded and finely chopped
450 g (1 lb) boneless, skinless chicken, cut
   into 2.5 cm (1 in) pieces
450 g (1 lb) raw prawn tails
2 fresh bay leaves, thinly sliced, or 2 dried
   bay leaves, crushed
1 sprig of thyme, chopped
1 teaspoon fresh oregano or ½ teaspoon
   dried
450 g (1 lb) long-grain rice
1.2 litres (2 pints) *Chicken Stock* (see p. 37)
1 teaspoon salt
3 spring onions, sliced
Chilli powder to taste

Heat the oil in a large frying pan or any other large shallow skillet-type dish and gently fry the *cabanos*. Add the paprika and stir to colour the oil. Toss in the garlic and sweat a little then add the onion, green peppers, celery and the red chillies. Cook over a medium heat until the moisture has been driven off and the vegetables are beginning to colour. Add the chicken, prawns, the bay leaves, thyme and the oregano and cook over a medium heat for about 5 minutes.

Add the rice and stir for 2 minutes, then pour in the chicken stock and add the salt. Bring to the boil and simmer gently for about 15 minutes or until all the liquid has been absorbed by the rice. Stir in the chopped spring onions and check the heat. If you like things hot add some chilli powder.

Serve with a green salad.
Serve with some ice-cold beer.

CHAR-GRILLED TIGER PRAWNS WITH LEMON GRASS, CHILLI AND CORIANDER

Tiger prawns are now being farmed in large quantities in Thailand. They are easy to buy here and you should be able to get all the ingredients to make this first course, including some bamboo skewers for a really authentic touch at any oriental food shop. The lemon grass should be fresh rather than dried.

Fish sauce is one of the greatest introductions to Western cookery since soy sauce; its clean, salt and savoury taste is ideal as a base for salad dressings instead of oil.

I use a large, relatively mild Dutch green chilli; be wary of the small ones.

SERVES 4

20 raw tiger prawns, headless, or king
   prawns, each weighing about 25 g (1 oz)
25 ml (1 fl oz) groundnut oil
1 teaspoon salt
Freshly ground black pepper

FOR THE DRESSING

25 ml (1 fl oz) Thai fish sauce (*nam pla*)
150 ml (5 fl oz) water
1 green chilli
1 lemon grass stick
Juice of 1 lemon
½ teaspoon sugar

FOR THE SALAD

A small bunch of fresh coriander
½ iceberg lettuce

Light the charcoal grill at least 30 minutes before you want to start cooking. (The secret of successful barbecuing lies in getting the grill bars so hot that anything you put on it sears and carbonizes quickly and so doesn't stick.)

Remove the shells from the prawns except the last small piece on the end of the tail. Cut them in half lengthways leaving them joined at the tail. Using a pastry brush, paint the prawns liberally with seasoned oil. Thread five prawns onto each skewer and set aside while you make the dressing and salad.

Measure the fish sauce and water into a bowl. Remove the seeds from the chilli and chop finely. Add it to the dressing. Remove the coarse outer leaves from the lemon grass and finely slice the more tender centre; don't be too purist about this as all lemon grass is fairly stringy. Add it to the bowl with the lemon juice and sugar.

Pick off about 20 of the best coriander leaves to use in the salad and reserve. Chop the rest finely. Set aside.

Slice the iceberg lettuce finely and arrange on four plates. Sprinkle with the reserved coriander leaves.

Grill the prawns for exactly 5 minutes, turning them half-way through the cooking time. Meanwhile, warm the dressing through over a gentle heat and add the chopped coriander just before taking it off the heat.

Place the prawns, still on the skewers, on top of the lettuce. Spoon the dressing liberally over the prawns and salad and serve.

Gewürztraminer goes exceptionally well with Thai food. The wine is sufficiently spicy and powerful to stand up to the strong tastes of chilli, coriander and lemon grass.

FRUITS DE MER

Fruits de Mer or *Plateau de Fruits de Mer* as it is called in France is the spectacular creation of French seaside restaurants: lobsters, crabs, langoustines, prawns, mussels, oysters, clams, winkles, whelks, sea urchins and any other shellfish that are available are presented on a large platter normally on a base of seaweed and crushed ice, sometimes with some big chunks of cork beneath them to give extra height. The dish is served with accompaniments of lemon wedges, mayonnaise and shallot vinegar (see p. 52).

This dish is the centrepiece of all the dishes presented at my restaurant. Nothing induces good, lively conversation better than the *fruits de mer*.

There is something relaxing and animating about eating with your fingers, but the world is split evenly between those who enjoy it and those who regard the whole thing as a bore. It is this division, between those who enjoy the sensual side of eating and those who regard eating as something that must be got out of the way, which leads to some people being wonderfully enthusiastic and joyful customers and others frankly being a pain. I have a great affection for Jean-Anthelme Brillat-Savarin whose book, *The Philosopher in the Kitchen*, published in 1825, is as meaningful today as it was then and should be read by anybody interested in eating. He quite literally saw physical differences between those who do and those who don't enjoy eating and summed it up as follows.

'Individuals predestined to gourmandism are generally of medium height, they have round or square faces and bright eyes and small foreheads and short noses, full lips and well rounded chins. The women are buxom, pretty rather than beautiful with a tendency to run to fat. Such is the exterior beneath which to look for the most agreeable company for these are the guests who accept everything they are offered, eat slowly and savour each morsel thoughtfully. They are never in a hurry to leave the place where they have found true hospitality and they are invited to stay all evening because they know the games and pass times appropriate to gastronomical gatherings. Those on the contrary to whom nature has refused an aptitude for the pleasures of taste have long faces, noses and eyes, whatever their height there is something elongated in their proportions, their hair is dark and flat and they are never plump, it was they who invented trousers. The women whom nature has afflicted with the same misfortune are angular in body, are easily bored at table and only live for cards and scandal.'

But back to the *fruits de mer* … It is a totally wonderful dish. The great thing about it is that it gives importance to all those little, unloved shellfish and crustacea like winkles, whelks, shrimps and hermit crabs and even sea urchins. The sort of thing that you would never buy any amount of on their own, together make up a meal which most are quite happy to pick at over a long leisurely lunch with a bottle or two of Muscadet and some convivial company.

You might think that trying to assemble the ingredients for a *fruits de mer* is a little outside your scope but you can make it out of as few or as many species as you like. It is one of those dishes, when on holiday by the seaside, that you can build up from a day's wandering around rocky beaches, picking mussels and winkles, fishing for shrimps in rock pools, turning over stones for shore crabs and digging in the sand for cockles and clams. By adding all these bits and pieces to, maybe, two lobsters, a brown crab and a spider crab you can make up a more than acceptable *fruits de mer*.

Fruits de Mer (*see page 197*)

In France shellfish are usually opened and served raw, like oysters. There is quite a lot of skill involved in opening live shellfish like clams, cockles and mussels so you may find it easier to steam them briefly open, maybe with a little bit of white wine. The trick is just to remove them from the heat as soon as they pop open so that the meats are hardly cooked at all and will taste, to all intents and purposes, raw.

Sitting out here in the garden at Trevone Bay on this stunning April morning just before Easter, with the sound of the surf in the distance, I think I'll go and raid the restaurant's kitchen, get some friends over, plus half a dozen bottles of ice-cold Muscadet, and lose an afternoon to pure pleasure.

SERVES 6

3 lobsters, each weighing about 450 g (1 lb)
3 crabs, each weighing about 750 g (1½ lb)
36 mussels
36 unshelled prawns, Dublin Bay prawns if
   possible
450 g (1 lb) shrimps
18 oysters
36 winkles

Plus any of the following:
Shore crabs
All types of clam
Cockles
Scallops
Sea urchins
Whelks

TO SERVE

600 ml (1 pint) *Mustard Mayonnaise*
   (see p. 43)
150 ml (5 fl oz) *Shallot Vinegar* (see. p. 52)
2 lemons, cut into wedges

½ bucket of seaweed
Ice
3 lemons
2 or 3 lobster picks
A claw cracker

COOKING AND ASSEMBLING THE FRUITS DE MER

Blanch the seaweed in boiling water (unless it's from a clean beach) then rinse in cold water and chill.

LOBSTERS AND CRABS

Cook the lobsters and crabs in plenty of boiling water salted at the rate of 150 g (5 oz) to 4.5 litres (8 pints). This is the salinity of sea water. The crabs should be pierced with a skewer once between the eyes and once under the tail flap, through the body and up to the eyes to kill them before boiling (see p. 25). Both crabs and lobsters should be dropped into boiling water, brought back to the boil and simmered for 20 minutes then drained and left to go cool. They taste better if they are not refrigerated, so cook them the same day you intend to eat them.

MUSSELS, CLAMS AND COCKLES

Wash and scrub the mussels, clams and cockles. Place separately in a large pan and add a splash of water or white wine. Cook on a fierce heat with the lid on and let the shellfish open in the steam produced by the splash of water. As soon as they open, remove from the heat and drain through a colander into a bowl. Keep the cooking liquor for another dish. Remove the beards from the mussels.

PRAWNS, DUBLIN BAY PRAWNS AND SHRIMPS

You normally buy these cooked, but if they are raw, place them in a pan of boiling salted water, bring back to the boil and simmer for 1 minute for shrimps and 2 minutes for either type of prawn.

OYSTERS

Open by inserting the blade of an oyster knife or short, thick-bladed knife between the hinge of the two shells. Protect the hand which holds the oyster by wrapping it in a tea towel.

WINKLES, WHELKS AND SHORE CRABS

Place in a pan of boiling salted water. As soon as the water comes back to the boil, drain immediately for winkles, simmer for 4 minutes for whelks and 5 minutes for shore crabs. Drain.

SCALLOPS

Clean the scallops as described on p. 29 but leave the scallop in the deep bottom shell. Discard the top shell. Steam the scallop in a perforated tray over boiling water until it has turned from opaque to white.

SEA URCHINS

Cut in half and drain off the water.

TO ASSEMBLE THE FRUITS DE MER

Use a large tray such as a circular tin tea tray or a wooden tray to display the seafood. Take the cubes from about four ice trays, place them in a polythene bag and crush with a rolling pin.

Place the ice and chilled seaweed on the tray and arrange the shellfish, crustaceans and lemons as naturally as you can. Carry the tray out to your guests and be prepared to receive the sort of rapturous reception that such a display must inevitably cause.

There are a few wines that are ideal to serve with this dish. Muscadet is best but any light, acidic French wine would go well with a Fruits de Mer; Sancerre, Pouilly Fumé, Sauvignon de Touraine, or maybe if you like something a little sweeter a Pinot Grigio from Italy.

SHELLFISH: COCKLES, CLAMS, WINKLES, MUSSELS, OYSTERS, SCALLOPS AND SQUID

Mussels, clams, cockles and whelks are some of the best-loved and cheapest seafood to be found, and even scallops are not madly expensive. Oysters are a bit of a luxury and the recipes that use them reflect that. This chapter also contains recipes for squid, cuttlefish and octopus which, unexpectedly, are classed as molluscs. The last two recipes are a bit of fun.

COCKLES

To me cockles are one of the best-tasting bivalves (two-shelled molluscs) and yet they are so cheap. I imagine this is because they're, thankfully, so abundant. I'm a great fan of eating raw cockles. When I dig for cockles, I can open them by forcing the base of one cockle against another, then twisting them until one opens to give me the sweetest and most delicious-tasting morsel to eat. I always include cockles in all the mixed shellfish dishes, like the *Mussel, Cockle and Clam Masala* on p. 210, the *Fruits de Mer* on p. 197 and the *Hot Shellfish with Garlic and Lemon Juice* on p. 205.

CLAMS

Until recently it was virtually impossible to get any clams in Britain except the large, hard-shelled clam, which is only really useful for chowders. All the delightful little clams that you get in France, the *palourdes*, the *praires* and *vernis*, were unavailable. Now things are beginning to improve. The recipes for *Mussels in the Shell with Linguine Garlic and Parsley* and *Grilled Mussels with Pesto* can be made with clams.

WINKLES

I don't think I've ever seen winkles on sale in a fishmonger's shop in Britain. But they're very easy to pick on the sea shore; turn over the seaweed on any rocky beach and you'll find winkles underneath. They come in various colours: yellow or a browny green but normally black or grey. They're all the same species and all edible. Wash them in cold water, bring them to the boil in well-salted water then boil for just 2 minutes. Drain them and eat with some *Shallot Vinegar* (see page 52). Get yourself a pin or a winkle picker, hoik them out, dunk them in the shallot vinegar. I think it tremendously civilized that even in the cheapest restaurants in Brittany, they offer you a little *amuse-geule* (appetizer) of a pile of winkles with maybe a little bowl of mayonnaise or shallot vinegar. You could even try making up some hot garlic butter to go with them. Winkles are, after all, just sea snails.

MUSSELS

Thank goodness that mussels are becoming so easy to buy now. One of the main problems with writing a cookery book is that there are always some ingredients that are difficult to get hold of: take lovage or Japanese breadcrumbs, called *panko*, for example. I included the recipes with these difficult ingredients because they are easily replaced but the worry about whether people could get hold of mussels used to be a little depressing.

Most mussels available in fishmongers and large supermarkets with fish counters are rope-grown. That means the spats (that is the mussel seeds) are encouraged to attach their threads (called a byssus) to ropes suspended in the sea. You can tell whether the mussels you buy are rope-grown or not by the occasional strands of rope still attached to the mussel. A great advantage of rope-grown mussels is that they tend to be relatively clean and free of barnacles and weed. Those that are harvested from the rocks tend to be harder to clean. As to flavour, the rope-grown ones tend to be sweet and plump, the rock ones more seaweedy and ozoney in flavour. But for the best flavour there is nothing to beat the small mussels that you can gather at very low tides on the beaches in the West and probably elsewhere in the country. The problem with these mussels is that they're a bit too small for mussel dishes but we use them very effectively as accompanying shellfish in fish dishes.

Mussels can be picked anywhere around the British coastline but, because of the way we dump our sewage into the sea and seem to forget about it, there is always a risk of food poisoning from polluted water. For example, around Padstow we find that shellfish in the bays facing the open sea are pretty safe, but those in the estuary are not. Any pollution that goes into the open sea tends to be well diluted, whereas pollution in a partially enclosed estuary is far more concentrated. I am a bit of an optimist and I do feel that we are all now aware of the unacceptability of dumping sewage in the sea and that eventually, over the next ten or twenty years, we will see a revolution in the improvement of pollution levels in the sea around us.

But let's put things into perspective. Most of the time it is safe to pick, cook and eat shellfish from the beach – and there is nothing like it as far as I'm concerned. Leading what one might call a bit of a stressful life, I find there is nothing quite as relaxing as going down to the mouth of the estuary on a low spring tide looking for butterfish (a small type of clam), tellins (another type of clam), mussels, cockles and even the occasional razor-shell clam if the tide is exceptionally low.

OYSTERS

There are two types of oyster on sale in Britain, the Native oyster (*ostrea edulis*) and the Pacific oyster (*ostrea gigas*). The Native or European oyster usually costs about twice as much as the Pacific. The Pacific oyster is only called Pacific because that's where it originates from. It grows perfectly happily in British waters, though it doesn't reproduce here because the water is slightly too cold. Baby oysters are grown in oyster hatcheries and then sown into the water when they're about the size of your thumbnail. The Native oyster fetches a high price because it takes longer to grow. The Pacific oyster grows much faster and is therefore the variety favoured by commercial growers.

The Native oysters from the West of England are called Helford oysters. They are still dredged from natural beds and are not farmed. The supply is restricted by a very sensible conservation method whereby oyster fishermen are only allowed to use sail-powered dredgers to fish for oysters, which slows them down considerably.

Since the Native oyster costs twice as much

as the Pacific, it might be pertinent to make some observations as to the taste: does it taste twice as good as the Pacific? The answer is that it doesn't, any more than you can quantify the taste of a bottle of good white Burgundy as being twice as good as a bottle of Australian Chardonnay. However, after 20 years of running the restaurant, last autumn I managed to set up a comparative tasting which I consider to be exhaustive.

During the filming of the television series this book accompanies, we went down to the River Helford and the Duchy Oyster Farm where I buy Native oysters. About six dozen Native oysters were opened for us and three dozen Pacifics. We also had some wines to aid our tasting. We were aiming to establish what it was about the Native that set it above the Pacific. The Natives won hands down. While the Pacifics were fresh and sweet, the Natives had a sort of slightly bitter, slightly metallic finish to them which, in the end, proved subtle and exciting. Like a good wine, the complexities of the taste ended up being far more satisfying than the simple, straightforward flavours of the Pacific. As far as the wine was concerned, we found that Chablis was the best accompaniment.

SCALLOPS

The other day I was trying to decide what it is that makes me want to keep on cooking. After all it isn't the easiest way to make a living. But last night we'd just cooked for 90 (after about 60 I have this joke with the chefs where I say something to the effect that that was great fun now we'll go home, when we all know we've got another 30 to cook for), when a fisherman brought in a few scallops in a box with some red gurnards, weever fish, a few crab claws and a couple of small octopus. When I see a box like that of gleaming fish and the scallops tightly closed, damp with bits of seaweed and sand clinging to them, it doesn't matter how tired I am, I know it's all worth it. I see raw materials

like those and I just want to do justice to them. I'd hate to have to work with frozen, soaked scallops. I have an almost possessive attachment to those beautiful fresh shells. Scallops are one of our most delicious shellfish – sweet and firm and relatively cheap. Only buy fresh scallops and steer clear of frozen ones, since they have often been soaked in water before freezing to increase their size and make the price seem more attractive. When they defrost, the water drains out of them along with a great deal of their flavour.

SQUID

Squid, like cuttlefish and octopus, belongs to the group known as cephalopods which means 'head footed', referring to the way the tentacles come out of the head. Cephalopods are in fact molluscs, like mussels and oysters, not fish. They are much underrated and seem to be one of the few species of marine life that have not yet been over-fished. They all have a delicious flavour, more akin to lobster or crab than fish, and deserve to be much more popular. The general lack of familiarity with these excellent species reminds me of a Padstow boy who went to Spain for the first time, ordered a plate of deep-fried battered squid rings and remarked, totally astonished, to his friends, 'Funny sort of onions they have over here'.

Squid and cuttlefish can be cooked and eaten without any tenderizing (see p. 28 for preparing squid) but octopus does need something to help it. I think the easiest way to tenderize octopus is to simmer it gently in water (see p. 28).

There are various recipes for octopus stews in Mediterranean cookery books but I've never found them particularly satisfying. I think the best way of preparing octopus is in a salad as with the shark on p. 163 but you can just as successfully make the salad entirely with well-cooked, sliced octopus.

HOT SHELLFISH WITH GARLIC AND LEMON JUICE

This Italian dish is a sort of hot *fruits de mer*. The quantities of shellfish are merely a suggestion. You may like to make the dish out of fewer or more varieties, or include crab or lobster as well and make it into a main course. I have given cooking methods for all the shellfish but you may find that you can more easily buy it ready-cooked, in which case you will only need to warm it through.

SERVES 4

| 4 whelks
| 32 winkles
| 8 cooked langoustine or 8 cooked
| Mediterranean prawns
| 24 mussels
| A little dry white wine
| 20 cockles
| 4 large clams
| 16 small clams
| 8 oysters
| 85 ml (3 fl oz) extra virgin olive oil
| 2 garlic cloves, finely chopped
| 1 small bunch of fresh parsley, preferably flat
| leaf, roughly chopped
| 1 red chilli, seeded and finely chopped
| Juice of ½ lemon

You will need to make a steamer to reheat the shellfish that has been previously cooked. Take your largest pan and pour a couple of inches of boiling water into it. Place some sort of trivet in it; the flower-petal steamer mentioned on page 35 would be ideal. Reheat the cooked seafood in the steam for about 4 minutes.

If raw, cook the whelks and winkles in well-salted, boiling water. Add the whelks, allow the water to return to the boil then simmer for 4 minutes. The winkles should be added to boiling salted water, returned to the boil and then drained at once. Keep them both warm.

Place the winkles and whelks (if already cooked) and the langoustine or prawns in a pan of well salted, boiling water and warm them through.

Put the mussels in a large pan with a lid, splash in a little dry white wine. Place the pan over a fierce heat, cover and leave until they have opened. Remove with a perforated spoon and keep warm. Do the same with the cockles, the clams, large and small, and finally, the oysters. These will take the longest and will not open fully; you will need to lever them open with a short, thick-bladed knife or oyster knife.

Strain the cooking liquor into a small pan through a fine sieve to remove any grit.

Arrange the shellfish on four large, warmed plates or on one very large serving dish. Add the olive oil, garlic, parsley, chilli and lemon juice to the shellfish liquor, bring to the boil and pour over the shells. Serve with plenty of French bread or ciabatta.

(LEFT) Mussel, Cockle and Clam
Masala (*see page 210*), (BELOW LEFT)
Grilled Mussels with Pesto (*see page
209*) and (BELOW) Mussels in the
Shell with Linguine, Garlic and
Parsley (*see page 208*)

MOULES ET FRITES AND MOULES MARINIÈRES

Long have I tried to sell *Moules et Frites* (mussels and chips with mayonnaise) at the restaurant, but without much success. It has long been one of my favourite dishes. I love chips and mayonnaise far too much, I'm afraid, and this combination is, to me, exquisite. The mussels are cooked very simply. You can, of course, serve the *moules marinières* without the chips and mayonnaise, maybe with some fresh baguettes and a bottle of Muscadet.

SERVES 4

1.5 kg (3½ lb) or 3.9 litres (7 pints) mussels
50 g (2 oz) unsalted butter
1 medium onion, chopped
50 ml (2 fl oz) dry white wine
1 tablespoon roughly chopped fresh parsley
1 quantity *Mustard Mayonnaise* (see p. 43)

Wash the mussels in plenty of cold water. Scrape away any barnacles with a short-bladed knife. Pull off all the beards and wash the mussels again. Discard any that are open and do not close when tapped sharply.

Take a large lidded pan that is big enough to hold all the mussels. Add the mussels, butter, onion, white wine and half the parsley and set over a fierce heat. Turn the mussels over every now and then as they start to open. Keep the lid on the pan in between turning them. When they are all open, remove from the heat and leave for 30 seconds or so to let all the grit settle to the bottom of the pan.

Scoop out the mussels with a big spoon and divide between four large, deep plates. Wide soup plates are ideal but you can use deep bowls as well. Pour all the juices from the pan over the mussels holding back the last tablespoon or so which will be full of grit. Sprinkle the rest of the parsley over the mussels and serve with the mayonnaise and chips.

MUSSELS IN THE SHELL WITH LINGUINE, GARLIC AND PARSLEY

I used to think that *spaghetti alle vongole* was a second-rate pasta dish using small tasteless clams in a much reduced tomato, garlic and onion sauce, having ordered it more than once in restaurants who knew nothing about the importance of not overcooking shellfish. I'm afraid I'm an eternal optimist as far as food is concerned. My wife Jill often laughs at my soon-to-be-dashed enthusiasm in restaurants where she can see by the look of the place that we are going to be disappointed.

But not so long ago we went to the coast of Italy below Rome and spent a week eating the real *spaghetti alle vongole*; pasta with the sweetest of clams, the type we know as carpet shells. Sometimes the same dish was made with mussels, which I thought was possibly even better. We ate other seafood too, for a week we ate nothing else, but it was mussels and clams with pasta that really captivated us.

The most important part of this dish is getting the pasta just right. The Italian interpretation of the words *al dente* is much more severe than ours where pasta is concerned. You can get away with much more bite in pasta than you think and, in this dish, the slight hardness of the pasta against the soft shellfish is what makes it so special.

The pasta is part-boiled in salted water then the cooking is finished with the liquor from the shellfish. The shells are not removed from the mussels because it is not a problem to eat the pasta with the shells – and the dish looks so much more exciting with them. You can use thinner pasta for this dish, but reduce the initial boiling time of the pasta to about 3 minutes.

SERVES 4

900 g (2 lb) or 2.25 litres (4 pints) mussels
350 g (12 oz) *linguine*
50 ml (2 fl oz) virgin olive oil
4 garlic cloves, thinly sliced
½ red chilli, seeded and very finely chopped
3 tablespoons roughly chopped flatleaf parsley
2 tablespoons dry white wine

Wash the mussels in plenty of changes of cold water. Scrape the mussels with a short, thick-bladed knife to remove any barnacles or seaweed and pull out the beards. Wash again and discard any that do not close when given a sharp tap.

Bring a large pan of well salted water to the boil and cook the *linguine* for 5 minutes. Meanwhile, heat the olive oil in a small pan and soften the sliced garlic, then add the chilli and parsley. Remove from the heat.

Drain the pasta through a colander and return the pan to a high heat. Add the white wine, then the mussels and then the pasta. Cover the pan to trap the steam and speed up the cooking of the mussels but occasionally stir the mussels and pasta to redistribute them.

When the mussels have all opened, remove the lid and add the oil, garlic, chilli and parsley and let the juices reduce for about 2 minutes. The pasta should be just cooked, but if it is too hard for your liking, replace the lid and cook gently for a couple more minutes. Serve with plenty of bread.

Serve with a bottle of Vernaccia di San Gimignano or a Pinot Grigio.

~~~~~~

GRILLED MUSSELS WITH PESTO

The mussels are opened and served in one shell which is filled with a garlic, basil and pine kernel *pesto*. For this recipe the *pesto* should be made quite dry and coarse, more like a stuffing than a sauce. You can make various other grilled mussel dishes in the same way using various flavoured butters like *Garlic Butter* (see p. 49) or *Coriander and Roasted Hazelnut Butter* (see p. 49). Also try the recipe on p. 45 for *Charmoula* as a filling and mix with some finely chopped almonds, or the *Rouille* on p. 45 mixed with breadcrumbs.

SERVES 4

60 large mussels
A splash of dry white wine or water

FOR THE PESTO

15 g (½ oz) fresh basil
2 large garlic cloves
175 ml (6 fl oz) olive oil
15 g (½ oz) Parmesan
15 g (½ oz) pine kernels
2 slices white bread made into breadcrumbs

Wash the mussels in plenty of changes of cold water, swirling them round until the water is clear. Scrape the mussels with a short, thick-bladed knife to remove any barnacles or seaweed and pull out the beards. Wash again and discard any that do not close when given a sharp tap.

Open the mussels by steaming them with a splash of dry white wine (or water) covered in a large pan over a fierce heat. Remove from the heat as soon as they have opened and discard one side of the shell. Strain the liquor through a colander and pour off into a small pan holding back the last tablespoon or so of mussel liquor which will contain a lot of grit.

Reduce the rest of the liquor to about 1 tablespoon by rapid boiling. (This will be added to the *pesto* ingredients.)

Put all the *pesto* ingredients with the reduced mussel liquor in a mortar and pestle or food processor and pound or blend until roughly chopped.

Pre-heat the grill to high. Arrange the mussels on a grilling tray. Spoon the *pesto* into all the mussel shells, then sprinkle over the breadcrumbs and grill until the breadcrumbs are beginning to brown.

Serve an Italian Chardonnay from the North-eastern wine region of Trentino. They can be exceptionally good and are usually very reasonably priced.

MUSSEL, COCKLE AND CLAM MASALA

I have specified rather more *masala* paste than you may feel you need for this recipe as the chilli already makes it very hot but if you like your Indian food hot then add it all.

You will need a large pan, preferably a wok, to cook this dish.

SERVES 4

25 ml (1 fl oz) vegetable oil
1.5 kg (3½ lb) or 3.9 litres (7 pints) mixed mussels, clams and cockles
85 ml (3 fl oz) water

FOR THE MASALA

1 tablespoon coriander seeds
1 teaspoon cloves
2 tablespoons cumin seeds
350 g (12 oz) onions, finely chopped
8 large garlic cloves
50 g (2 oz) fresh ginger, chopped
Walnut-sized knob of dried tamarind pulp (seeded)
1 teaspoon turmeric powder
3 fresh red chillies
2 tablespoons red wine vinegar
3 tablespoons coconut cream

FOR THE GARNISH

2 tablespoons fresh coriander leaves, chopped

In a frying pan, dry-fry the coriander seeds and cloves over a medium heat for a few minutes, then add the cumin seeds, heating them for another 30 seconds. Grind in a clean coffee grinder or mortar, then put this mixture with the remainder of the *masala* ingredients into a food processor and blend to a paste. If the masala paste is too stiff add a little vegetable oil to loosen it.

Fry the *masala* in the vegetable oil until the spices separate from the oil.

Wash the mussels, clams and cockles and toss them in the *masala* paste then cover with a lid and, shaking from time to time, steam-cook until the shells open. If you feel the mussels haven't produced enough liquid add a little water. The recipe contains no salt as mussels are salty, but taste to check the seasoning. Throw in a generous amount of chopped coriander and serve in bowls.

OYSTERS WITH BEURRE BLANC AND SPINACH

The oysters in this dish are hardly cooked at all. This combined with the *beurre blanc* is fresh and pleasing.

SERVES 4

16 oysters
16 spinach leaves, stalks removed
25 g (1 oz) shallot or small onion, finely chopped
1 tablespoon white wine vinegar
1 tablespoon white wine
50 ml (2 fl oz) water
150 g (5 oz) unsalted butter

Prepare a steamer to cook the oysters (see p. 205). Thoroughly wash the oysters and steam for about 4 minutes. Remove and open, keeping the liquor that comes out of them. Put the spinach leaves in the steamer and steam for 2 minutes.

Put the shallot or onion, vinegar, wine and water into a small pan. Add the juice from the oysters and simmer until only about 2 table-spoons of liquid are left. Cut the butter into small squares and whisk it in a little at a time, off the heat, building up a light emulsion.

Remove the oysters from their shells. Lay a folded leaf of spinach in the bottom of each shell. Place the shells on a suitable serving dish and push briefly under the grill to warm the spinach. Put the oysters on top and pour the *beurre blanc* over each. Place under the grill again to warm through then serve.

OYSTERS CHARENTAIS

This is a seemingly odd combination: freshly opened oysters with hot spicy sausages. The idea is that you eat an oyster, take a bite of the sausage then a good gulp of cold white wine like Muscadet. We use caul fat for the sausages – a membrane laced with fat which comes from around a pig's stomach lining. It should be reasonably easy to order half a pound or so from the butcher.

SERVES 4

20 Pacific oysters

FOR THE SAUSAGES

350 g (12 oz) belly pork
½ teaspoon salt
½ teaspoon paprika
½ teaspoon black pepper
½ teaspoon thyme
½ teaspoon cayenne pepper
75 g (3 oz) *chorizo* sausage, skin removed
100 g (4 oz) caul fat for wrapping the sausages

Put all the sausage ingredients into a food processor and blend until the mixture is coarse, that is the bits in it are about the size of demerara sugar. Remove and portion the sausages into balls about the size of a golf ball and mould into rough sausage shapes. Wrap them in 10 cm (4 in) squares of caul fat.

Twenty minutes before serving open the oysters but keep them flat, taking care not to spill too much of the salty liquor. (Refer to the notes on p. 29 for instructions on opening oysters.) Divide the oysters between four plates.

Pre-heat the grill to high and grill the sausages. Place three sausages beside each serving of oysters – don't forget the Muscadet.

Steamed Scallops with Ginger, Soy, Sesame and Spring Onions

This recipe came to me as a result of a visit to a restaurant in Gerrard Street, Soho.

It is fascinating to me how the Chinese restaurants in London's Soho have grown in everyone's estimation in the last 30-odd years. I can recall in the early days seeing dark red ducks hanging in every front window and wondering how anyone except the Chinese would dare to eat such frightening looking food. The smell was enough to scare you rigid and the look of the stuff – wow!

Then about 25 years ago I went with a more adventurous friend to the Lido in Gerrard Street. He said I should try anything, it would all be good. So I ordered the most dreadful sounding dishes on the menu, *Boiled Eel in Black Bean Sauce* and, I think, *Steamed Fish Heads*. It was all totally wonderful and I've been back many times since.

My early reserve about foreign food is not something I feel very proud of, but I do use my own former reluctance to try things as a reminder that if I can become a convert, anyone can, including my youngest son, Charles, who won't touch much more than spaghetti hoops. Very vexing for a father who is a chef, but maybe he'll change.

This dish is a classic. It's incredibly easy to cook and a reminder to all cooks to keep it simple. Scallops are usually ill-treated by over-creative cooks because they seem to go well with almost anything; consequently, they are combined with almost anything. But if, as a result of such a combination, you can't really taste the scallop, why waste money? Why not use something like tofu instead?

SERVES 4

16 scallops in the shell
1 teaspoon finely chopped fresh ginger
120 ml (4 fl oz) sesame oil
2 tablespoons soy sauce
1 tablespoon roughly chopped fresh
  coriander leaf
3 spring onions, finely sliced

Prepare a steamer following the suggestions on p. 205.

Sprinkle the scallops with the ginger. Place in the steamer and steam for about 4 minutes until only just set. While they are cooking, put the sesame oil and soy sauce in a small pan and warm through. Lay the scallops on four plates and pour over the sesame and soy sauce. Sprinkle on the coriander and sliced spring onions then serve.

Scallops with Noisette Butter

This is the simplest of recipes but *noisette* butter needs to be made correctly to taste really good. It goes very well with grilled or fried fillets of any flat fish and any number of the cod family like whiting, hake or haddock.

If you are making this as a starter, it would be more appropriate to use queens. Queens are a type of small scallop. The only difference between it and the larger bivalve is that it has two concave shells whereas the scallop has one concave and one flat shell.

SERVES 4

16 scallops (or 24 queens) in their shells
225 g (8 oz) unsalted butter
Juice of ½ lemon
1 small bunch of fresh parsley
Salt and freshly ground black pepper

Pre-heat the grill to high.

Cut up the butter and place in a small pan. Set the pan over a medium heat until the butter has melted and started to brown. This is the important bit of the recipe – the butter needs to go a delicate but not dark shade of brown. The word *noisette* means nutty and that is how you can tell when it is cooked enough – when it smells of warm nuts. Remove from the heat as soon as the butter has reached that stage and keep warm.

Brush the scallops with a little of the *noisette* butter and grill for 5 minutes. Remove and place on four warmed plates. Squeeze over the lemon juice and season with salt and freshly ground black pepper. Pour the *noisette* butter over all the scallops and scatter with parsley.

Serve with plenty of fresh crusty bread to mop up the juices.

Sautéed Scallops with Basil, Saffron and Pasta

Scallop shells make excellent containers for seafood. You will need 20 scallop shells for this recipe. If it is at all possible, buy the scallops and shells together, though you will need to buy a few extra empty scallop shells as well.

SERVES 4

12 good-sized scallops
600 ml (1 pint) *Fish Stock* (see p. 36)
50 ml (2 fl oz) white wine
A good pinch saffron
150 ml (5 fl oz) double cream
50 g (2 oz) unsalted butter
100 g (4 oz) thin pasta such as vermicelli or
   fedilini
6 basil leaves, sliced

Slice the scallops in half. Put the fish stock, the white wine and the saffron in a pan and boil rapidly to reduce by three-quarters. Add the cream and the butter and reduce further until the sauce coats the back of a spoon.

Boil the pasta in salted water until tender but firm to the bite (*al dente*). Toss it in a little butter with the sliced basil leaves.

Warm the 20 scallop shells under a moderate grill and arrange on 4 plates. Distribute the pasta between the shells and bring the sauce to the boil. Add the scallops and cook for 2 minutes. Spoon the scallops and sauce into the 20 shells and serve.

(TOP LEFT) Oysters Charentais (*see page 211*), (BELOW LEFT) Scallops with Noisette Butter (*see page 212*) and (BELOW) Sautéed Scallops with Basil, Saffron and Pasta (*see page 213*)

SAUTÉED SCALLOPS WITH LENTILS AND CHARDONNAY

I use oaked Australian Chardonnay in large quantities for this dish, along with a pinch of spice normally associated with Indian cookery.

Serve with a heavily oaked Australian Chardonnay. You only need about an eighth of a teaspoon of spice to go into the sauce so I have had to specify the quantities as small pinches and large pinches.

SERVES 4

| 12 scallops

FOR THE SAUCE

A small pinch of ground allspice
A small pinch of ground cloves
A small pinch of ground nutmeg
A large pinch of curry powder
10 g (½ oz) unsalted butter
25 g (1 oz) onion, chopped
25 g (1 oz) carrot, chopped
300 ml (10 fl oz) oaked Chardonnay
600 ml (1 pint) *Fish Stock* (see p. 36)
50 ml (2 fl oz) double cream
50 g (2 oz) unsalted butter, cut into cubes

FOR THE LENTILS

50 g (2 oz) green lentils, preferably Puy lentils
175 ml (6 fl oz) *Fish Stock* (see p. 36)
1 clove
1 fresh or dried bay leaf
2 slices of onion
½ teaspoon salt

To make the sauce, put the spices, 10 g (½ oz) butter, the onion and carrot in a pan and cook over a gentle heat for about 4 minutes. Pour in the Chardonnay and stock and bring to the boil. Simmer until the volume has reduced by about two-thirds. Strain the stock, add the cream and simmer again until the volume has reduced by about two-thirds.

While the sauce is reducing, simmer the lentils with the fish stock, clove, bay leaf, onion and salt until tender. Drain.

Cut each scallop into three discs. Put a frying pan over a high heat. When hot, rub a little of the butter over the pan then put in half the scallops. Cook for 30 seconds only on one side to caramelize, then turn and cook for a further 30 seconds on the other.

Remove and keep warm. Pour any juices into the sauce. Heat the pan again, add a little more butter and fry the second batch of scallops.

Place a pile of lentils on each of four warmed plates and arrange the scallops on top. Whisk the rest of the cubes of butter into the warm sauce and pour round each plate.

CHAR-GRILLED SQUID WITH A PEPPER MARINADE

Squid marinated in olive oil with black pepper, Szechuan pepper and red chillies. The squid is best cooked on a barbecue grill but you can also get good results using a ribbed grill pan. I got the idea for this dish from the River Café in London.

This recipe can be equally well made with cuttlefish.

SERVES 4

½ teaspoon black peppercorns
½ teaspoon Szechuan peppercorns
1 red chilli, seeded and finely chopped
50 ml (2 fl oz) virgin olive oil
Juice of ½ lemon
½ teaspoon salt
1 tablespoon soy sauce
1 garlic clove, finely chopped
350 g (12 oz) squid, cleaned (see p. 28)

75 g (3 oz) rocket leaves
Lemon wedges to serve

Grind the black and Szechuan peppercorns coarsely. Use a mortar and pestle or put the peppercorns on a chopping board, cover them with a clean tea towel and roll over them with a rolling pin. Put them in a bowl with the red chilli, olive oil, lemon juice, salt, soy sauce and garlic.

Light the barbecue. Cut the bodies of the squid into 7.5 cm (3 in) pieces then cut each tentacle in half. Put the squid into the marinade and leave for 30 minutes, turning over once or twice. Remove the squid from the marinade and grill for 1 minute. Turn and grill for another minute.

Arrange the salad leaves on four plates. Place the squid on top and drizzle over the rest of the marinade. Serve with a wedge of lemon.

SAUTÉED SQUID WITH OLIVE OIL, GARLIC AND PARSLEY

I am very enthusiastic about quick and simple recipes. This recipe was inspired by a dish in a charming little book called *The International Squid Cook Book* by Isaac Cronin. I love the way Americans get bees in their bonnets about things. He's a complete fanatic about every aspect of squid and he says this recipe is the easiest and, many people think, the best way to cook it. Serve with chips.

SERVES 4

450 g (1 lb) squid
2 garlic cloves, finely chopped
25 ml (1 fl oz) olive oil
A pinch of crushed dried chilli
1 tablespoon roughly chopped fresh parsley
Juice of ¼ lemon
Salt and freshly ground black pepper
Lemon wedges to serve

Clean the squid (see p. 28) and cut the body section into rings.

Quickly fry the garlic in hot olive oil and add the squid just as the garlic is beginning to brown. Add the seasoning and a pinch of chilli. Turn over and sauté for 2–3 minutes. Add the parsley and lemon juice. Serve with more lemon wedges and the chips.

I think that in the not too distant future we will all be enjoying seafood in Britain with the same general enthusiasm as the Americans from Maine, the Portuguese, French and Spanish. I want to be able to go to a beach and find someone grilling fish over a driftwood fire to sell to me. In any country where seafood is valued, there is someone selling good things from the sea to eat right by the beach. In Britain you can buy ice-cream, windbreaks and surfboards but I want grilled pilchards with a simple salad or fresh spiny lobster just out of the sea, as I had once on a beach in Greece.

The last two recipes in this book encapsulate everything I love about seafood, cooked simply with no fuss straight from the sea.

PILCHARDS GRILLED OVER DRIFTWOOD WITH A TOMATO, RED ONION AND BASIL SALAD

SERVES 4

    12 absolutely fresh pilchards
    Olive oil for brushing the fish
    6 tomatoes
    1 red onion
    A bunch of basil
    30 ml (2 fl oz) olive oil
    1 tablespoon white wine vinegar
    ½ teaspoon salt
    Freshly ground black pepper

You will need some sort of grill wire on which to cook the pilchards. Make a fireplace with beach pebbles, something you can rest the grill wire on. Build up a driftwood fire, then let it burn down to hot ash. Remove the guts from the pilchards and scrape off the scales. Brush with oil and season well inside and out. Slash them three times on either side down to the bone. Grill them for about 4 minutes on each side. Meanwhile slice the tomatoes and thinly slice the onion. Chop the basil. Make a dressing with the olive oil, white wine vinegar, salt and black pepper and mix with the salad. Serve the fish straight from the grill.
Sit with a glass of Australian Chardonnay and watch the sun set.

THE CLAMBAKE

Every July we hold a large barbecue on one of the beaches near Padstow for all the staff. We end up with well over 100 people. We load the old charcoal barbecue (which we used to have in the restaurant) into the fish van, make lots of tandooried monkfish, teriyaki mullet fillets, shark steaks marinated in charmoula and a bucketful of Thai prawns. We then fill an old tin bath with ice and bottles of beer and off we go.

This year we're going to have a clambake too. We'll dig a shallow pit in the beach, about 6 feet by 2 feet and about 18 inches deep, and line it with large smooth rocks. Then we'll build a large driftwood fire on it to heat up the rocks and leave it burning for 2 hours. When it's burnt right down we'll brush the hot ash off the stones, put a layer of seaweed on top of the baking hot rocks and pile on the clams, small lobsters, crabs, langoustines, some plump mackerel, corn on the cob and some small new potatoes. We'll cover them with more seaweed and an old damp sack and leave everything to cook gently in the steam of the seaweed for about an hour. They'll taste so good with all that ozone-iodine flavour of the seaweed – a real seafood extravaganza!

LISTING OF AMERICAN, AUSTRALIAN AND NEW ZEALAND FISH

The following list gives local names, where necessary, or suggests a similar fish as an alternative.

British Isles	USA	Australian and NZ
Anchovies	Anchovies	Anchovies
Brill	Petrale sole, Brill sole	Sole, Flounder
Cod	Cod, Pacific cod	Blue cod
Coley	Haddock	Hoki
Conger eel	Conger eel	Blue grenadier
Dabs	Flounder	Flounder
Dover sole	English sole, Gray sole	Sole, Flounder
Eel	Eel	Eel
Flounder	Flounder	Flounder
Grey mullet	Mullet, Striped bass	Groper, Coral trout
Gurnard	Searobin	Gurnard, Coral trout
Haddock	Haddock	Blue cod, Hoki
Hake	Hake, Silver hake	Hake
Herring	Herring	Sardine
John Dory	John Dory, Oreo Dory	John Dory
Lemon sole	English sole, Flounder	Sole, Flounder
Ling	Cusk, Cobia	Jewfish
Mackerel	Atlantic mackerel	Mackerel
Megrim sole	Flounder	Flounder
Monkfish	Monkfish, Anglerfish	Monkfish
Octopus	Octopus	Octopus
Parrot fish	Parrot fish	Parrot fish, Snapper
Pilchards	Sardines	Sardines
Pollack	Pollock	Rock cod
	Walleye pollock	Hoki
Pouting	Cod, Whiting	Hoki
Ray	Skate	Ray
Red bream	Red snapper	Snapper
Red mullet	Goatfish	Red mullet, Barbounia
Salmon	Salmon	Atlantic salmon
Sand eels	Sand launce, Smelt	Smelt
Sardines	Sardines	Sardines
Sea bass	Sea bass	Groper
Sea trout	Steelhead trout	Atlantic salmon

British Isles	USA	Australian and NZ
Shark	Shark	Shark
Skate	Skate	Skate
Snapper	Snapper	Snapper
Sprats	Smelt	Sprats
Squid	Squid, Calamari	Squid, Calamari
Swordfish	Swordfish	Swordfish
Tuna	Tuna	Tuna
Turbot	Flounder	Sole, John Dory, Flounder
Whitebait	Whitebait, Smelt	Whitebait
Whiting	Whiting	Whiting
Witch	Flounder	Flounder, Sole

SHELLFISH

British Isles	USA	Australian and NZ
Blue crab	Blue crab	Blue crab
Brown crab	Dungeness crab	Blue swimming crab
Clams	Hardshell clams	Clams
	Littleneck clams	Littleneck clams, Pipi
	Cherrystone clams	Clams
Cockles	Cockles	Pipi, Cockles
Crayfish, Crawfish	Crayfish, Spiny lobster	Yabbies
Langoustine	Norway lobster, Lobsterette	Scampi
Lobster	Lobster	Rock lobster
Mussels	Blue mussels	Mussels
Oysters	Oysters	Oysters
Prawns	Shrimp	Prawn
Queens	Bay scallop	Queen scallop, Tipa
Razor-shell clam	Razor clams	None
Scallop	Sea scallop, Bay scallop	Scallop
Sea urchin	Sea urchin	Sea urchin
Shore crab	Green crab	Spanner crab
Shrimp	Shrimp	Shrimp
Soft-shell crab	Soft-shell crab	Soft-shell crab
Spider crab	Spider crab, snow crab	Blue swimming crab
Spiny lobster	Spiny lobster, Crawfish	Crayfish, Spiny lobster
Swimming crab	Green crab, Blue crab	Blue swimming crab
Whelk	Whelk, Conch	Whelk
Winkles	Periwinkles	Winkles

ALTERNATIVE FISH

The following is a list of all the fish and shellfish used in the book giving an alternative to use if you can't get hold of the one in the recipe. The alternatives are not necessarily the most similar fish biologically but rather ones that work almost, if not equally, as well.

EEL: MACKEREL

CONGER EEL: SHARK, SWORDFISH OR TUNA

HERRINGS: MACKEREL OR PILCHARDS

POLLACK: COLEY, OR LARGER WHITING

WHITING: HADDOCK OR COD

MACKEREL: HERRING

SALMON: LARGE SEA TROUT

SEA TROUT: SALMON OR TROUT

SPRATS: SARDINES

WHITEBAIT: SAND EELS

JOHN DORY: BARBECUED DISHES – SEA BASS: OTHERS – TURBOT OR BRILL

RED MULLET: ANY OF THE BREAM FAMILY OR SEA BASS

SEA BASS: GREY MULLET OR RED MULLET

RED BREAM: JOHN DORY

COD: HADDOCK

GURNARD: SEA BASS OR WEEVER FISH

MONKFISH: CHAR-GRILLED RECIPES – SWORDFISH; OTHERS – TURBOT OR JOHN DORY

HADDOCK: COD OR HAKE

HAKE: HADDOCK OR COD

LING: MONKFISH

SWORDFISH: SHARK OR TUNA

SHARK: TUNA, SWORDFISH OR CONGER EEL

TUNA: SWORDFISH OR MONKFISH

DOVER SOLE: WITCH SOLE, SAND SOLE

FILLETS OF DOVER SOLE – MEGRIM SOLE, LEMON SOLE, WITCH SOLE

LEMON SOLE: MEGRIM SOLE, WITCH SOLE, PLAICE

BRILL: TURBOT, LARGE JOHN DORY

HALIBUT: TURBOT

PLAICE: LEMON SOLE, DABS, WITCH SOLE, FLOUNDER

TURBOT: BRILL, JOHN DORY

SKATE: ANGEL SHARK, PORBEAGLE SHARK

SQUID: CUTTLEFISH

OCTOPUS: LARGE CUTTLEFISH

CUTTLEFISH: SQUID

BROWN CRAB: SPIDER CRAB

SHORE CRAB: SWIMMING CRAB

SPIDER CRAB: BROWN CRAB

SWIMMING CRAB: SHORE CRAB

WHELKS: OCTOPUS

SCALLOPS: SLICES OF MONKFISH

QUEENS: SCALLOPS

PRAWNS: ANOTHER SPECIES OF PRAWN

SHRIMPS: SMALL PRAWNS

LANGOUSTINE: LARGE PRAWNS

RAZOR-SHELL CLAMS: ANY OTHER SPECIES OF CLAM

CLAMS: COCKLES OR MUSSELS

MUSSELS: CLAMS OR COCKLES

WINKLES: SMALL MUSSELS

COCKLES: MUSSELS OR SMALL CLAMS

OYSTERS: MUSSELS OR CLAMS

LOBSTER: SPINY LOBSTER

SEA URCHINS: SCALLOP ROE

INDEX

Page numbers in italics refer to the photographs